D0677380

HATE PREJUDICE AND RACISM

SUNY SERIES, THEORY, RESEARCH, AND PRACTICE
IN SOCIAL EDUCATION

PETER H. MARTORELLA, EDITOR

HATE
PREJUDICE
AND
RACISM

MILTON KLEG

STATE UNIVERSITY OF NEW YORK PRESS

Published by
State University of New York Press, Albany

© 1993 Milton Kleg

All rights reserved

Printed in the United States of America

No part of this book may be used or reproduced
in any manner whatsoever without written permission
except in the case of brief quotations embodied in
critical articles and reviews.

For information, address State University of New York
Press, State University Plaza, Albany, N.Y., 12246

Production by Diane Ganeles
Marketing by Bernadette LaManna

Library of Congress Cataloging-in-Publication Data

Kleg, Milton.
    Hate prejudice and racism / Milton Kleg.
        p.   cm. — (SUNY series, theory, research, and practice in
    social education)
        Includes bibliographical references and index.
        ISBN 0-7914-1535-X (alk. paper). — ISBN 0-7914-1536-8 (pbk. :
    alk. paper)
        1. United States—Race relations.   2. United States—Ethnic
    relations.   3. Racism—United States.   I. Title.   II. Series.
    E184. A1K49   1993
    305. 8'00973—dc20   92-28115
                                                                  CIP

10 9 8 7 6 5 4 3 2 1

162075

Belmont University Library

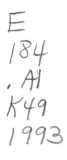

E
184
. A1
K49
1993

AAX–6509

To Anna Rae
and to the memory of Ann Kleg and Dora Wolff.
They made dreams come true.

CONTENTS

PREFACE

It's not so much the prejudices, we all got those. It's the
hate, the hate prejudice that does us ill.

As I perused a map showing the villages, towns, and cities with
their names and the number of people deported to concentration
camps during the Second World War, a haunting and unnatural
feeling came over me. The village of Berezno seemed to stand out,
and the number of one thousand indicating those deported or executed ran through me like a sudden shock of electricity. It was there
in Berezno that my cousins were forced to dig their own graves before they were summarily executed.

Almost fifty years later, my twelve-year-old daughter awoke
trembling from a nightmare. Just prior to retiring, she had seen a
televised news report on David Duke, former Imperial Wizard of the
Knights of the Ku Klux Klan and neo–Nazi. Would her world be any
different from the past?

This book was written with the belief that if future generations
are to achieve a better world, it would require a concerted effort on
the part of today's citizens. We can ill afford to either ignore or remain passive bystanders in a world divided into hostile camps.

Although some chapters focus on the role of educators, the work
should provide a background for all concerned citizens. Regarding
the area of education, my goal was to address educators at two
rather distinct levels, the teacher and teacher of teachers. In doing
so, I was faced with the stereotype that teachers of school children
and young adults seem to be of a practitioner whose interest is limited to the mechanics of instruction. It is a stereotype that I find
totally unwarranted and repugnant.

How in the world can we expect teachers to encourage students
to be reflective and concerned citizens if we maintain the notion
that a teacher is nothing more than a technician? As early as 1904,
John Dewey noted that teachers must "continue to be students of

subject-matter and students of mind activity."[1] He also stated that "Unless a teacher is such a student, he may continue to improve in the mechanics of school management, but he can not grow as a teacher, an inspirer and director of soul-life." Therefore, I rejected the notion that teachers are neither able nor interested in exploring the new challenges regarding critical social issues. The rejection of this idea also includes the rejection that treatises presented to teachers must be in the format of texts or guides to instruction— often so sterile and unchallenging they make a mockery out of the concept of sapience, the very root of which distinguishes humankind from other members of the animal kingdom. I have attempted to integrate these oft perceived dichotomous populations as fibers of the same rope and as equally and intellectually capable of discerning what best challenges apply to each.

As for the structure of this work, I have attempted to address those topics that form the foundation of the study of race and ethnic group relations. This involved the examination of hate prejudice and violence, past and present—near and far, the foundation of race as scientific concept and the foundation of racism, race as a social concept. In addition, the attempt has been made to reexamine the meaning of ethnicity and ethnic groups, attitudes, stereotyping, and the manifestations of hate prejudice—discrimination, aggression, and scapegoating.

I do not expect the reader to agree with all of my analyses or perceptions. To do so would require a return to mental sterility. Rather, it is hoped that substantive content will be informative, and the perceptions and paradigms presented will be challenging and subject to challenge; for where there is challenge, there is growth.

ACKNOWLEDGMENTS

I should like to take this opportunity to express my gratitude to those individuals who assisted and encouraged the development of this work. I must thank Ravay Snow whose assistance was most helpful. Ravay questioned and challenged various points, and this no doubt assisted in clarifying issues. Secondly, it should be noted that chapters three and four contained some aspects of an earlier work, *Race, Caste, and Prejudice*, that was co-authored with Marion J. Rice.

I should like to express my gratitude to the following individuals for their support, patience, and/or suggestions: Peter H. Martorella, Nathaniel Lauer, Marc Mahlios, William Carter, Timothy Huffman, Dan Malloy, Danny Welch, Joe Roy, Maurice Holt, Kaoru Yamamoto, and William F. Grady. A word of appreciation is extended to Priscilla Ross, acquisitions editor at SUNY Press, and Diane Ganeles, production editor of SUNY Press. Finally, I must thank Anna Rae, Rachel, Esther, Devorah, and Itamar for their just being there. Ok, Iti, it's done.

CHAPTER 1

ON HATE AND SOCIAL EDUCATION

In the desert
I saw a creature, naked, bestial,
Who, squatting upon the ground,
Held his heart in his hand,
And ate of it,
I said, "Is it good, friend?"
"It is bitter—bitter," he answered,
"But I like it
Because it is bitter,
And because it is my heart."
    —Stephen Crane

In the past five thousand years, much of humankind has progressed from the hunting and gathering stage to an age of space exploration, from using onions and abracadabra to using electrocardiographs and chemotherapy. We also have become more efficient in expressing and acting upon our fears, prejudices, and rivalries. The subspecies homo sapiens sapiens has replaced stones and clubs, spears and arrows, with gas chambers and thermonuclear devices designed for total annihilation.[1] But whether one is killed by a stone, potassium cyanide, or a nuclear device is of little consequence. Death is finality.

Today racial and ethnic prejudices, discrimination, scapegoating, and other forms of aggression continue to characterize the human experience. The irony of history has been the failure of so many to realize, as did Stephen Crane in the above poem, that the destruction of other humans is a form of suicide at the subspecies level.

Social and behavioral scientists attempt to examine and explain these self-destructive experiences with heuristic models based upon inferences of statistical probability drawn from many examples. Poets and novelists observe the same social phenomena, but their reflections, based more upon introspection and personal encounters, attempt to create an emotional and intellectual experience for the individual reader and the larger society.

1

In education, social studies instruction became one logical component of the curriculum for the study and examination of critical social issues with a goal, among others, of creating humane and intelligent decision makers. Yet, on the whole, some of the very basic roots of social, political, and economic conflicts have been continually ignored within many social studies curricula. All too often, children receive instruction on the story of humankind without addressing the fears, hatreds, and frustrations that often underlie the causes of conflict at personal and group levels. If social studies education is to contribute toward improving interpersonal and intergroup relations, the learning experiences of students must somehow penetrate the superficiality of the content in current curricula. It should seek to explicate the root causes of social conflict.

There is no one intersection of time and geographical place where hate prejudice and racism dominate the history of humankind. These phenomena are intricately woven into the tapestry of the human experience. The lives of Leizer Richtol, Eugene Williams, and others illustrate these phenomena. Their stories provide the backdrop to our treatment of the ever present, ever raging violence that teachers must somehow address. And address it they must, if we are to achieve a more civilized and humane world.

Before the Holocaust

The Ukrainian village of Pyasechno was part of Russia until after World War I. During the war it was taken by the Germans and eventually turned over to Poland. It was a small village with about seventy-five families. The houses were simple, made of wood, and usually consisted of a kitchen, two small bedrooms, and a living room that was used as a sleeping area as well. Here in Pyasechno resided young Leizer Richtol with his mother, sister, and grandmother.

Like so many others in the early twentieth century, Leizer Richtol's father, Aaron, had left his family behind in Russia as he attempted to establish himself in America. Finally, in 1914, the young Leizer, his mother, Chia, and three-year-old sister, Leba–Devorah, obtained their ship cards and were preparing to join Aaron in a world far beyond their imaginations. But the cousins, Kaiser Wilhelm II and Tsar Nicholas II, had other ambitions, and their war interfered with the Richtol family's plans.

The Night of Bayonets

For two more years, as the war raged on the Eastern front, the Richtols remained in Pyasechno. On the evening of Wednesday, February 2, 1916, eleven-year-old Leizer, his mother, and Leba–Devorah were in their frame home entertaining relatives and guests. The events of the night were a living nightmare to Leizer and remain to this day indelibly etched in his memory.

> At night, soldiers would come, stalking and attacking villages and homes. On this night, they came to Pyasechno and stormed into our home. All told, we were twelve that night. The soldiers tied our hands and ravaged the house, taking what food and other items they thought useful. They were careful not to shoot us because it might arouse the authorities. Instead, they ran their bayonets through my little sister, mother, relatives, and guests. I could hear whimpering, cries, and screams. Suddenly, there was a sting and the hurt of a bayonet cutting into my side, another stab entered my back, and another, and again until I had received six wounds. I began gasping for air. A bayonet had penetrated one of my lungs.
>
> As we lay bleeding, the soldiers threw straw onto the floor and set fire to the house. They left. My grandmother, my mother, Chia, and sister, Leba–Devorah, died that night. Three generations murdered in an instant that seemed like forever.
>
> Cousin Label managed to free himself from the bonds. Noticing that I was alive, he untied me. The flames licked upward over the furniture and wall, blocking our passage to the door, so we escaped out the window. Label managed to assist six others out. Some died later from their wounds.
>
> A Ukrainian peasant, our neighbor, took us in, and it was not long before the police arrived. But before their arrival, I remember the peasant's son standing over me taunting, "You are going to die, and I shall have those fine shoes you are wearing." After the police came, we were taken to the hospital in Kovel [30 kilometers southeast of Pyasechno] and treated for our wounds.[2]

According to Leizer Richtol, "The police were Germans. The killers were Russians. In those days the German authorities protected us. They were good to us." German forces had invaded this area and had set up a temporary military government until a Polish civilian government could be established. Nevertheless, small bands of Russian soldiers and stragglers behind German lines preyed upon Jews—objects of hate.

Following an investigation, the German authorities learned that the Richtols' neighbor had collaborated with the Russians and encouraged them to attack the Richtol house. Three of the Russians were captured, brought to trial, and found guilty of murder. Leizer reflected, "I was able to witness their execution. As the firing squad's volley echoed in the cold air, there was no feeling, no joy. Their execution did not and could not return my sister and mother."

As the ravages of World War I continued, Leizer and his cousin moved to Chevel, just a few kilometers west of Pyasechno. There they remained with Leizer's uncle. By 1919, the civil war or counter–revolution between the communists and the anti-communists was flaring in Russia, and in this year alone, Jews were the target of 1,326 pogroms in the Ukraine.[3] Thousands of men, women, and children were indiscriminately murdered in their homes or as they fled. Murdered—not because they were communists or anti-communists—but because they were members of the Mosaic faith, pariahs among Christians in Eastern Europe.

That is how it was, before the world had heard of concentration camps, gassings, and ovens. The hate and violence directed against Jews during this period was rooted in centuries of anti-Semitism. The same sets of prejudices and stereotypes that led to the murders of these people in the Ukraine would spawn the Holocaust. The Holocaust was not an anomaly—not a quirk that appeared and passed in the history of Europe. It followed in logical sequence from a history of hate prejudice and persecution.

After the Holocaust

World War II had just ended, and the world was shocked, no, horrified, as the camps of Belsen, Buchenwald, Flossenberg, Mathausen, Natzweiler, Neuengamme, Ravensbruck, Dachau, Treblinka, Maidanek, and Sachenhausen were opened. The mass murder of six million Jews, as well as six million other nationals and ethnic minorities, seemed almost unimaginable. Near the town of Oswiecim (Auschwitz), Poland, alone, more than three million Jewish children, women, and men had been murdered—systematically exterminated. One might suppose that such murder—such hate would have been cause for a world to hang its head in shame. However, this was not so.

On July 4, 1946, in the city of Kielce, less than ninety miles from Auschwitz, a rumor is spread by nine-year-old Henryk Blaszczyka. He claims he saw Jews kill fifteen Christian children and that he, himself, had been held captive but was able to escape. The murders allegedly were for ritual purposes—the age-old blood libel that had haunted Jews in the Middle Ages. Police are called to investigate while the townspeople are steaming with hate and delirious for revenge.[4]

Before the police can dispel the false rumor, Jews are attacked with knives and clubs. Eventually, the young Henryk will admit that he was told by a Polish peasant to spread the rumor, but it comes too late for the forty-one men, women, and children murdered—this, less than eighteen months after Auschwitz has been liberated. The massacre at Kielce is not an isolated event. Sporadic anti–Semitic outbursts occur throughout Eastern Europe during this post-Holocaust period.[5]

More than fifty years later, and across the Atlantic, the blood libel cropped up in America in the form of a flier. (See the following page.) It did not result in mass demonstrations or murders, and this must be an encouraging sign. But the fact that it did appear at all should signal a warning that racial and ethnic hate prejudices are no less a critical issue today than twenty, fifty, or one hundred years ago. The roots of prejudice endure from generation to generation, across cultures and national borders. The United States is no exception.

The American Dilemma

Leizer Richtol survived the pogroms and slaughter before the Holocaust. After making his way back to Kovel, where he remained for another year, he managed at age sixteen to arrive in America in late 1921. While trying to survive in eastern Europe, he had no knowledge of the racial and ethnic hatreds permeating the United States. He only knew what he had heard people say, that it was a place where one could be free and safe. Indeed, this is the same image that the majority of Americans have been taught and have shared since the founding of the nation.

In this bastion of Western democracy, it is difficult to conceive of a people dedicated to the propositions of equality and human dignity on one hand, and actively engaged in genocidal acts and inhumane indignities on the other. Yet, this is exactly what Gunnar Myrdal perceived as the "American Dilemma".

> The "American Dilemma" ... is the ever-raging conflict between, on the one hand, the valuations preserved on the general plane

WHERE ARE OUR
Missing Children?

"Each year, 50,000 Children are Murdered within 48 hours of abduction." *(Major City Police Dept.)* This amounts to 137 children per day in America.

"If a Jew does not drink every year the blood of a non-Jewish man, then he will be damned for eternity." — *(National Review, March 8, 1985.)*

"As the blood is drained into cups, the Jewish leaders raise the cups and drink from them, while the Gentile Child slowly expires in an atmosphere of unrelieved horror." *(History of the Jews, Mullins.)*

"I believe our Children are being Sacrificed in Ritual Murder." — *(Chief of Detectives, Metropolitan County Sheriff's Dept.)*

WHERE ARE OUR
Missing Children?

JEWISH
RITUAL MURDER

Flier accusing Jews of ritual murder, St. Cloud, Minnesota area, circa 1990.

which we shall call the American Creed, where the American thinks, talks, and acts under the influence of high national and Christian percepts, and, on the other hand, the valuations on specific planes of individual and group living, where personal and local interest; economic, social, and sexual jealousies; considerations of community prestige and conformity; group prejudices against particular persons or types of people; and all sorts of miscellaneous wants, impulses, and habits dominate his outlook.[6]

Racism and other prejudices combined with greed to virtually destroy Native American nations and establish one of the most execrable forms of captivity—chattel slavery. Some can attempt to explain away the earlier acts committed against Indians as events which must be set in the perspective of the time and beliefs of a people who did not understand the unity of the human species. Certainly much has changed since 1872, when, for example, Francis Walker, Commissioner of Indian Affairs, described his policy regarding the treatment of American Indians. According to Walker,

> There is no question of national dignity, be it remembered, involved in the treatment of savages by a civilized power. With wild men, as with wild beasts, the question whether in a given situation one shall fight, coax, or run, is a question merely of what is easiest and safest.
>
> No one certainly will rejoice more heartily than the present Commissioner when the Indians of this country cease to be in a position to dictate, in any form or degree, to the Government; when, in fact, the last hostile tribe becomes reduced to the condition of suppliants for charity. This is the only hope of salvation for the aborigines of the continent. If they stand up against the progress of civilization and industry, they must be relentlessly crushed. . . . They must yield or perish; and there is something that savors of providential mercy in the rapidity with which their fate advances upon them . . .
>
> Whenever the time shall come that the roving tribes are reduced to a condition of complete dependence and submission, the plan to be adopted in dealing with them must be substantially that which is now being pursued in the case of the more tractable and friendly Indians . . . This is the true permanent policy of the Government.[7]

Such a policy statement, along with massacres of American Indians, can be neatly set aside by explanations that the white dominant group really did not understand the Native American. But how do we explain the textbook account of the Osage Indians published in 1967, some ninety-five years after the Walker policy?

> They were said to be greasy, and disgusting objects with dirty buffalo robes thrown over their shoulders. The women, if possible, were more filthy and disgusting than the men. The Indians never cleaned their food before cooking and eating it. Wild game would often be cooked and eaten with the blood and dirt of the hunt still upon it.[8]

Nor can we dismiss the constant racial and ethnic violence which has persisted throughout the twentieth century. The events of today or any day, for that matter, are rooted in the events of the past. In order to develop a perspective of the intense hostility encompassing race relations in America, it is necessary to examine the history of racial violence. Yet when we merely look at the statistics of murders, riots, and lynchings since the Civil War, they fail, as statistics often do, to describe what racial violence means at a personal level. Therefore, notwithstanding that to describe all of the events in detail would be too much to ask, I shall provide a select few for purposes of illustration. These accounts may provide a better insight in helping us realize more fully from where we have come in the arena of intergroup relations.

Racial Conflict Across America

CROSSING THE LINE

It is Sunday, July 27, 1919. While Leizer Richtol is struggling to remain alive and join his father in America, a black youth, seventeen-year-old Eugene Williams, is trying to keep cool on a hot and muggy Chicago summer afternoon. For Eugene and others in the Midwest metropolis, Lake Michigan is a recreational oasis. Eugene enters the lake from the 29th Street beach at about 4 o'clock in the afternoon. Although he swims opposite the "white" section of the beach, he is not concerned. He is some distance from any white bathers, and no one seems to mind. What Eugene does not know is that four black youths have crossed the imaginary line into white territory on the beach.[9]

White bathers immediately order the youths to return to their "Negro" section. The youngsters retreat, only to return shortly in greater numbers and accompanied by adults. The two races clash, first limiting their violence to verbal threats, then escalating with volleys of stones. As one group attacks, the other retreats and then counterattacks. Some of the stones are pitched beyond the beach, and Eugene, now apparently aware of a bad situation, begins to swim further out into the lake to avoid being pelted. He grabs onto a railroad tie floating in the lake. A white youth enters the water and begins swimming toward him. Eugene lets go of the drifting wood, takes a few strokes, and disappears beneath the surface.

Although a coroner's jury will eventually determine that the youth had drowned out of "fear" of swimming toward the shore, a rumor spreads among blacks at the scene that a white man had stoned Eugene and caused his death. Immediately, black bystanders accuse a white man of hitting Eugene with a stone. A policeman, called to the scene, refuses to arrest the accused, and for about two hours, the situation remains tense but not violent. The rumor regarding the alleged stoning of Eugene and the refusal of the officer to arrest the accused now spreads throughout the nearby black neighborhood, bringing more people to the scene. At about this time, the officer arrests a black man on the complaint of a white. Infuriated blacks immediately attack the officer; shots are fired by James Crawford, a black, who is then felled by the return fire of a black police officer. Fights break out along the beach and rumors spread among both racial groups. Indiscriminate attacks by both whites and blacks break out along Chicago's south side and continue into the early morning hours.[10]

By 3 A.M. five whites have been stabbed, and one has been shot. Seven blacks have received knife wounds, and four are shot. Full-scale rioting continues throughout Monday and Tuesday. The rioting spreads from South Chicago to the predominantly Italian west side. By Wednesday, the death toll reaches thirty-one, with 500 wounded; 6,000 soldiers of the state militia are called into action to quell the riot.[11] Before the rioting ends on Saturday, August 2, thirty–eight people are killed, 537 hurt, and 1,000 of Chicago's citizens are left homeless by fires.[12] All for crossing an imaginary color line.

Immediately following the Chicago riot, described by John Hope Franklin as "the nation's worst race war"[13] to that date, rioting broke out in Knoxville, Tennessee; Omaha, Nebraska; and Elaine, Arkansas. The Knoxville and Omaha riots included lynchings, which have played a major role in the history of American race relations.

THE OMAHA RIOT

Will Brown, black and forty-five years old, is arrested for allegedly assaulting a white, nineteen-year-old woman, Agnes Lobeck. Brown is placed in the county jail, located on the top floor of the Douglas County courthouse in Omaha.[14] On the afternoon of Sunday, September 28, 1919, a number of white citizens appear at the courthouse to demand that Brown be turned over to them. Omaha's mayor, E. P. Smith, had rushed to the scene at the first sign of trouble and is in the courthouse as the crowd's number increases to five thousand. While Mayor Smith and County Sheriff Michael Clark discuss the situation, some whites break into stores, stealing weapons and explosives. Others stop a streetcar and drag blacks onto the pavement where they are beaten. Rumors begin to spread, and one rumor that Dean Ringer, the police commissioner, had shot a young child, so excites the crowd that some take off to the commissioner's home with yells to lynch the commissioner.[15]

At 10 P.M., the mayor exits the building and begins to appeal for calm. Before he can back away, Smith is seized and dragged down the street. Amidst cries of, "Give us the key to the jail," "If we can't get the nigger, we'll lynch you," "He's no better than the nigger," and, "He's a nigger lover,", some members of the mob place a rope around the mayor's neck and hoist him on a streetcar pole. As blood begins to exude from Mayor Smith's mouth, police arrive and cut the rope. Smith falls to the ground and is carried to a patrol car. He is rushed to the home of a surgeon. Contrary to early reports that he had been killed, Smith survives the attempted lynching.[16]

At about the same time that members of the crowd had taken the mayor, someone had pitched a fire bomb through a window of the courthouse. This was followed by cans of gasoline. Within minutes, the first four floors of the building are ablaze. The police retreat to the fifth floor as rioters enter the building. When some of the crowd try following the police, the officers open fire, causing a momentary retreat.

During this respite and with the fire still not under control, panicky prisoners attempt to throw the accused Brown to the mob. The police restrain this attempt. For an hour the situation is one of continued mob cries and sporadic shooting from both sides. Firemen are unable to battle the flames due to threats and attacks. Then at about 11 P.M., a small band of rioters manages to climb into the building through a window and reach the fourth floor. At this time, they storm the stairwell to the fifth, and someone, either a fellow prisoner or guard, shoves Brown toward the attackers who pull him outside.[17]

By the time the mob gets its first view of Brown, he is entirely naked. He is grabbed and dragged across the street from the courthouse. Someone places a rope around his neck, and he is hung from a lamp post. Just as he is hoisted up, shots are fired into Brown's body. The shooting continues for some time until the body has been riddled by over one thousand bullets and shotgun pellets. Not content with the hanging and shooting, the mob cuts Brown's body down from the post and his remains are burned. With only the torso remaining, they then string it up to a streetcar pole where it is left.[18] The next day, federal troops are called into Omaha and much of the rejoicing over the lynching among many participants turns to fear as arrests are made and more threatened.[19]

The events leading to this lynching and the lynching itself were not extraordinary. As noted earlier, the Omaha lynch riot was only one of several which took place during the late summer and fall of 1919. On October 6, 1919, two black men, Jack Gordon and Will Brown, were burned at the stake and riddled with bullets near Lincolnton, Georgia. Following the burning, leaders of the mob insisted that the lynching in no way reflected hostility toward other blacks in the community.[20]

Since the Civil War, there have been approximately five thousand lynchings across the country.[21] Many of these have been community affairs; others have been by small bands of individuals or hate groups. The Omaha riot and lynching was not dissimilar from many of these.

TURBULENT SIXTIES

By the middle of the twentieth century, the struggle for racial and ethnic equality became known as the civil rights movement. The Supreme Court decision in *Brown versus Board of Education* (May 17, 1954), the Montgomery bus boycott in December of 1954, and other subsequent Supreme Court rulings and demonstrations thrust the American Dilemma before the public. It could no longer be ignored. The civil rights movement reached its climax on Tuesday, August 27, 1963, with the March on Washington. Blacks, Whites, Hispanics, Native Americans, Protestants, Catholics, Jews, the poor and the wealthy—more than two hundred thousand attended, demonstrated, and heard the address of Dr. Martin Luther King. As Dr. King stood before the Lincoln Memorial, he delivered the famous "I have a Dream" speech. It is interesting to note, however, that he did not begin with "I have a dream," As can be seen below, he stated, "I *still* have a dream." One cannot help but to reflect upon the effects of what seemed to be a protracted and often frustrating effort to achieve equality.

> I say to you today, my friends, though, even though we face the difficulties of today and tomorrow, I still have a dream. It is a dream deeply rooted in the American dream. . . .
>
> I have a dream that one day on the red hills of Georgia sons of former slaves and sons of former slave owners will be able to sit

down together at the table of brotherhood. I have a dream that one day even in the state of Mississippi, a state sweltering with the heat of injustice, sweltering with the heat of oppression, will be transformed into an oasis of freedom and justice.

. . .

When we allow freedom to ring—when we let it ring from every city and every hamlet, from every state and every city, we will be able to speed up that day when all of God's children, black and white men, Jews and Gentiles, Protestants and Catholics, will be able to join hands and sing in the words of the Negro spiritual, "Free at last, Free at last, Great God a' mighty. We are free at last."[22]

For millions of Americans, Dr. King's words were a source of inspiration. For others, they were a source of increased bitterness. Among some of the latter, the expression "Martin Lucifer King" was used to describe the civil rights leader. Even twenty–five years later, pejorative references to King can still be found. In the *Aryan Territorial Alliance News Letter,* Dr. King is referred as " . . . the big black nigger."[23]

But racist reaction did not need to wait twenty-five years. Less than three weeks after the March on Washington, on the morning of Sunday, September 15, children at the Sixteenth Street Baptist Church in Birmingham, Alabama, were just completing their Sunday school lesson when an explosion ripped through the classroom. Windows blew out, parts of walls and ceiling tore away, and chairs and tables went flying in every direction. Parents and friends rushed to aid those who had been in the wake of the blast. There the lifeless bodies of four young black girls were found. At least fifteen others had been hurt.[24] Fourteen years later, on Monday, September 26, 1977, Robert Chambliss, a former Ku Klux Klan member, was charged with the bombing and was subsequently convicted on four counts of first degree murder.[25]

The year following Dr. King's "I have a Dream" address, Congress enacted the Civil Rights Act of 1964 that prohibited various forms of discrimination. In the same year, urban violence erupted in at least seven cities—New York, Rochester, Jersey City, Paterson, Elizabeth, Chicago (Dixmoor), and Philadelphia. Five people were killed, 952 injured, and 2,484 arrested. Over 1,000 stores were damaged.[26]

The Watts Riot. In Los Angeles on another hot summer's night, August 11, 1965, Lee Minikus of the California Highway Patrol arrests Marquette Frye for driving recklessly and under the influence of alcohol. While Ronald, Marquette's brother, fetches his mother in order that she might claim the car, Minikus is joined by another patrolman. When Ronald and his mother return to the scene, Mrs. Frye chastises Marquette for drinking. At this moment, Marquette becomes hostile and resists arrest. Ronald joins his brother in resisting the officers. Now, Mrs. Frye, who a moment earlier had expressed disdain for Marquette's behavior, jumps on an officer's back. The scuffle ends with the arrest of all three Fryes.[27]

By 7:25, twenty minutes after Marquette's arrest, 1,000 or so citizens of the black area of Watts converge on the scene. As the police prepare to leave, someone spits on one of the officers. The officer moves in amongst the crowd; there is name–calling, threats, shoving, and pushing. A woman and a man are arrested. Again the police attempt to leave, but now one stone, then another, is hurled, rumors spread, and rioting ensues.[28] At riot's end, the results of Watts were similar to that of the Chicago riot forty–six years earlier. Thirty–four persons were killed, 1,032 reported being injured, and 600 buildings had been damaged by fire—200 totally.[29]

Newark, Detroit and the Nation. In the summer of 1967, rioting occurred in numerous cities throughout the United States. In Newark, New Jersey, 23 persons were killed during the rioting. Of these twenty–one were black, six were women, and two were children.[30] In Detroit, rioting resulted in 43 deaths.[31] Thirty–three were black and ten white. The deaths in Newark and Detroit accounted for approximately eighty percent of the fatalities from riots. As violence erupted throughout the United States, President Lyndon B. Johnson appointed a commission to investigate the civil unrest. Two days later, on July 29, he issued Executive Order 11365 directing the Commission to carry out its task and to report its findings.

The *Report of the National Advisory Commission on Civil Disorders* (also referred to as the Kerner Commission report) listed 164 disturbances during this hot summer of Sixty–seven.[32] Following an exhaustive investigation, the Commission stated in its summary:

> This is our basic conclusion: Our nation is moving toward two societies, one black, one white—separate and unequal.[33]

Almost a decade earlier, the Commission on Civil Rights (originally set up by President Harry S. Truman in 1948) had reported:

> What is involved here is the ancient warning against the division of society into Two Cities. . . . America . . . must succeed

where others have failed. It can do this not only by resolving to end
discrimination but also by creating through works of faith in freedom a clear and present vision of the City of Man, the one city of
free and equal man envisioned by the Constitution.[34]

The National Advisory Commission on Civil Disorders concluded with an excerpt from one of its early witnesses, Kenneth B.
Clark:

> I read that report . . . of the 1919 riot in Chicago and it is as if I
> were reading the report of the investigating committee on the
> Harlem riot of '35, the report of the McCone Commission on the
> Watts riot.
>
>   I must again say in candor to you members of the Commis-
> sion—it is a kind of Alice in Wonderland—with the same moving
> picture re-shown over and over again, the same analysis, the same
> recommendations, and the same inaction.[35]

Then in its own words, the Commission finishes its report with the
following:

> These words come to our minds as we conclude this Report. . . .
> we have uncovered no startling truths, no unique insights, no sim-
> ple solutions. The destruction and the bitterness of racial disorder,
> the harsh polemics of black revolution and white repression have
> been seen and heard before in this country.
>
>   It is now time to end the destruction and the violence, not only
> in the streets of the ghetto but in the lives of people.[36]

The decade of the sixties witnessed more civil rights legislation
than at any time since the end of slavery. But this period of turmoil
also included the assassinations of John F. Kennedy, Martin Luther
King, and Robert Kennedy, as well as numerous racial riots, murders, and bombings. The friction created by the American Dilemma
seemed to be overshadowed by other events. King, the main civil
rights leader, was dead, and his assassination began a chain of
events that led to the decline of the movement. With the advent of
the seventies, public attention was focused elsewhere, on Vietnam
and Watergate. As the decade of the eighties approached, the
stigma of having lost a war, international terrorism, hostage taking, inflation, and a recession dominated the national scene. Racial
violence occurred intermittently but not on the same scale as during the sixties.

A Kinder, Gentler America

Except for an occasional riot, the American public was virtually unaware of continued racial and ethnic murders, beatings, vandalism, and cross–burnings. When George Bush became President in 1989, he spoke of a kinder, gentler America. In this final year of the eighties, anti-racial and anti-ethnic prejudices accounted for no less than eight murders, eight bombings, eight arsons, 51 assaults (at least 20 by Skinheads), 30 cross–burnings, and over 110 acts of vandalism.[37] Of these, only two killings made national news and raised the hue and cry of increasing racial hatreds. These were the black powder–pipe bombing deaths of U.S. Circuit Court of Appeals Judge, Robert S. Vance in Mountain Brook, Alabama, on Saturday, December 16th, and Robert Robinson, a black attorney and alderman in Savannah, Georgia, on the following Monday.

Finally, on Wednesday, April 29, 1992, south central Los Angeles exploded into the worst rioting that had occurred since the sixties. The spark that ignited this riot was the acquittal of four Los Angeles police officers who had been charged with beating Rodney King. King had led police on a high speed chase. Upon apprehending him, King was not only beaten excessively, but someone actually taped the beating on a home video camera. When word of the acquittals was publicized, violence erupted in the south central area of Los Angeles.

The pattern was somewhat similar to riots of the past in terms of looting, burning, and fatalities. The rioters appeared to consist primarily of Latinos and blacks. Vengeance was exacted upon Korean store owners, whites, and other Latinos. A major target, at least verbally, was the police. By the time the riot was quelled approximately forty-five individuals had been killed and between 1500 and 2000 wounded. More than 1,200 businesses were destroyed.[38] Looters carried clothing, furniture, food, and anything else that they desired.

Since a number of looters (as many as four in five according to some estimates[39]) came from other areas of the city, and a number of whites appeared among them, the rioting appeared to be less racial. The fact is that racial and ethnic hatreds and its long range effects were indeed at the core of much of the violence. The violence was not limited to south central Los Angeles. Fires, rioting, and robberies spread to Hollywood, Beverly Hills, Westwood, and Koreatown. In downtown Los Angeles, violent demonstrations also occurred at the city hall and police headquarters. Beyond

Los Angeles, violence broke out in Las Vegas, Atlanta, and other cities.

One important aspect of the Rodney King case and riots is how Americans responded to both the verdict and the violence. Most Americans regardless of race and ethnicity indicated that the verdict of acquittal was a miscarriage of justice. But the responses of blacks were mainly emotional and tended toward overgeneralizing. Norman Amaker, a professor of law at Loyola University (Chicago), may have epitomized the feelings of many blacks and other minorities when he commented: "African–Americans will draw from this the lesson we've always known. Our lives aren't worth shit."[40] On the other hand, Roy Innis, Chairman of the Congress of Racial Equality stated,

> I don't believe that this one incident—the beating of Rodney King in Los Angeles and the miscarriage of justice . . . will turn back the real social revolution that we should be so proud of . . . I'm convinced that the romance America had with overt racism is over. . . . The justice system has protected and shielded us from the worst effects of prejudice and hate in the '50s and '60s. The judiciary has been the bulwark of black freedom in this country. Black America, and the rest of America, needs to hear from honest black leaders who will not attempt to alibi for the pillagers.[41]

Although Innis's remarks may appear more rational, he seemed to represent a minority view within the black leadership as well as the rank and file. Resentment and racial hatreds seem to have a stranglehold on race and ethnic relations in America, and violence continues through to the present. Could this be the kinder, more gentle world of which Mr. Bush spoke?

Let America Be America Again

Approximately 3,000 years ago, Koheleth wrote, "That which was, will be, and that what was done, it will be done, and there is nothing new under the sun."[42] In 1938, Langston Hughes wrote:

> Let America be America again
> Let it be the dream it used to be.
> Let it be the pioneer on the plain
> Seeking a home where he himself is free.
>
> (America was never America to me)

•••

O' let my land be a land where Liberty
Is crowned with no false patriotic wreath,
But opportunity is real, and life is free,
Equality in the air we breathe.

(There's never been equality for me,
Nor freedom in this "homeland of the free.")

Say who are you that mumbles in the dark?
And who are you that draws your veil across the stars?

I am the poor white, fooled and pushed apart,
I am the Negro bearing slavery's scars.
I am the red man driven from the land,
I am the immigrant clutching the hope I seek—
And finding only the same old stupid plan.
Of dog eat dog, of mighty crush the weak.

•••

Let America be America again—
The land that never has been yet—
And yet must be—the land where every man is free.[43]

America, a nation struggling to be free, and yet, somehow tied to an unforgiving past, a confused presence, and an uncertain future. All because of an imaginary line? Because of rumor, a spat? Or is it because of what we find in the hearts, minds, and hands of people regardless of when and where they are?

The roots of hate extend deep, round about the sinew and marrow of mankind—from the villages of Poland and Russia to the major cities and hamlets of America, from the now-vacated concentration camps of Europe to—it seems—every inhabited place on this planet. The legacy of the twentieth century will be whatever people select—from advanced technologies to landing men on the moon and beyond. But no civilized people can ignore the fact that genocide is a concept coined in this century. Now there is a label by which to categorize the mass murders of the Armenians, Jews, Kampuchians, and others—whose death tolls defy comprehension. A civilized people cannot ignore the groundswell of prejudice and the need to reduce these hatreds.

Any attempt to resolve the problems of prejudice and its manifestations—acts of bigotry—will require a thorough and somewhat painful exploration into the nature of prejudice and racial and ethnic violence—past and present, near and far. And perhaps most painful of all, it will require a look at who and what we are, as a society, as individuals, and as teachers. If this is not done, then surely there will be "nothing new under the sun," and we shall continue to be faced with "the same old stupid plan of dog eat dog, of mighty crush the weak."

Teaching About Hate

Some Missing Pages of History. Racial and ethnic prejudices and hatreds are deeply rooted in the American experience. To a large extent, these prejudices, hatreds, and acts of discrimination and violence form some of the missing pages of our history texts.

In 1629, the Massachusetts Bay Charter provided the framework for a colony which was to discriminate on the basis of religion.[44] In 1647, the colony prohibited Catholics from settling in Massachusetts Bay and called for the execution of any Jesuit who, once having been ousted, should return.[45] On the other hand, in predominantly Catholic Maryland, the Toleration Act of 1649 provided freedom of religion to all Christians,

> noe pson or psons whatsoever within this Province . . . belonging professing to believe in Jesus Christ, shall from henceforth bee any waies troubled, Molested, or discountenanced for or in respect of his or her religion nor in the free exercise thereof . . . thereunto belonging nor any way compelled to the beleife or exercise of any other Religion against his or her consent, . . . [46]

Nevertheless, this act was repealed after the colony became predominantly Protestant. Rights of Catholics were eventually restored, and only Jews and Unitarians were left without civil rights until the Blasphemy Act extended protection to all Christians.[47] It was not until 1826 that Jews were enfranchised.[48]

Historical figures, indeed American heroes, whom school children are taught to admire, held strong racial and ethnic prejudices. Inventor Samuel F. B. Morse became a staunch anti–Catholic and proposed that, to stem the threat of foreign Catholic immigrants, a law be passed that "No foreigner . . . ever be entitled to the right of suffrage."[49] Concerning American Indians, Teddy Roosevelt remarked, "I don't go so far as to think that the only good Indians are dead Indians, but I believe that nine out of every ten are, and I shouldn't like to inquire too closely into the case of the tenth." Then he added, "The most vicious cowboy has more moral principle than the average Indian."[50]

Before becoming president, Woodrow Wilson cautioned against diluting the white race in America by allowing southern and eastern Europeans into the United States.[51] Later as president, Wilson was invited to a private showing of *Birth of a Nation,* possibly the most racist anti-black film ever produced—depicting blacks as oversexed savages and the Ku Klux Klan as the savior of white civilization and women. After the showing, he reportedly commented, "It's like writing history with lightening, my only regret is that it is all so terribly true."[52]

During the early 1940s, Earl Warren, who, as Chief Justice of the Supreme Court, was to become the target of racists and segregationists, sounded the alarm of having Japanese-Americans on the western coast of the United States. Years later, Warren conceded, "I have since deeply regretted the removal order and my own testimony advocating it. . . . It was wrong to react so impulsively. . . . It demonstrates the cruelty of war when fear, get–tough military psychology, propaganda, and racial antagonism combine with one's responsibility for public security to produce such acts."[53] At this juncture, we well may ask how many children have been given the opportunity to learn about the treatment of Japanese Americans and to reflect upon the guilt expressed by such as Warren? Furthermore, how can children be expected not to repeat past mistakes and injustices if they are not privy to them?

In addition to neglecting these facts, most history texts fail to provide any comprehensive treatment of the social history of the United States. As the United States heads toward its third century, in all likelihood we can expect history textbooks to become more encyclopedic regarding details of earlier events and problems. Furthermore, given the commercial nature of texts, it is not surprising that they ignore less favorable aspects of the American experience. Few, if any nations, find it appealing to hang out their unsightly past. Consequently, when social problems are examined by students, it will be left to their teachers to compile, construct, and execute appropriate curricula on these issues.

PREJUDICE AND THE SOCIAL STUDIES

Indoctrination versus Freedom of Choice. Teaching about prejudice brings two goals to mind. One includes having students learn concepts and facts regarding prejudice and its effects. The other goal includes reducing prejudiced attitudes and changing behavior in a positive direction with regard to minorities or other groups. This latter goal implies a possible change in values and attitudes. In a multiethnic, democratic society, the teaching of values and attitudes presents a dilemma. It is a dilemma between the individual's right to have and maintain a set of personal values, regardless of social acceptance and expectations, and those values which society supports. The following is an attempt to identify this dilemma and to see how social studies educators have attempted to come to grips with it.

A primary role of education in any society is the socialization of children. This is nothing more nor less than indoctrination—a term which many American teachers associate with autocratic or totalitarian regimes. But the fact is that all societies indoctrinate. As Marion J. Rice notes,

> All societies indoctrinate—both in and out of school. This is the process of socialization. Socialization is prerequisite for an individual to live in a society; the vast majority of individuals must agree upon the rules and observe them or there would be no society. Undoubtedly there are many changes which need to be made in American society. But public schools are held in trust for all citizens, not just for the advocates of the status quo or of reform.[54]

In a homogeneous folkculture, there is no dilemma on what should be included in the educational curriculum for children. The members of such societies share the same Weltansehen, and divergence from the norm is controlled by a variety of social pressures placed upon the individual. Furthermore, contact with the outside world or with other cultures is often highly superficial and diffusion of cultural traits into the society are carefully screened. Finally, folkcultures are maintained by the lack of social change. The folkculture in its purest form is so alien to Americans that life within such a culture is almost inconceivable.

In a multicultural, democratic society there is a constant dilemma as to what children should learn and how they should be socialized. The dilemma would not be as acute if the society were democratic but not multiethnic, or if it were multiethnic but not democratic. An autocratic state can resolve the problem of diverse values and customs among different ethnic or racial groups by segregation and other acts of discrimination. A democratic society which is totally monolithic has no need to consider divergent folk-ways as there are no other groups present.

In the United States, there inevitably arises the problem of what Donald W. Oliver referred to as cultural unity versus cultural pluralism. Like Rice, Oliver points out that,

> Whether the teacher likes it or not, he is a socializing agent. He teaches the student how to work out his problem as an individual and makes him aware of the extent to which he must consider a common group framework and common group norms in approaching his individual problems.[55]

Oliver then defines a dilemma as it applies to American education,

> One dilemma is basic to this issue. The more common values we accept and teach and the more often we express an accepted cultural response at a particular point of choice, the greater cohesion there probably will be within the culture. On the other hand, the greater the variety allowed in expressing answers to cultural problems, the wider will be the area for individual choice and individual freedom.[56]

It is within the framework of this dilemma that teachers of social studies have had to somehow determine the operational goals of the curriculum, that on the one hand must foster socialization designed to actualize the American Creed, and on the other hand must permit the individual those freedoms of choice to accept any set of values or beliefs he/she desires.

If we were to operationalize the American Creed into goals for social studies education, that is, to seek to instill values expressed in the American Creed—liberty, justice, equality, self-determination, mutual respect, and so on—it may result in losses of these freedoms and rights as suggested by Oliver,

> To make American ideals a reality is to translate broad, vague, statements of liberty, equality, human dignity, achievement, and the like, into specific actions to be desired. Once this is done, ideology emerges, and education becomes the imposition of that ideology. The actual implementation of liberty and equality in terms of "action and skill" might well mean considerable losses in the very liberty we are trying to preserve.[57]

Oliver's proposed solution to the dilemma is to have students understand the American Creed at a general plane and permit them to reflect upon this at the personal level, thereby resulting in

"enlightened self-interest within a multivalue society."[58] He justi-
fies this bi-level or dual approach, as he calls it, by "the assumption
that, although liberty cannot be made a sacred value to all men, the
nation and form of government which will support and protect that
liberty can."[59]

This argument suggests that the best teachers can do is to
present students with the facts regarding prejudice and racism and
hope that their prior socialization in learning about, identifying
with, and integrating the American Creed into their attitudinal
structure will result in a less prejudiced set of attitudes. As we examine the goals offered for social studies education, we find an emphasis on decision–making skills, reflective inquiry, and, at the
same time, the expressed desire to have the student develop and accept democratic values. However, a straightforward indoctrination
of these values appears to be rejected outright by many educators.

THE GOALS OF SOCIAL STUDIES.

The current thought regarding the goals of social studies education is reflected by Peter H. Martorella among others. He speaks
of developing reflective, competent, and concerned citizens, to
whom he applies the metaphor of social studies as a matter of the
head, hand, and heart.[60] According to Martorella, the concerned citizen has

> an awareness of his/her rights and responsibilities, a sense of so-
> cial consciousness, and a well-grounded framework for deciding
> what is right and what is wrong. In addition, the concerned citizen
> has learned how to identify and analyze issues and to suspend
> judgment concerning alternate beliefs, attitudes, values, customs,
> and cultures.[61]

As for the competent and reflective citizen, Martorella suggests
that he/she have "social skills related to ... multicultural understanding" and "a knowledge of concepts, facts, and generalizations ... concerning individuals, groups, and societies. Also the
reflective citizen understands the processes of ... problem solving
and decision making."[62] Although his goals for social studies education are consistent with most social studies' curricula, they do not
address the problems teachers must face in challenging prejudiced
attitudes based upon a set of faulty and emotional "facts," "concepts," and "generalizations" held by the student prior to instruc-

tion. Martorella's notion of a multicultural understanding assumes a realistic understanding, not one distorted by misconceptions.

Not dissimilar from Oliver, Martorella falls back on core values previously learned by students. He presents a partial list of core values of American culture that Milton Rokeach reports are shared among people.[63] Among these is the value of equality. As an illustration, Martorella suggests that students might closely examine their attitudes toward minorities in conjunction with the commonly held value of "equality under the law." Displaying caution, his discussion falls short of asserting that if the student believes and feels strongly that all people should be treated equally under the law, then it follows that the student will oppose inequalities for minorities.

Core values also may include racist and/or ethnocentric values. It may be thought of as an Orwellian–like principle that all people are equal, but some are more equal than others. To many this principle is totally irrational, contradictory, and makes no sense at all. But to those holding conflicting values about equality for all and special cases for some, the principle makes all the sense in the world. Educators often act on the assumption that people are, by and large, rational, logical individuals. To the contrary, I would suggest that people like to think of themselves as rational and logical, but in matters of interpersonal and intergroup relations this often is not so.

According to Theodore Kaltsounis, "the main goal of social studies is to develop the student's ability to make decisions."[64] Kaltsounis assumes the rationality of people and more. He addresses the problem of racism by quoting from the 1973 yearbook of the National Council for the Social Studies,

> Institutional racism is pervasive in America. It adversely affects its perpetrators and victims. Racism causes majority groups to develop a sense of false superiority and confused identities and ethnic minority groups to inculcate feelings of inferiority and deflated self-concepts. In a racist society, all groups are unable to develop positive attitudes toward self and others. Racism is a dehumanizing and destructive social phenomenon which must be critically analyzed in the classroom if we are to develop a more just society.[65]

Kaltsounis ignores the concepts—prejudice, discrimination, and scapegoating, and instead, focuses his discussion on the need for learning about various ethnic groups. This is the same approach taken in the yearbook, *Teaching Ethnic Studies: Concepts and*

Strategies.[66] Although it is not explicitly stated in his treatment of the problem of racism, the following suggestions for multiethnic studies imply that Kaltsounis would have us believe that merely learning about other cultures will somehow tackle the problem of racism. On the other hand, Martorella has intimated that students should examine problems of discrimination and racism against the student's values of equality and justice. While neither may be sufficient, the latter is probably the best we can expect from a general discussion on the goals of social studies education in a multiethnic, democratic society.

The dilemma for educators is more apparent when one examines the work of Shirley H. Engle and Anna S. Ochoa. They stress the need for citizens in a democracy to be "skilled and responsible decision makers."[67] They even state that children "should come to have a more reasoned understanding of democracy, including such ideas as . . . the protection of minority rights and opinions; freedom of press, freedom of religion, . . . "[68] However, as for teaching values, Engle and Ochoa state that "Indoctrination of values is the mode of authoritarianism."[69] Yet, as noted earlier, all societies indoctrinate. Although Engle and Ochoa hold that human dignity is the most basic value in a democracy,[70] they seem ambivalent about directly imposing this value upon students.

What we gather from these social studies educators is a commitment toward the democratic ideal that precludes the teaching of values in catechistic manner. As for teaching about prejudice, it seems the treatment these educators would embrace is to present information, have students reflect upon it, and resolve what is right or is wrong on their own. Of course, this requires that the children will have to be provided with instruction in developing the critical thinking and study skills that permit reflective inquiry. It also requires that teachers insure sufficient time for reflection. Unfortunately, under the pressures of time constraints, many teachers substitute discussions for reflection. Notwithstanding that educators have encouraged the teaching of reflective inquiry and critical thinking, many classrooms in America continue to neglect these topics of instruction.

Another problem seldom addressed is that some students will adhere to a set of propositions which will guide their thinking on all aspects of an issue. For example, some students may attach themselves to the belief that any foreign intervention by one country into the affairs of another is wrong. Therefore, regardless of the facts of a given conflict situation, these students constantly will seek information which supports their convictions. Social studies educators who support the development of rational and objective decision makers are speaking of an ideal goal and not one that is necessarily a reflection of the current state of our curriculum and the educational development of our children.

When it comes to teaching about prejudice or any critical social issue, perhaps the best we can do is to accept the reality of the situation and give it our best effort. The bottom line is simply that students who have accepted strong racist beliefs may or may not modify them after examining and reflecting upon evidence related to prejudice and racism. This is especially true when a student's religious dogma is the basis for such beliefs. When this is the case, the teacher has no right to chastise or ridicule the student. For example, a student may believe that all people must be treated equally. But the student also may believe that this only applies to the off-spring of Adam and Eve and not to Jews, who, according to some racist beliefs, are the offspring of the Devil when he raped Eve. Or a student might hold the belief that equality does not apply to blacks because they are sub-human and descended from apes.[71]

TEACHING ABOUT PREJUDICE

Resolving the Dilemma and Identifying Values. As social studies teachers committed to resolving the American Dilemma, to creating a better world, a more kind and gentle world, we might ask how social education can work toward achieving these goals if we fail to explore the roots of intergroup rivalries and hatreds. Do we expect a doctor to prescribe a cure for an illness without a knowledge of the causes? Of course not.

At its most rudimentary level, education designed to understand and reduce racial and ethnic prejudices requires at least two areas of emphasis. One is an examination of the feelings, beliefs, and behaviors of members of ethnic and racial groups for the purpose of understanding how and why groups and individuals of different creeds interact. The other area of emphasis seeks to achieve a reduction of prejudiced attitudes and behavior and to engage the student in critical inquiry into the causes, condition, and effects of racism and other forms of prejudice, discrimination, and scapegoating.

Values. If education is to improve social relationships, it must serve as a change agent. By definition, any goal which seeks to change some aspect of society implies a value judgment and a value base. Undergirding the study of prejudice for the purposes mentioned above is the basic value that all people, regardless of race, creed, gender, national origin, and religion have the basic human rights to life, dignity, and equal worth.[72]

The fact cannot be hidden that, in the study of intergroup relations and the nature of prejudice, there inevitably emerges the question of rights and wrongs. Prejudice, aggression (from name-calling to genocide), and discrimination in employment, housing, education, and public accommodations, are wrongs. Nevertheless, it must be stressed that students must be given the opportunity to discover this on their own within a value analysis mode. However, for students with very limited understandings, there should be no objection if the teacher indicates that the negative aspects of prejudiced beliefs and behavior are "wrongs" when such beliefs lead to violations of human dignity or the law. Not every child is a reflective, concerned, or competent citizen.

Goals and Needs. In empirical and applied educational research, the goals of a given educational treatment (novel curriculum design or unit of study) often are designed to create a change in the student. In fact, some, but certainly not all, teachers hold that that is what teaching is all about—changing a student by providing her or him with new knowledge, skills, or attitudes. The goals of teaching about prejudice include cognitive (knowledge), affective (feeling), and conative (behavior) objectives. The latter consists of both the development of critical thinking skills and behavioral changes in the students' interaction with members of other groups.

In order to bring about these changes, the teacher is faced with an exciting and complex task. Unlike teaching about a historical event that largely is limited to adding to the students' cognitive structures, teaching about prejudice involves changing fixed beliefs and feelings. For many teachers this task requires (1) developing a new knowledge base regarding the nature of prejudice, discrimination, and aggression, as well as the roots of racism and other related beliefs; (2) coming to grips with various levels of prejudices from the mild to the extreme; (3) learning how to deal successfully with combined student prejudices and sensitivities without threatening the student; (4) understanding the nature of attitudes and attitude change from a social–psychological perspective; and (5) being able to develop and execute teaching strategies designed to help students examine and critically evaluate hardcore hate groups, their literature, actions, and philosophies.

Overview of the Remaining Chapters

This book was structured to provide a conceptual framework and knowledge base regarding ethnic groups, the nature of race and racism, prejudice and stereotyping, discrimination and aggression, and hate groups and individuals who promote ethnic and racial hatreds. In order to accomplish this, chapter 2 deals with ethnicity and the nature of ethnic groups. For it is groups of people and their individual members who constitute the perpetrators and victims of ethnic and racial violence. In the discussion of ethnicity and ethnic groups, a paradigm will be presented that offers an alternate way in which to define and analyze the nature of ethnicity. To some extent this paradigm and the meaning of ethnicity may challenge the preconceptions of some. And while it may not be flawless, it does attempt to come to grips with one of the most elusive and yet basic concepts in intergroup relations.

The concepts of race and racism have played a salient role in the development of ethnic and race relations over the past centuries. Yet few people really understand race and its limitations as a scientific concept, and the word racism has been so widely and carelessly used during the preceding decade that its meaning and usefulness have been greatly diminished. Nevertheless, racism is one of the greatest causes of intergroup strife and dissension. For these reasons, chapters 3 and 4 are dedicated to the exploration of race as a scientific and as a social concept (racism), respectively.

Chapters 5 and 6 discuss the topics of prejudice, attitude, stereotyping, and related concepts. These topics and related concepts form the basic foundations of understanding one's perceptions of reality and her or his predisposition to act toward others. These chapters provide both, theoretical perspectives and empirically researched findings, related to the topics discussed.

Chapter 7 addresses problems of racial and ethnic discrimination and aggression. It is the acting out of prejudiced attitudes that scars the body, mind, and soul of its victim. At the same time, the overt expression of hostility guides the perpetrator closer to becoming an ignoble creature, not unlike the one described in Crane's poem as naked and bestial. This chapter will address various forms of aggression stemming from prejudices and ranging from jokes and name–calling to murder.

Once we have explored the nature of ethnic groups, race and racial thought (racism), prejudice, attitudes and stereotyping, and discrimination and aggression, we shall be able to move into the circle of hate in its more virulent forms. In chapter 8, we leave the theoretical and historical and come face to face with hate groups and individual purveyors of racial and ethnic hate—from the teen-age Skinhead to the Pastor of an Identity Church, from the school teacher teaching children that the Holocaust was a "Holohoax" to the rise and fall of the Silent Brotherhood, who committed robbery and murder in the name of racial purity.

These chapters should not be regarded merely as background material for teachers. The concepts, events, and stories described can be useful in identifying material for classroom use by students. Indeed, even the accounts presented in this chapter may be considered for reflective inquiry among students. Therefore, I have attempted to include a healthy number of illustrations and short case studies. In addition, I have taken the liberty to include a number of endnotes that supplement the main text.

Throughout the book most case studies and examples will focus upon the black and Jewish experience. Although there are many groups that have been victimized, blacks and Jews remain the most salient and sustained targets of organized and individual hate. In 1979 there were 129 acts of vandalism, harassments, threats, and assaults reported against Jews. By 1991 this annual total reached almost 2,000.[73] Furthermore, approximately ninety percent of all hate literature published during the past 15 years has been directed at blacks and Jews. Indeed, a 1992 issue of the *White Patriot* published by the Knights of the Ku Klux Klan lists 28 recommended publications. Of these, four are anti-black racist publications and twenty-one are unmistakably anti-Semitic.[74]

The main function and purpose of this book is to deal conceptually with prejudice and its various manifestations. It is not designed to be a case study approach covering all acts, perpetrators, and victims of hate. For those seeking detailed case studies and background information on particular groups and their experiences the reader should refer to works dedicated to particular groups or events such as the genocide of Armenians, Kampuchians or the events of the Holocaust. As for detailing the literature of hate groups and their activities, this is provided in greater depth since such information is seldom or readily found in libraries.

The final chapter is entitled "Teaching about Hate Prejudice and Violence." Here we shall attempt to reexamine the issues and concepts presented in the earlier chapters and to reflect upon their implications for social education. Some suggestions will be presented as guidelines for developing instructional experiences related to the central problems addressed in this work.

Earlier in this chapter, I stated that any attempt to resolve prejudice and its manifestations—acts of bigotry—will require a thorough and somewhat painful exploration into the nature of prejudice and racial and ethnic violence—past and present, near and far. And perhaps most painful of all, it will require a look at who and what we are as people. Upon the completion of this book, the challenge for presenting students with the problems stemming from hate prejudice and racism will be in the hand, the mind, and the heart of the teacher.

CHAPTER 2

ETHNIC GROUPS

Ethnic is an adjective, and English never adopted a noun from the Greek ethnos [native or race]. The lack of a convenient substantive form has induced many writers to coin a number of makeshifts, all of which have their drawbacks.

—William Petersen
"Concepts of Ethnicity"

In order to deal intelligently with the nature of hate prejudice as a critical social issue, it is necessary to understand the human targets of hate prejudice and violence. These targets consist of racial and ethnic groups. In this chapter we shall explore the nature and social processes of ethnic groups whose members at one time or another may be victims or perpetrators of hate prejudice and violence. Race will be discussed both as a biological and a social concept in the following chapters.

After more than a half-century of use among social scientists, the concept of ethnic group remains without a universally accepted definition. This chapter, therefore, begins with a brief discussion of the lack of consensus on the meaning of ethnic group followed by an attempt to offer a definition that is both meaningful and useful.

The Lack of Consensus on the Meaning of Ethnic Group

In 1989, Ringer and Lawless suggested that, given the large number of examples of ethnicity, " . . . it would seem that the question, 'What is an ethnic group?' would be easy to answer by now. And yet, the opposite is true. Shorn of its denotative and descriptive concreteness, the term takes on an elusive, mystical, and frequently romanticized character."[1]

In order to present the problem of defining ethnic within a meaningful context, it is helpful to note Harold A. Larrabee's observation that, when dealing with social issues, there is a constant collision of the cognitive and the affective.[2] The study of any social issue, then, may be perceived as involving a combination of knowledge and feelings as if they are different fibers of the same rope. This is especially true when dealing with such concepts as ethnicity, pluralism, race, prejudice, and discrimination.

Possibly the most complete compendium on ethnicity in America is the *Harvard Encyclopedia of American Ethnic Groups,* published in 1980. In their introduction, editors Thernstrom, Orlov, and Handlin, readily admit the work required a definition of an ethnic group, but this was "no simple matter because there is as yet no consensus about the precise meaning of ethnicity . . . "[3] Although failing to offer a precise definition of ethnic group, Thernstrom, et al. identify fourteen attributes used in their selection of groups for review in the encyclopedia with the following qualification: "All groups treated here are characterized by some of the following features, although in combinations that vary considerably." These include:

1. common geographic origin;
2. migratory status;
3. race;
4. language;
5. religious faith or faiths;
6. ties that transcend kinship, neighborhood, and community boundaries;
7. shared traditions, values, symbols;
8. literature, folklore, and music;
9. food preferences;
10. settlement and employment patterns;
11. special interests in regard to politics in the homeland and the United States;
12. institutions that specifically serve and maintain the group;
13. an internal sense of distinctiveness;
14. an external perception of distinctiveness.[4]

Although they made a definite contribution to the literature on ethnicity and ethnic relations, the editors were criticized by Simpson and Yinger, who suggested that Thernstrom, et al. were too inclusive and possibly motivated by the socio–political climate of the time in treating racial groups as ethnics. They state, "This doubtless expresses [on the part of Thernstrom et al.] a desire to oppose racial discrimination . . . "[5]

This also seems to be the concern of William Petersen. Within the *Harvard Encyclopedia of American Ethnic Groups,* Petersen's discussion on the "Concepts of Ethnicity" also supports Larrabee's observations regarding the dilemma of seeking precise meanings in the social studies. Petersen's response to his rhetorical question, "Why, contrary to almost every informed opinion, have recent years seen a reassertion of ethnicity?"[6], further illustrates a concern that social concepts and processes often are subject to the political orientations of social scientists. Further, he notes that the definition and nature of ethnicity have been manipulated in an attempt to conform with political "policy, to disguise the very existence of racial differences."[7]

It is also useful, in attempting to define ethnic group, to cite Kaplan's suggestion, as does Petersen. According to Kaplan, problems stemming from the lack of precise meanings should not prevent attempts to pursue novel explanations and to establish models for understanding. Social scientists are often obsessed with defining concepts precisely. In doing so, they often ignore phenomena which may challenge this precision. Kaplan states,

> There is a certain kind of behavioral scientist who, at the least threat of an exposed ambiguity, scurries for cover like a hermit crab into the nearest abandoned logical shell. But there is no ground for panic. That a cognitive situation is not as well-structured as we would like does not imply that no inquiry made in that situation is really scientific. On the contrary, it is the dogmatisms outside science that proliferate closed systems of meaning; the scientist is in no hurry for closure. Tolerance of ambiguity is as important for creativity in science as it is anywhere else.[8]

Ethnic Groups: In Search of Meaning

One commonly accepted, albeit general, definition of ethnic group is *any group sharing a common culture and feeling of kind or oneness.* Just what this might include is expressed in Brewton Berry's definition from the early 1950s. Berry defined an ethnic group as, a human group bound together by ties of cultural homogeneity. Complete uniformity, of course, is not essential; but here does prevail in an ethnic group a high degree of loyalty and adherence to certain basic institutions, such as family patterns, religion, and language. The ethnic group often possesses distinctive folkways and mores, customs of dress, art, and ornamentation, moral codes and value systems, and patterns of recognition. . . . Above all, there is a consciousness of kind, a we–feeling.[9]

Following his definition, Berry points out that many groups will focus on some but not all of the above-mentioned characteristics. In some cases, these one or two salient features may be the only major differences between groups. Religion may be the salient binding attribute for some groups, while language or a common recent history serve to unite others. Religion plays a significant factor among some ethnic Mormons, Moslems, Hutterite Brethrens, Armenians, and Old Order Amish. Often this salient factor is most apparent when two groups are in conflict. In Northern Ireland, the political struggle between Catholics and Protestants keys on the religious salient to the point that Jews are categorized as either Protestant Jews or Catholic Jews.[10]

In the case of blacks or African Americans, the salient is neither religious nor racial, although select physical traits may be used as social indicators of group membership. Rather, it is a common, relatively recent, historical experience that has resulted in the creation of this group. In actuality, African Americans have a diverse African ancestry, and an estimated eighty percent of African Americans have some white or Native American ancestry.[11] Yet many members of this group have little or no factual knowledge of their specific African heritage.

General labels such as Negro, African American, or black did not come into common usage among African slaves until after their arrival in America. Even white slaveholders in South Carolina demonstrated a preference for Bambara and Malinka ethnics over the Igbo, indicating an awareness that not all Africans were the same.[12] Nevertheless, a common history of victimization, including chattel slavery, followed by segregation, discrimination, and acts of violence, provides a salient bond among many of today's African Americans. This bond, of course, is reinforced by an imposed social concept of race.

In search of a precise meaning of ethnic group, one finds Berry's definition to be virtually synonymous with Henry Pratt Fairchild's composite definition of nationality. Is ethnic group merely a new term for an older and more traditionally used concept? And if so, why? As Ringer and Lawless suggested, the concepts of ethnic group certainly seemed to take on "an elusive, mystical, and frequently romanticized character." The relationship between ethnic group and nationality may provide a basis for delineating the meaning of ethnic group.

Ethnicity and Nationality

One of the most comprehensive definitions of nationality based upon a variety of sources is provided by Fairchild:

> A human group bound together by specific ties of cultural homogeneity. A true nationality is animated by a consciousness of kind (q.v.) and has a fundamental similarity in its mores (q.v.). There need not be, and seldom is, complete uniformity in all cultural traits; but there must be conformity, or at least sympathy and cooperation, with reference to a number of the basic institutions such as language, religion, dress, and ornamentation, recreation, moral code, political system, family pattern and ethical ideas (q.v.). The members of a nationality feel a bond of sympathy to each other different from that they experience toward the members of another nationality. They desire to share a common life. This desire may not be realized, but as long as it exists it serves to give reality to the nationality. . . . Political unification is not an essential component of nationality.[13]

If we accept Berry's definition of ethnic group and compare it with Fairchild's concept of nationality, the two concepts can be treated as interchangeable. However, Fairchild distinguishes between nationality and nation. He states that a nation would consist of a nationality or ethnic group which has founded or achieved statehood—a political structure within a defined geographic area.[14] Within the context stipulated by Fairchild, a nationality may be spread over a number of states with various degrees of concentration.

In the United States, some nationalities are more heavily concentrated in specific regions. Hispanics from Mexico are most prominent in the Southwest and West, including Texas, New Mexico, Arizona, Colorado, and California. The bulk of German communities extends across the northern United States with relatively few communities found in the southeastern states. Norwegian communities are found primarily in the northern Midwest. Notwithstanding these concentrations, members of various nationalities are found throughout most of the United States.[15]

In what was formerly the Soviet Union, specific norady (ethnic groups or nationalities) tended to be more concentrated in previously independent territories, including the Union Republics of Latvia, Lithuania, and Estonia. Twenty Autonomous Soviet Socialist Republics (ASSR's) or subdivisions of Union Republics were established upon ethnic lines. All but the ASSR of Dagestan reflected ethnic names (e.g., Mari, Mordovia, Yakut, Tatar). The Dagestan area of the Caucasus contained so many diverse groups that the geographic name of the area was used to identify it. A number of ASSRs had experienced ethnic changes to the point that some of the formerly dominant ethnic groups numbered in the minority.[16] On the other hand, the relative lack of diffusion of other nationalities became apparent at the Union Republic level during the beginning of 1990 when Latvia, Lithuania, Armenia, Georgia, Azerbaijan, and other former and quasi–states asserted their independence, causing fear among non-nationals in these territories.

The origin of the use of ethnic group among social scientists seems to stem either from a common popular misunderstanding of nationality or the desire to distinguish between a larger society and distinct cultural groups residing within it. Although a nationality may be divorced from the concept of state, it often is thought of as a political concept. In addition, an individual may belong in some measure to a mass-nationality within a political territory (e.g., the United States) and still retain a sense of nationality based upon other cultural traits or ancestry (e.g., second generation Italian–Americans). With the introduction of "ethnic group," social scientists and historians could classify individuals according to cultural distinctions within a larger society.

Ethnic Group as a Subsociety

As early as 1937, a definition of ethnic group expressed the notion of a subsociety " . . . living together within an alien civilization but remaining culturally distinct."[17] In his seminal work, *Assimilation in American Life,* Milton Gordon stipulates the meaning of ethnic group "to refer to a type of group contained within national boundaries of America, I shall mean by it any group which is defined or set off by race, religion, or national origin, or some combination of these categories."[18] This concept of an ethnic group as a subsociety raises the question as to how one treats an entire nation or state society. For example, are Saudis a nation and not an ethnic group? Or are they both—an ethnic group that has achieved statehood?

Twenty-five years following Gordon's work, Ringer and Lawless point to the confusion between a nation and an ethnic group. Referring to Gordon and others, they state, "A number of these observers however seem to be inconsistent in this usage [of nation as a state society, and cannot quite make up their minds whether to include or to exclude the nation from the category of ethnic group."[19] Without resolving the problem, Ringer and Lawless elect to "confine the term ethnic group to subgroups, subsocieties, or even subnations within the more general state society or nation–state."[20]

The implication of this selection is that the mass culture of the United States, or the dominant, mass culture of any other state, would not be regarded as an ethnic group. By disregarding the mass culture, one can argue that a multiethnic state is merely a conglomeration of many cultural or ethnic groups. In turn, this assertion could be politicized by special interest groups representing various ethnicities, each striving for domination within the political, economic, and social structure. However, there seems to be no apparent reason why an ethnic group cannot be regarded as either a distinct subsociety or a dominant, mass culture that has achieved statehood.

In the following section, a model is provided that disregards the ideation that ethnic group only refers to distinct subsocieties within a larger society. Furthermore, while the discussion and controversies over the nature and meaning of ethnic group probably will not be resolved in the near future, the paradigm attempts to move us beyond the definition stage and toward an examination of the complexities of ethnicity and ethnic affiliation.

A Paradigm: Defining Ethnic Group

Earlier, we noted Kaplan's view of the social scientist who, "at the least threat of an exposed ambiguity, scurries for cover like a hermit crab into the nearest abandoned logical shell." A number of scholars seem to have taken this route by shying away from the problems and complexities of attempting to expand and improve upon what we mean by an ethnic group. In the following paradigm, the definition of ethnic group is essentially the same as stipulated by Berry in the fifties. This definition provides the infrastructure for the paradigm.

The paradigm consists of five categories and an explanation of how they are interrelated. The categories are, (a) ethnic group, (b) subethnic group, (c) composite ethnic group, (d) individuals or groups of heritage, and (e) groups of faith. A major caveat regarding the model is warranted. Since groups and individuals are in the process of change, definitive categorization may be difficult at a given time and place.

Ethnic Group: First Category

ETHNIC GROUP DEFINED.

An ethnic group or "ethnos" consists of individuals who share a distinct culture and are "bound together by ties of cultural homogeneity"[21] that result in a common way of perceiving, thinking, feeling, and interacting with reality. By distinct culture, we include a group's cultural traits and complexes such as language, religion, mores, moral code, ethical ideals, dress, ornamentation, recreation, diet, family patterns, political orientation, social roles, stratification, and status. Cultural homogeneity is the collective and organized body of cultural traits. It creates strong social and psychological bounds that influence cognitive, affective, and behavioral processes among group members. These processes combine with life experiences (often involving contact with outgroups) to influence cultural traits and complexes.

Group of Inclusion and Unitary Membership. This definition of ethnic group is exemplified by such groups having strong, viable bonds within distinct cultural pockets (Italian, Arab, Vietnamese, etc.). It also includes distinct national groups that are dominant in a society as ethnic groups (e.g., Saudis in Saudi Arabia, Americans in the United States, Poles in Poland).

Furthermore, according to this definition, membership in one ethnos precludes membership in other ethnic groups. However, this does not deny individual loyalties for more than one group. For example, in the Middle East, ethnic Druze traditionally maintain strong political loyalties in their state of residence. Those in Syria are loyal to the Syrian government, and Israeli Druzes hold strong Israeli loyalties. As a consequence, the Druze have engaged in combat on opposing sides. At the same time, these people have strong in-group ties; endogamy is enforced, and outsiders are not permitted membership. Local autonomy is a major factor among Druze and, if threatened, may result in alienation from their state of residence.

Nor does membership in one ethnic group deny the fact that an individual may *feel* or *believe* that he or she is a member of two or more groups. In a given social context, a member of one ethnic group may share strong other-group loyalties and a sense of oneness of kind. Although a person can identify with the heritage of one or more ethnic groups in addition to his/her own, it does not make that person a member of the other ethnos.

Mixed Heritage: A Hypothetical Illustration. None of the above situations means that the individual is actually a member of two distinct ethnic groups. For example, if "I–P" were the offspring of an Irish and Polish couple, the extent to which "I–P" is Irish or Polish will be determined by "I–P" 's cultural cohesiveness or the cultural homogeneity to one group or the other. "I–P" cannot maintain cultural homogeneity with both groups simultaneously. If this were possible, the two cultures, Irish and Polish, would not be distinct from one another. The fact that "I–P" may have learned the ways of both groups may result in this individual being able to "pass" as a member of either group, but "I–P" probably will be Irish of Polish heritage, Polish of Irish heritage, or, in the United States, American of Irish–Polish heritage. Of course, there are other possible outcomes as will be discussed later under subethnic and composite ethnic groups.

Dual Loyalties. Even when a member of an ethnic group holds two sets of loyalties, one for the state with its dominant culture or ethnos and one for the individual's immediate ethnic group, this does not constitute membership in two ethnic groups. Political citizenship and loyalties should not be confused with ethnicity. Satmar Hassidim, of the Williamsburg section of New York City, are American citizens and engage when necessary with other Americans, but they share little or no salient cultural traits with members of mass–American society.[22]

Nor does the individual switch back and forth between groups from one moment to the next. However, it is possible for a person to "appear" to switch ethnic roles or "wear the mask."[23] Furthermore, a member of an ethnic group can have a positive attitude toward a somewhat alien mass–society whose values, beliefs, and behaviors are not acceptable within the individual's immediate ethnic group.

Symbolic and Pseudo Ethnicity. When the social order permits people to assimilate without restrictions, it is possible for individuals to voluntarily identify with a particular ethnos. This seems to be the case with many white Americans. Herbert Gans coined the term, symbolic ethnicity, to refer to the selection of an ethnic identity based upon one's real or imagined heritage.[24] In such cases, individuals choose to identify with a particular group "as more or less a leisure activity."[25] They also select those folkways that are convenient and do not interfere with their normal life–styles or goals.[26] Gans views symbolic ethnicity as an illusion that does not reduce the process of assimilation and the eventual absorption of ethnic groups into the American mainstream.

According to J. Milton Yinger, Gans's concept of symbolic ethnicity is synonymous with his, Yinger's, concept of "imagined ethnicity" and McKay's "pseudo–ethnicity."[27] However, McKay distinguishes between symbolic ethnicity and his concept of pseudo–ethnicity by pointing out that the latter is often a political tool, "[these] more closely resemble interest groups or social movements than ethnic groups per se."[28] This distinction and the fact that groups may claim ethnicity for political reasons may have serious implications in studying the socio–political landscape in the United States.

The test of one's ethnic valency to a group, whether that valency is symbolic, pseudo, or real often occurs when major conflicts surface between ethnic groups (e.g., one's immediate group and a mass–society). In such conflict situations, some individuals may opt to abandon their immediate group, leave the field—flee, or resist— even to the point of martyrdom. Finally, social interaction between or among ethnic groups may lead to the formation of subethnic, composite, or entirely new ethnic groups.

SUBETHNIC GROUPS: SECOND CATEGORY

Subethnic groups exist within dominant ethnic groups or along-side other subethnic groups **of the same genera.** Subethnic groups share a common culture and maintain a sense of cultural homogeneity, but they vary to the extent that one sub–group may be distinguished from another in some cultural traits. The nature of subethnic groups can be rather complicated, as in the case of Anabaptists.

Old Order Amish, Mennonites, and Hutterites may be viewed as separate ethnic groups or as subethnic groups of Anabaptists, depending upon how particular communities view themselves in relation to others. In some cases, Old Order Amish might be considered a subethnic group of the Mennonite.

Within the Hutterite community, Schmiedeleut, Dariousleut, Lehrerleut, and Arnoldleut make up four subethnic groups. Each of these subethnic groups is made up of colonies unified under a Leut. The Leut is "the largest unit within which there is both a means and a moral obligation to settle disputes."[29] Separate subethnic groups (e.g., Schmiedeleut) prefer endogamous or in–Leut marriages.

As these groups are quite distinct from mass-American culture, they would not constitute a subethnic group of the American ethnos. On the other hand, there are some more "liberal" Mennonite communities that might be more accurately regarded as subethnic American, Mennonite Americans, or Americans of the Mennonite Faith (see Groups of Faith, below) than within the traditional Mennonite community.

Formation of Subethnic Groups. A subethnic group may be formed as a result of breaking from a main ethnic body. This may be due to political, social, or ideological, internal conflicts, or it may occur as a result of geographic isolation. In any case, the subethnic group **must maintain cultural homogeneity with the larger, more general group or lateral group.** This is much different from the concept of a particular ethnic group being a sub-group of a larger **alien** mass society or culture.

Members of an ethnic group, who migrate to a new land, may adopt cultural traits that distinguish them from their original generic ethnic group. Yet, if cultural homogeneity with the original group is maintained, these people may form a subethnic group of the original. For example, an American *Cambodian* would be Cambodian but distinguished from Cambodians residing in other states by certain American traits. Should these American *Cambodians* or their descendants continue to assimilate into American culture, they might form what is best described as Cambodian *Americans*. This group would be primarily American—culturally homogeneous with Americans—but would retain a sufficient number of Cambodian traits to make them somewhat distinctive from other Americans. As a group, they may be regarded as an American subethnos— Cambodian *American*.[30] Traditional Cambodian culture at this level of assimilation would be somewhat alien to such people, and there would be little basis for viewing them as belonging to the Cambodian ethnos. When these people assimilate and amalgamate (biological assimilation) even more, they may become Americans of Cambodian heritage or they may form a composite ethnic group.

The more an ethnic or subethnic group integrates the cultural traits of an alien ethnos into its own structure, the more its distinctiveness will be obscured until the group becomes culturally extinct or emerges as an entirely new group. The interaction between distinct groups may lead to the formation of composite ethnic groups.

THE COMPOSITE ETHNOS: THIRD CATEGORY

From the earliest times, people have lived in groups, set off from others. They also have engaged in both violent and peaceful means of crossing group boundaries. Whenever and wherever ethnic groups encounter each other, some form of cultural and biological assimilation and the diffusion of cultural traits usually occurs.

Intergroup contact over a period of time often results in exogamous marriages and offspring of mixed ethnicity may constitute a composite ethnic group. As long as ethnically mixed individuals of the composite group do not assimilate into another existing ethnic group, a new ethnos or subethnic group may emerge. The new ethnos will be characterized by the development of customs, institutions, and other social and cultural traits.

Individuals of mixed ethnicity may assimilate into one of the original ethnic groups, or they may assimilate into a dominant, state or mass ethnos—totally disassociating themselves from one or both former groups. In another instance, a person might assimilate into one group and maintain a sense of identity with the other. (See Individuals or Groups of Heritage, below). In the United States, most individuals and groups have tended to follow the latter course of assimilation rather than form a new ethnos.

American Ethnos and Cultural Change. Finally, and perhaps the most difficult to comprehend, is the transition of a major, dominant ethnos into a composite ethnos and back into itself. American culture in the United States represents what might be a composite ethnic group. In the past, it may have been possible to define American culture with some accuracy as predominantly white, English (or Western European), and Protestant, with a set of basic monolithic values, beliefs, and social patterns. Today, this is hardly the case. As the recipient of cultural traits from a variety of cultures, a constant influx of ethnic group members from throughout the world, and the influence of rapid technological advances, American mass culture is in an intense state of social and cultural change.

A complete and accurate description of American ethnicity is probably impossible. Certainly one can identify a variety of current basic institutions, beliefs, values, traditions, and customs that seemingly are shared by Americans. But the extent to which these actually are shared by the masses, and the extent to which they will remain somewhat stable for any appreciable length of time is unknown. What differentiates this type of composite ethnos from others is the fact that, as a mass dominant culture, the American ethnos appears to be experiencing a voluntary metamorphosis. This may explain why some observers have attempted to refute the current understanding of America as a "melting pot" and have suggested the concept of a multicultural state void of any dominant or national ethnos.

INDIVIDUALS OR GROUPS OF HERITAGE: FOURTH CATEGORY

The descriptions of ethnic, subethnic, and composite groups do not address all of those who identify with a particular ethnic, national, or religious heritage. Nor do they address the mass of individuals who are in the process of assimilating into other groups. Millions of American citizens are primarily members of the dominant American culture but regard themselves as members of some other ethnic group. These are individuals who maintain an affinity for their heritage of past generations but who think, value, behave, and perceive reality as members of ethnos Americanus.

These individuals are Americans of whatever other cultural heritage with which they identify—e.g., American of Hispanic heritage, Greek heritage, etc.. Similarly, Amish, Jews, and Mormons, who are assimilated to the level that they perceive, think, value, and behave American, are identified as Americans of Amish, Jewish, or Mormon heritage.

Subethnics and Of Ethnic Heritage. The subethnic Italian in America would maintain Italian cultural homogeneity and traits— perceive Italian, value Italian, and interact with reality primarily as an Italian. One may have Italian ancestry and maintain an Italian name such as Vitale. But this does not make a person an ethnic Italian. By the definition stipulated in this paradigm, ethnicity involves much more than a name or ancestry—it requires greater social and psychological dimensions, as previously discussed. Conversely, one who has neither Italian ancestry nor an Italian name may become an ethnic Italian through acculturation. A caveat to all of this is that some groups do not permit outsiders to become members (e.g., Druze); others may not recognize disassociation (e.g., Jews and Catholics); and, in the case of prejudices and hatreds, membership or at least full membership may be denied (e.g., the status of African Americans).

Symbolic and Of Heritage Ethnicity. Those who symbolically identify with a particular ethnic group may fall into the "of heritage category." Symbolic ethnicity permits individuals to select attributes of their heritage that are regarded as non-threatening and socially acceptable to others. While acknowledging that not all ethnics are permitted the option to select their ethnicity, Mary Waters suggests that "the ultimate goal of a pluralistic society should be a situation of symbolic ethnicity for all Americans."[31] Waters continues,

> If all Americans were free to exercise their "ethnic option" with the certainty that there would be no costs associated with it, we could all enjoy the voluntary, pleasurable aspects of ethnic traditions . . . There are parts of these past ethnic traditions that are sexist, racist, clannish, and narrow–minded. With a symbolic ethnic identity an individual can choose to celebrate an ethnic holiday and refuse to perpetuate a sexist tradition that values boys over girls or that channels girls into domestic roles without their consent.[32]

Waters's perception of symbolic ethnicity may well be what most white Americans view as ethnicity when proclaiming multiculturalism in America and decrying the melting pot concept. What they fail to see is the fact that such symbolic multiculturalism is part and parcel of the assimilation process. In other words, everyone shall be Americans while sharing aspects of distinct heritages as quaint remembrances of the past.

GROUPS OF FAITH: FIFTH CATEGORY

The fifth category in the paradigm, groups of faith (or more simply religious groups), consist of groups that are identified with a particular religion or belief system. This category is somewhat complicated by the fact that some belief systems actually define an entire socio–cultural system. When this is the case, the group may be regarded as an ethnos. However, Ware, in 1937, and Gans, in 1991, seem in agreement that a difference exists between ethnicity and religious groups even when the latter defines a socio–cultural system.[33] Nevertheless, there seem to be some inconsistencies in their discussions of ethnic groups as opposed to religious groups. Both treat Jews as an ethnic group, but Ware does not regard Mormons as such, and Gans uses the word cult to describe the Satmar.

Many Americans identify themselves with some form of Protestantism. Yet for many of these individuals, all but a few of their salient cultural traits would be regarded as secular and unaffected by religion. In this case, they would be regarded in the "of Heritage" category. Others of the same Protestant denomination, even attending the exact same church, might be considered under the "Groups of Faith" category.

It is uncertain whether Jews belonging to the Reform Jewish Movement would be more appropriately regarded as Americans of Jewish heritage or Americans of Jewish faith. The Movement, whose structure is assimilationist and in some cases rejects the concept of religious dogma, adjusts to the norms and trends in American society. However, practicing members of the Jewish Conservative Movement may be categorized as Americans of Jewish Faith. Some Orthodox and so-called "ultra–Orthodox" Jewish groups are most likely to comprise a Jewish ethnos.[34]

As noted, only when a system, usually regarded as a religion, permeates the entire cultural life of a group, can we define the group as an ethnos (as with Old Order Amish). In the United States, we find a number of religious groups that have evolved from a culturally oriented gemeinschaft toward one more aptly resembling a gesellschaft within a dominant social structure. Therefore, a particular group might be regarded as an ethnic group at one time and a "Group of Faith" at a later time.

APPLYING THE PARADIGM

The paradigm, thus presented, identifies five categories: ethnic group, subethnic group, composite group, individuals or groups of heritage, and groups of faith. The category of groups of heritage usually, but not always, is composed of individuals acting and feeling on their own without an organized social group. When the paradigm is applied, an individual's identification of his or her group membership may not be as meaningful as it appears.

Identification, Meaning and Needs. For instance, when in common parlance one states that he or she is Greek, this could mean ethnically Greek or of Greek heritage. When one says he or she is Moslem, this might indicate an ethnic Moslem, Moslem of heritage, or Moslem of faith. Likewise, the label Hispanic may mean American of Hispanic heritage or ethnically Hispanic. By being aware of these possibilities, the teacher, student, researcher, or other recipient of such messages should attempt to avoid stereotyping or over generalizing.

A given label merely may indicate one of a number of possibilities. Further inquiry would be necessary to determine just what is meant by the label. This additional information can be used to understand a person's perspectives, predilections, expectations, and behaviors. It also provides information regarding individual, special needs predicated upon ethnic necessities.

Persons in Transition. With the exception of the category "of heritage", the paradigm focuses primarily on groups rather than individuals. In other words, some, but not all individuals, may be identified as belonging to a particular group under the more general category. At a given point in time, an individual may be in transition between ethnic groups (assimilating from a distinct ethnic group to another—e.g., from Amish to American). Still other individuals may be in transition from one category of a group to another, as from Irish to "of Irish heritage."

Just how an individual may wish to identify her or himself is another matter that requires discussion beyond the scope of symbolic ethnicity that has already been discussed. If we are to understand the dynamics of ethnicity and intergroup relations, it is important to examine ethnicity in terms of ingroup and outgroup perceptions. Indeed, some observers, such as Shibutani and Kwan, more broadly define ethnic group based upon the perception of self and others: " . . . those who conceive of themselves as being alike by virtue of their own common ancestry, real or fictitious, and who are so regarded by others."[35]

Ethnic Ingroup and Outgroup Identification

The paradigm, presented above, is largely independent of how one identifies the group to which he or she claims to belong. Nor does it consider the judgments of others—including group members and nonmembers. Ingroup or outgroup sources of identification and classification have been used, but often they are cloaked by distortions. These distortions may result from any number of considerations, political, social, economic, or psychological. Even scholars have permitted the political, social, and economic conditions of a time to thwart their own perceptions. The case of Louis Wirth illustrates the effects of social and political conditions at an intersection of time and place, as well as the scholar's negative perceptions of his group of origin.

Self Identification: A Scholar's Dilemma

University of Chicago sociologist Louis Wirth authored *The Ghetto* in 1928. Notwithstanding his reluctance to define a Jew explicitly, Wirth described Jews as a group that would qualify as an ethnic group and a religion.[36] Twelve years later, on January 28,

1940, during a University of Chicago Round Table program on NBC radio, Wirth, John A. Wilson, director of the Oriental Institute of the University of Chicago and Malcolm Wiley, Professor of Sociology from the University of Minnesota discussed the topic entitled, "The Jews."

During the exchange, Wirth agreed with Wiley that assimilation was a reciprocal process on the parts of both Gentiles and Jews. Wirth stated:

> Yes, and some of us in the Jewish group have been working just to that end; to indicate that an archaic, ancient ritual which is different from what the rest of the world does cannot be preserved without the Jew being regarded as an alien and a stranger. That is in the course of being modernized.[37]

A few moments later, Wirth remarked that biological assimilation (intermarriage and interbreeding) is beneficial to intergroup relations and indeed, this explains "how America has grown into the kind of polyglot, rich, cultural nation that it is."[38]

In this dialogue, Wirth is suggesting nothing less than the extinction of the Jewish ethnos through cultural assimilation and amalgamation (biological assimilation). On October 5, 1941, in another Round Table, Wirth, along with Anthropologist Robert Redfield, and Arthur H. Compton, Dean of the Division of the Physical Sciences at the University of Chicago, discussed the topic "Anti–Semitism: A Threat to American Unity?" During the broadcast on the Red Network of NBC radio, the discussion centered on the definition of a Jew.

Redfield pointed out that Jews are not a race in the biological or scientific sense.[39] Wirth stated that if Jews " . . . are not a race, neither are they a religious group, because there are a lot of people among Jews who do not belong to the Jewish Church [sic]."[40] Following this comment, Wirth added that "Jews are not a nation or nationality because they have no state."[41]

Finally, Redfield asked, "So 'who is a Jew' is something which may be changed by a political edict or event?"[42]

Wirth answered, "Exactly. A Jew is a person who thinks of himself as a Jew and is treated by others as a Jew; but that has varied throughout history and in different parts of the world."[43]

These discussions indicate that Wirth would regulate Jews to an abstract non-people—something residing in the minds of individuals. All of this may have been related to Wirth's conception of what is needed to make the Jew more acceptable in the mass society during a period of extremely high anti–Semitism. In doing so, Wirth presents some highly irregular arguments. For example, he does not regard Jews as a religious group, on the basis of the fact that "many Jews do not belong to the Jewish Church [sic]." However, it is doubtful that he would reject Catholics or Methodists as religious groups simply because some of their members do not attend church.

Another non sequitur is the notion that Jews are not a nationality (ethnic group) because they do not have a state. We have already noted that a nationality need not have achieved statehood. Hopi, Sioux, and other Native American groups have been recognized as Indian nations. Yet, they have no independent state. Polish nationality (or ethnicity) did not dissolve during periods when Poles did not have political autonomy. Nor did the nationalities (or ethnicity) of peoples under Soviet hegemony dissolve.

What Wirth totally ignores are the cultural traits and complexes that make up Jewish nationality—civil and criminal laws, courts of justice, religious beliefs, mores, morals, traditions, dress, language, and customs. Even in Eastern Europe, especially Poland, Jews were permitted at various times to have local autonomy. In the Act of Kalisz of 1264, Boleslaw Pobozny, Boleslaus the Pious, guaranteed a "creation of a Yiddish–speaking autonomous Jewish nation based on the Talmudic Law (until 1795) . . . [44]

Could any such edict or act of government be conceived to apply to a non–people? Could anything be more clear that this act pertained to a nationality? What then explains Wirth's push to denationalize, dereligiousize, and fictionalize the Jew? The answer may be found in Wirth's own background and experiences.

With war raging in Europe and reports of violence against Jews being received, Wirth may have felt that it was politically and socially expedient for Jews to survive as individuals rather than as a nationality. This, of course, is speculation based upon what he said.

On the other hand, Wirth's position might be explained by his personal biases. He was quite assimilated and indeed had exceeded the limits of exogamy, having wed Mary Bolton, a Southern Baptist.[45] Mary's father, an itinerant preacher, sent Mary to the University of Chicago because it had been founded by Baptists. He thought Mary would be safe from foreign and secular influences.

Louis and Mary met at a German Club meeting, and it was love at first sight. Throughout most of married life, Louis claimed to be agnostic, and Mary became an atheist. Whether or not Wirth allowed his personal life experiences and the events of the times to influence his **"sociology of the Jew"** can only be inferred, but his definition of a Jew was used by sociologists and appeared in sociology texts for years following.

Lessons from Wirth. Wirth's comments suggest three items for consideration. First, social concepts and definitions of groups or other social systems are subject to redefinition to fit a given place, condition, or time. Second, the work of scholars, upon whom teachers and others rely for substantive and reliable knowledge, may be subject to biases resulting from personal experiences. Third, the Wirth case illustrates the complexities involved when individuals attempt to define their own group and at the same time attempt to find their own place in or out of the "ethnic sun."

Marginality and Between Walls

Individuals living in a state whose mass culture (national ethnic group) differs from their own are subject to forces of assimilation to varying degrees. People seek to be accepted and treated indiscriminately and without prejudice. Cultural and racial differences have been the catalyst almost universally for ethnocentric and xenophobic reactions. These reactions have created barriers to social acceptance, mobility, economic advancement, and political efficacy. Therefore, ethnically and racially different group members are under constant pressure to seek some degree of assimilation. The constant tension between conforming to a mass national ethnos and maintaining one's cultural identity has served to move individuals toward "marginality" and what we shall describe as "between walls."

Many individuals are between walls or marginal. Between walls indicates the individual is in transition, moving slowly from one ethnos to another, such as from Ukrainian to American. As an individual acculturates and assimilates, he or she moves further away from the core of his/her group, becoming a marginal member. Within the above paradigm, the marginal person is usually heading toward becoming a member of the dominant ethnos and "of heritage" of the original group. Figure 1 indicates the movement toward the American ethnos category.

There are a number of possibilities aside from the one illustrated in Figure 1. Subethnic groups may form from one generation to the next, and individuals of different generations may appear in different categories over generations. It also is possible for an individual to move through categories over the course of a lifetime. In

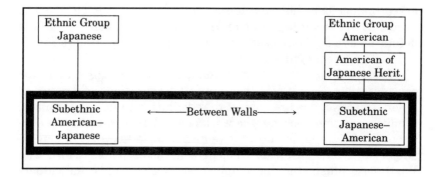

Figure 1. A pattern of movement toward another ethnos within one or more generations. Shaded area indicates zones of expected or possible marginality among individuals and of expected or possible formation of composite groups.

addition to movement away from one's group of origin, there may be a nativistic movement to rediscover and establish one's own roots. According to Marcus Lee Hansen, this movement is most likely to occur among third generation descendants of immigrants, but Gans questions whether this is not merely a symbolic, as opposed to authentic return, to ethnicity.[46] It may be noted that the "of heritage" category materializes only when one *enters* a new ethnic group, as illustrated in Figure 2. This figure illustrates the movement from the American ethnos to the Japanese ethnos.

When individuals are at different stages of assimilation or within a particular ethnic or subethnic category, attitudes toward one another may vary. Those who remain within a given ethnos may view marginal or assimilated group members as modern, vulgar, wild, or disrespectful of tradition. The more assimilated or marginal individuals often regard the hard core ethnics as backward, disgusting, or harmful to progress. On the other hand, there may exist little or no enmity—each resigned to accept the other. Indeed, some of the more assimilated or marginal individuals may consider more traditional individuals "quaint" or even describe their own situation in terms like "I know I should keep the old ways, but it is just not for me." During the 1880s, Reform Movement Jews viewed "observant Jews [as] 'old fashioned,' 'bigoted,' and 'unreasonable.' "[47] As noted in the case of Louis Wirth, he intimated that Orthodox Jewry must assume some responsibility for prejudices against them because of attending to "archaic" and "ancient rituals."

It is during the period of marginal existence that an individual may fluctuate between the acceptance of one identity over another,

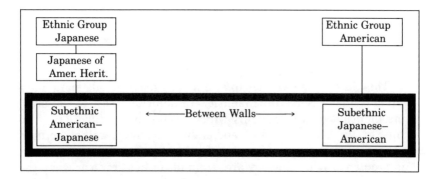

Figure 2. Pattern of movement from American ethnos to Japanese ethnos within one or more generations.

rejection of any or all ethnic identity, or merely remaining in a state of uncertainty without any overt concern as to what they are or are not. In some cases, this may lead to a love–hate relationship between one's original group and the national ethnos. At one moment, the individual may feel pride and love for his ancestral group and disdain for the national ethnos. At another time, the feelings and beliefs may be reversed, and he/she may seek positive identification with the national ethnos. This is especially true of individuals whose immediate group has been the victim of prejudice and discrimination. This love–hate relationship may lead to a lack of group identity.

EFFECTS OF LACK OF GROUP IDENTITY

Members of ethnic and subethnic groups that have a history of being victimized by discrimination and scapegoating may reject their ethnicity and at the same time be regarded as an outgroup by the mass society or dominant ethnic group. A history of severe victimization may result in structural normlessness or anomie. For the individual, this can be accompanied by a lack of group identity and alienation or anomia. The American Psychiatric Association touches upon anomia in its description of "identity disorder."

> The essential feature of this disorder is severe subjective distress regarding inability to integrate aspects of the self into a relatively coherent and acceptable sense of self. . . . Conflict regarding friendship patterns may be expressed in an inability to decide the kinds of people with whom to be friendly and the degree of

intimacy to permit. Conflict regarding values and loyalties may include concerns about religious identification, . . . and moral issues. . . . Frequently, the disturbance is epitomized by the person's asking, "Who am I?"[48]

This description alludes to and indeed may include one's questioning of his or her ethnic identity. In addition, most of the problems mentioned are problems which relate to the function of an ethnic group. That is, one's membership within an well structured and stable ethnic group often sets forth solutions to such questions and problems. When one deviates from his or her group or when the group structure is impaired and not stable, the problems may become serious. It has been suggested that Native American children in certain areas have suffered anomia which has been linked to suicide, and it is not surprising that in dealing with Native Americans in the educational filmstrip series of the seventies, *Minorities USA,* the authors entitled a particular filmstrip *Native Americans: Who Am I?.*[49]

Unrecognized Ethnicity. Generally, when an individual, who is not a member of a minority ethnic group in the United States, comments that he or she does not identify with any particular ethnic group, the individual would be more accurate to state that he or she is an American (ethnically). These people often are neither marginal nor between walls. They are members of the dominant ethnic group within a society.

The popular notion that ethnics are somewhat different or exotic, along with the fact that members of the national ethnos do not perceive anything special about their own culture, probably contributes to this lack of specific identification. The cliché of not being able to see the forest for the trees may be quite appropriate in this case. Furthermore, members of the national ethnos may feel disassociated from a particular ethnic group when the ethnicity of the latter is being stressed and romanticized. This can create feelings of resentment for others and, at the same time, stimulate an awareness of one's national ethnos.

Although we shall not delve further at this time into the problems arising from anomie, anomia, and marginality, it is important to note that, when the traits of ethnic groups and subethnic groups clash with the norms of a national ethnic group, the consequences can be psychologically as well as socially damaging. This is especially true when the ethnic group or subgroup 1) is a minority (a victim of discrimination), 2) does not have a set of alternative values or norms which are successfully competitive with the norms of the mass society, or 3) permits its members to seek conflicting ingroup and outgroup goals simultaneously.

Outgroup Identification

Ethnic groups may be identified by nonmembers of the group or by those who claim to represent a group but who are themselves marginal or "of heritage." Such classifications are usually political in nature. The most common instances of outgroup classification are those by governments. In Nazi Germany, the definition of a Jew was set forth on November 15, 1935. It specified the following:

> 1. A Jew is anyone who descended from at least three grandparents who were racially fully Jews. Article 2, par. 2, second sentence will apply. [This states: "One grandparent shall be considered full blooded if he or she belonged to the Jewish religious community."]

> 2. A Jew is also one who descended from two full Jewish parents, if: (a) he belonged to the Jewish religious community at the time this law was issued, or who joined the community later; (b) he was married to a Jewish person, the time the law was issued, or married one subsequently; (c) he is the offspring from marriage with a Jew, in the sense of Section 1, which was contracted after the Law for the protection of German blood and German honor became effective (RGBI. I, page 1146 of 15 September 1935); (d) he is the offspring of an extramarital relationship, with a Jew, according to Section 1, and will be born out of wedlock after July 31, 1936.[50]

Unlike the Third Reich and South Africa where the creation and use of racial classification was and, in the case of the latter, still is used to create subordinate and superordinate groups, the United States has used ethnic and racial classification to combat discrimination. But even in the United States, the use of racial classification has led to charges, not totally unwarranted, of discrimination against non-minority group members. Furthermore, in the United States, we find federal standards both general and highly subjective for determining the nature of a group and how one is to be classified as a member of a particular ethnic or racial stock. The major thrust in this area concerns employment practices. The Federal government's Equal Opportunity Commission's instruction booklet for employers provides the following classification:

White (Not of Hispanic origin)—All persons having origins in any
of the original peoples of Europe, North Africa, or the Middle East.
Black (Not of Hispanic origin)—All persons having origins of the
Black racial groups of Africa.
Hispanic—All persons of Mexican, Puerto Rican, Cuban, Central
or South American, or other Spanish culture or origin, regardless
of race.
Asian or Pacific Islander—All persons having origins in any of the
original peoples of the Far East, Southeast Asia, the Indian Sub-
continent, or the Pacific Islands. This area includes, for example,
China, Japan, Korea, the Philippine Islands, and Somoa.
American Indian or Alaskan Native—All persons having origins in
any of the original peoples of North America, and who maintain
cultural identification through tribal affiliation or community
recognition.[51]

In practice, the determination of a person's race or ethnicity is
left to "visual surveys of the work force, or from post–employment
records as to the identity of the employees. Eliciting information on
the race/ethnic identification of an employee by direct inquiry is not
encouraged."[52] The guidelines further state that "Race/ethnic designations as used by the Equal Employment Opportunity Commission do not denote scientific definitions of anthropological origins."[53]

In contrast to the United States' criteria and method of determining group membership, the Germany of the Third Reich was
pseudo–scientifically oriented. The scientific, pseudo–scientific,
and social dimensions of race and ethnicity will be discussed more
thoroughly in the chapter on race and racism. At this time, it may
suffice to say that political entities are not reliable sources for determining racial or ethnic groups.

The Emergence and Extinction of Ethnic Groups

New ethnic groups may emerge while others change or even
cease to exist. The concept of African Americans illustrates an ethnic group that has developed from a common recent history of Africans from various distinct groups. Indeed, even in terms of a racial
gene pool, many blacks have white ancestry. In South Africa, co-
loureds also make up a relatively recent ethnic group. A seldom-
noted, newly developed ethnic group is the American.

This can be highlighted by examining American communities
in other countries. In Israel, one can find American settlements as
well as urban or suburban enclaves, as in Ra'anan, near Tel-Aviv.

The reason most observers fail to notice the ethnic American is that relatively few Americans seek resettlement outside the United States, where the contrast is readily apparent.

James Baldwin's *Notes of a Native Son* provides a social–psychological landscape of the struggle to be both an American and a Black American. He relates that being an American and having a common bond with white Americans did not reveal itself until he had lived in Paris for two years.[54] According to our paradigm, Americans are a generic group of which African Americans are a subethnic group and, theoretically, there should be no problem for a subethnic member to identify with the genera. Nevertheless, victims of racism and ethnic prejudices often are denied the opportunity to perceive this logical connection.

Ethnic groups may form from other groups due to political conditions within a geographic area. Conquest, forced migration, forced political and social minority status, and involuntary and voluntary isolation of a previously non–distinct group may result in the creation of a new ethnic group. The emergence of a new belief system, combined with external persecution, may also lay the groundwork for a new ethnicity.

On the other hand, political, social, and economic repression may contribute to the extinction of an ethnic group. Finally, the lack of repression combined with modern technological conveniences and intergroup contact can achieve a breakdown of ethnic folkways. In other words, political and social structural changes in a given area may result in either the maintenance, resurgence, or extinction of an ethnic group. Notwithstanding occasional irredentist movements, an examination of technological and social changes throughout the world seems to indicate a trend toward cultural extinction of more traditional ethnic groups.

Ethnic Minorities

Ethnic groups that are not in the mainstream of society and that are the victims or prejudice, discrimination, and scapegoating are referred to as ethnic minorities. A problem that emerges in the United States and elsewhere is to determine when a particular ethnic group is an ethnic minority. For example, is a Hispanic living in a community in which no racial or ethnic discrimination is present a member of an ethnic minority within the particular community? At the community level, the answer should be no. Yet, at the national level, the response might be yes. Most studies and texts on ethnic minority and majority relations avoid this question by examining ethnic group relations at the national level.

An even more complicated issue arises when a member of the majority group is prevented from an equal opportunity to compete for employment due to a quota system. In some cases, the Affirmative Action program in the United States and norming, the process whereby government tests for employment assign different passing levels for blacks, Hispanics, and whites, does result in regulated discrimination, albeit imposed by the majority group upon its own members. Some majority group Americans believe they have or are becoming a sociological minority—victims of discrimination. In attempting to compensate for past injustices and in order to insure equal opportunity for minorities, the government has created an anomaly that can be perplexing for social scientists and others. This issue of affirmative action will be discussed in a later chapter.

MINORITY ETHNICITY AND SOCIETAL PROCESSES

The goals of an ethnic or racial minority may be viewed in terms of social processes of assimilation, pluralism, isolationism, separatism, secession, or revolution. Furthermore, within a given group, there many be subgroups with differing goals. There are African Americans who seek to assimilate totally. Then there are those whose goals are pluralistic, seeking to maintain some sort of ethnic symbolism. Still there are others who seek a degree of isolationism or separatism.

Assimilationism. An assimilationist goal is one in which a group seeks to achieve equality with a dominant group by becoming amalgamated through intermarriage or sufficiently integrated as to give up any distinctiveness. Many Japanese, Chinese, Black, Italian, Polish, and Jewish Americans as well as others have followed this process. Intermarriage, leaving the cultural pocket, changing names, and religion have been used to achieve assimilationist goals. For those who are identified as "racially different," the goals are often more difficult to achieve due to racial prejudices.

Pluralism. Pluralistic goals of an ethnic minority include a desire to maintain cultural identity including any of the following: religion, language, traditions, core cultural values, or national heritage. In addition, these goals include obtaining economic, political, and social equality in the mass–society. Unless limited by prejudice and discrimination, this form of pluralism is probably terminal since over the long haul groups seeking this state will most likely assimilate into the majority.

Although the United States is regarded as a pluralistic society, it would seem more accurate to describe it as an open assimilationist society—permitting people to freely assimilate and to maintain their ethnicity for as long as they wish. The results have so far been that various ethnic groups continue to assimilate at a constant rate so long as they are not hindered by racial or ethnic discrimination.

Similarly, the former Soviet Union consisted of numerous ethnic groups, but ethnicity was maintained by the establishment of ethnic republics. As a result, the U.S.S.R. was fractionalized along ethnic lines and maintained the appearance of a unified state under the hegemony of a strong central government.

Isolationism and Separatism. The distinction between isolationists and separatists may be regarded as a matter of degrees. An isolationist group may seek partial withdrawal from a mass–society in terms of social and cultural affairs. Such groups seek a communal territory where they may conduct their social affairs with only very marginal influence from the outside. In the area of politics and economics, these may be moderately active participants in the general society. Groups seeking to isolate themselves will tend to set up their own schools, charitable organizations, remain aloof from institutions, organizations, and community activities involving the general society. Children in isolationist groups will tend to learn their own group's version of history as well as that taught to children in the mass culture. Unlike those in groups seeking pluralistic goals, the isolationists will tend to assimilate at a slower rate.

Separatists constitute a more extreme form of isolationism. They tend to view themselves as totally independent from other groups, especially the mass–society. Interaction with the outside world is kept at a minimum and conducted only out of necessity. Usually, the necessity is due to economic needs or to political pressure imposed by the dominate society. Like isolationists, separatists will maintain their own institutions and teach their own brand of history as a part of the socialization process of children. Both, isolationist and separatist groups, may view themselves as living in a dimension other than that known to the remainder of the larger society. But at the same time they may remain quite aware of what is going on in the outside world. For such groups, assimilation is viewed as a constant threat.

Today, in America, certain Moslem, Black, Indian, Anabaptist, and Jewish groups seek a somewhat isolationist existence. Leaning toward the separatist end of the spectrum are Hutterite Brethren who tend to live in rural areas and some Hassidic Jews such as the

Satmar who have established urban colonies (e.g., Williamsburg in New York). Black Muslims also advocate separatism, but the extent to which this separatism is realized is questionable.

Ethnic isolationism and separatism may be imposed from without as well as from within. Either way, it often creates a ghetto or "pale of settlement" type condition, causing a rise of xenophobia, prejudices, and scapegoating on the part of the outsiders (the outgroup). On the flip-side, negative stereotyping, prejudices, and discrimination on the part of members of isolationist and separatist ethnic groups against outgroup members are not uncommon.

Secession and Revolution. Some ethnic minorities may seek secessionist or revolutionary goals. In the case of the former, there is a desire to achieve total independence. Secessionist movements may be achieved by leaving the geographic area and resettling in a place where the ethnic minority can assert its own destiny. The secessionist goal also might include a civil war as in a case where the group seeks independence without moving to another location.

The revolutionary goals among minorities include an attempt to gain dominance over the existing majority group. Select conflicts in the Middle East, Africa, and the conflict in Northern Ireland may illustrate revolutionary goals on the part of ethnic minorities.

LIMITED PLURALISM

While particular minorities may have their own agenda as to what the socio–economic–political structure should be, these decisions are usually defined and approved by the majority. Some states may permit a degree of pluralism that allows ethnic minorities to remain isolated or even separated. Periodically, in Poland, Russia, and North Africa, Jews were permitted to maintain their own courts, police force, schools, and other institutions within their community. At other times they were totally disenfranchised and forced to live in select areas.

In the United States, pluralism is tolerated to a limited degree but with a strong undercurrent of assimilationist policy. Isolationist and separatist goals among minorities may be achieved only within the confines of a general national policy. The United States has not permitted what it views as revolutionary or intra–state secessionist movements. However, secessionist movements that call for an exodus of ethnic or racial minorities to another alien territory or state have not been opposed by the United States.

The American War of Rebellion (1861–1865) established the principle that secession from the United States would not be tolerated. Any movement that is perceived, whether correctly or incorrectly, as a threat to the fabric of American society and the political structure will be challenged. This threat has not been limited to dramatic revolutionary activities of extremist groups. On a number of occasions, the issue of the right of the state to mandate the socialization of minority children through education has been brought before the courts. As a democratic republic, the United States has struggled to determine the line between separatism (isolationism) and secessionist movements.

Pluralism and Assimilation in America

Many Americans have come to recognize the presence of distinct ethnic and racial groups and their democratic right to maintain a distinct ethnic character. Nevertheless, a state requires some degree of cohesion—a sense of national unity. The assimilation of various groups into what has been called the melting pot serves this end. Two problems emerge regarding this situation. First, one might ask how a group can maintain its special ethnicity and still assimilate to a level that supports a sense of national unity? Second, is it feasible for an ethnic minority to assimilate successfully only to a partial extent?

The study of distinct ethnic groups within a larger mass-society indicates that, when barriers of discrimination are removed, the ethnic groups tend to assimilate into the mass–society. While American educators speak of multicultural education and a pluralistic society, they fail to provide comprehensive thought as to the inherent contradiction between the processes of assimilation and maintaining distinct ethnic identity.

Teachers provide students with instruction and experiences that illustrate the diversity of American ethnic groups by having their charges experience "ethnic" foods, view traditional clothing, or read or listen to stories about this group or that. However, when an ethnic group's values or behaviors conflict with those of the American ethnos, the particular ethnic group's folkways may be rejected outright. For instance, we have many elementary teachers who find it very disturbing that children who are Jehovah's Witnesses refuse to say the pledge of allegiance, participate in birthday parties or other commonly accepted events.

American Norms: The Standard. The degree of support for a pluralistic society is limited by established societal norms. This is no different in the United States today than it was two decades ago. In other words, while promoting the rights of cultural minorities to be distinct and co–exist within American society, this initial tolerance among educators often is limited by anything they perceive as uncommon or unacceptable by mass American standards. The result is that many Americans may think of themselves as supportive of a pluralistic nation, but in practice this concept often is rejected. America is indeed a "melting pot" and must be if there is to be a viable American nation within the United States. As noted earlier, American society seems to be open assimilationist—permitting a limited degree of autonomy to ethnic groups.

Assimilation versus Multiculturalism. While attempting to come to grips with two dynamically opposed processes, assimilation and retention of ethnicity, the process of assimilation continues. Fourth and fifth generation western European Americans have, for the most part, little or no ethnic identification of their particular old world ancestry. As one American of Irish heritage noted, "I really don't know much about Ireland, but I wear green on Saint Pat's Day." On the other hand, the assimilation of racial minorities is much slower due to the stigma of racism and the obtrusiveness of physical differences. Notwithstanding some fairly large cultural pockets in cities like Chicago and New York, most European ethnics have melted—totally assimilated into the American ethnos. The same has occurred among old, Hispanic families in Florida and the Southwest.

Ethnic groups may change over time within a particular area. Most often these changes are movements toward assimilation. The problem faced by students, teachers, and scholars when attempting to understand these changes is to determine the extent to which a group is seeking to assimilate. Some groups may seek total assimilation. Others may seek to assimilate only to the point of achieving certain perceived benefits of the mass–ethnos.

THE ETHNICITY: INSIDER–OUTSIDER

The complexity of identifying ethnic groups, subethnic groups, individuals of faith or heritage and their perceived needs should not appear meaningless or futile. Only when we become sensitive to these complexities are we better able to understand the social dynamics needed to improve intergroup relations and the problems of stereotyping and prejudices in a changing and complex multiethnic society.

The needs of American Hispanics, Hispanic Americans, and Americans of the Hispanic heritage are not necessarily the same. A child from a traditional American Indian background may have distinctly different needs and aspirations than a child whom we would describe as American of Native American heritage. A teacher might point out to her students that wearing a hat indoors is not appropriate. This may not affect the American of Jewish heritage but would certainly be an affront to an American Jewish child.

Furthermore, teachers and others will receive mixed signals from ethnics, depending upon the category of ethnicity. For example, a teacher may find that children who are Americans of Hispanic heritage (Hispanic Americans) are more likely to provide eye to eye contact, while the American Hispanic child will tend to look down when being addressed by an adult as a gesture of respect. An employer may find it difficult to understand why one Jewish employee may not object to working on a Saturday, and another Jewish employee will absolutely refuse to work on this day, even at the expense of losing his or her job.

In order to deal intelligently and appropriately with the variety of ethnic groups and their members, we need to understand the nature of ethnic groups and the variety of ways people perceive and value their ethnic membership. In addition, we should seek to understand how the ethnic group members perceive what for them is the "outside world," and in turn how they are perceived by others—including ourselves.

Ethnicity is a complex concept and exists in varying degrees for different individuals and groups. A member of an ethnic group is influenced by the internal structure and folkways of the group. He or she is also influenced by individual personal experiences as a member of the group and the collective experiences of the group in relation to other groups. These individual and collective experiences are related to the prejudices, fears, aggressions, and racist beliefs that have plagued intergroup relations from time immemorial. With an understanding of ethnicity and the nature of hate prejudice and racism, we can hope to develop the necessary skills and suppleness of mind that will permit individuals of different ethnic and racial backgrounds to work, learn, and share as equals.

CHAPTER 3

RACE: A BIOLOGICAL CONCEPT

If we were to select the most intelligent, imaginative, energetic, and stable third of mankind, all races would be represented.

—Franz Boas

In recent years and especially during the mid to late 1980s, the term racism became a popular descriptor for both acts of prejudiced attitudes and behaviors. Racism has been so broadly applied that its actual meaning has been lost. When a concept becomes so broad that it can be used for almost any purpose, its utility diminishes and sometimes, as in the case of racism, it leads to absurdities.

There are numerous examples of the emotional and often irrational misuse of the term, racism. According to some, it is racist to discriminate against women; yet women do not constitute a racial group. During 1991, a State of New York Task Force on Minorities reported that "African–Americans, Asian–Americans, Puerto Ricans, Latinos and Native Americans have all been the victims of an intellectual and educational oppression . . . "[1] They recommended a rewriting of history textbooks that included dropping the word slave, allegedly a racist expression, for enslaved persons. The Task Force even recommended that pictures showing the Conestoga wagons be eliminated from textbooks because they allegedly represent racist oppression by white pioneers. Such absurdities abounded during the early nineties in a wave of what became known as political correctness.

The rise of politically correct thought has ominous overtones for racial and ethnic relations. Being politically correct has come to mean holding liberal, anti-racist, pro-minority views even to the point of derogating other ethnic and racial groups. Although on the surface this did not seem terribly problematic, the advocates of political correctness have no tolerance for views that challenge their

specific beliefs. On occasion, they will use the labels of racism
or racist to thwart open intellectual inquiry that may question
their tenets.

One aspect of politically correct thought was to attack Western
culture as primarily racist. This provided a climate in which ethnocentrism on the part of minorities gained respectability. One illustration of this was the development of the Portland Public School
District's *African–American Baseline Essays* that contained both in-
accurate and ethnocentric material. It was not until late 1991 that
political correctness and such works as the Portland curriculum
units began to receive criticism from academicians and teachers.

Arthur M. Schlesinger Jr.'s *The Disuniting of America* severely
criticized the political correctness movement and those multiculturalists that espoused the politically correct line.[2] Others such as
Mary Lefkowitz,[3] Lawrence Hyman,[4] Barbara Dority,[5] and Oritz de
Montellano[6] began to recoil from the excesses of political correctness and the new wave of ethnocentric multiculturalism. In Washington, D. C., public high school teacher, Eric Martel, collected and
began disseminating scholarly material that exposed the deficiencies of minority ethnocentric curricula.[7]

By virtue of its general application to anything regarded as distasteful, racism (or racist) has become little more than a denigrat-
ing label, void of its original meaning. In actuality, racism refers
to those beliefs and behaviors that focus upon the concept of race.
Although it may appear adequate to discuss racism without a
thorough understanding of race, such discussions may lead to misapplication and undeserved labelling. In order to rise above the
emotional and near irrational level of discourse, it would be prudent
to initiate one's understanding about racism by obtaining an understanding of the concept of race and its development. Therefore, in
this chapter we shall trace the development of race as a scientific
concept. This should offer a basis upon which to examine the development of race as a social or popular concept and the nature of racism in its proper context, that is, its relationship to the concept
of race.

The Nature and Dimensions of Race

The word race is one of the most misunderstood and explosive
words in any language—so much so that one anthropologist, Ashley
Montagu, suggested that, "The idea of 'race' represents one of the

most dangerous myths of our time, and one of the most tragic."[8] It tends to trigger irrational and emotional behavior that is based, in most instances, on insufficient or untrue information. On the other hand, there are variations in the physical appearance of people in different parts of the world. Some anthropologists find it useful to use either typological (categories based on type) or geographical (categories based on location) classifications to refer to the biological differences among people.

Because misunderstandings about race have often led to violence and bloodshed, it is important to define the concept of race clearly and to examine its effect on people's behavior. The concept race is of particular importance in the United States where there have been constant conflicts among ethnic and racial groups. Many of the larger and poorer minority groups have been the objects of systematic discrimination and targets of hate violence because of their race. Furthermore, minority groups have nurtured their own brands of hate and discrimination along racial lines. Physical differences have been and continue to be the basis of different social treatment. Because of skin color and other biological traits, millions of Americans have not had the same opportunities for schooling, housing, and job opportunities as those Americans exhibiting more socially acceptable characteristics.

Awareness of Physical Differences

From time immemorial, groups of people have been aware of the physical and cultural differences which set them apart from others. Group names and creation stories alike have emphasized such differences. Thus, when the Cheyenne of the Western Plains referred to themselves, their name emphasized their unique self-perception. Cheyenne simply means "the people." The names of the Yahgan of South America and of certain Papuan groups likewise mean "the people."

Self-praising names are an important means of group identification, emphasizing ties of kinship, marriage, and common heredity or group traits (often referred to as "blood"). The sense of ingroup identity emerges in such ways, and from this sense it is an easy step to view all other groups as outsiders. In fact, are they not outsiders—those who do not look, speak, or behave as we do? It is not surprising then to see why Greeks and Romans of the ancient world regarded other peoples as barbarians, even though ancestors of some of these "barbarians" had built great cities and empires long before there was Greece or Rome.

Creation stories frequently describe a creator god forming humankind from primordial mud. The Yaqui of the American Southwest and Mexico made explicit a physical standard based on color. According to these Indians, their god formed man from clay and placed him in the oven to harden. Alas, upon removing the clay from the oven the god found that man was not yet finished; he was too light. On the second attempt, the god left the clay in the oven too long; man was too black. The third attempt was successful. Out came a brown Indian color—just right. The physical characteristics of the dominant group are those which are generally singled out in a culture for approval.

In the western world, the creation stories of Genesis gave a theological rationale for regarding humankind as entity. The period of exploration and conquest beginning in the 1500s brought Europeans into wider contact with people of different physiques and cultures. The increased consciousness of physical and cultural differences also coincided with the rise of the scientific movement in Europe.

In the eighteenth century, application of the principles of scientific observation and description led to a vast extension in information about the flora (plant life) and fauna (animal life) of the world. Organizing this information into a systematic body of knowledge required systematic categories of thought. Applying Aristotelian principles of classification according to similarities and differences, the science of biology made tremendous strides. With new information about other places, peoples, and cultures gleaned from the reports of explorers and travelers, it was inevitable that scientists also would place humankind into a classificatory system.

Development of Race as a Biological Concept

One of the early classifications of people was by the Swedish botanist, Carl von Linné, more popularly known as Carolus Linnaeus, founder of the binomial system of classification of plants and animals. In a fourfold 1738 classification, Linnaeus classified people into the following groups and identified what he perceived as their distinguishing characteristics:[9]

1. *Europaeus albus:* White, ruddy, muscular.
   Abundant yellow hair; blue-eyed.
   Light, lively (active), ingenious (inventive).
   Covered with tailored clothes,
   Governed by customs (ruled by rites).

2. *Americanius rubesceus:* Reddish, choleric, erect.
Straight, dense, black hair; wide nostrils; freckled face; chin almost beardless.
Persevering, contented, free.
Paints himself with skillful red lines.
Ruled by custom.
3. *Asiaticus luridus:* Yellow, melancholic, inflexible.
Black hair; dark eyes.
Stern, haughty, stingy (miserly).
Covered with loose garments.
Ruled by opinion.
4. *Afer niger:* Black, phlegmatic, indulgent.
Black hair, kinky; skin smooth, flat nose, tumid lips.
The women with a natural apron, the breasts lactating abundantly.
Crafty, lazy, negligent.
Anoints himself with oil.
Governed by whim (caprice).

Although Linnaeus never employed the term race in his work, he not only classified people into categories based upon physical likeness, but he ascribed behavioral traits to each group, creating a structure of stereotypes. This ascription of personality traits to various groups was not unique. Even Aristotle claimed that,

> Those who live in a cold climate and in Europe are full of spirit, but wanting in intelligence and skill;. . . . Whereas, the natives of Asia are intelligent and inventive, but they are wanting in spirit . . . But the Hellenic race, which is situated between them, is likewise intermediate in character, being high–spirited and intelligent.[10]

Within the scientific community, the term race appears to have been first introduced by Comte de Buffon in his work, *Histoire Naturelle, Generale et Particulere,* that began to appear in 1749. Buffon used race to describe and compare different groups of humans based upon the accounts of travelers and explorers. He used race as a descriptive category to simplify the presentation of data about different peoples. Buffon did not attempt to classify humans into subgroups. Buffon's work antedated Darwin's explanation of evolution and the rise of the science of genetics, and his explanation of racial variation is remarkably perceptive. According to Buffon:

... there was originally only one species, who, after multiplying and spreading over the whole surface of the earth, has undergone various changes by the influence of climate, food, mode of living, epidemic diseases, and the mixture of dissimilar individuals; that, at first, these changes were not so conspicuous, and produced individual varieties; that these varieties became more afterwards specific because they were rendered more general, more strongly marked and more permanent by the continuation of the same causes; that they transmitted from generation to generation—and that, lastly, as they were originally produced by a train of external and accidental causes, it is probable that they will gradually disappear or at least ... differ from what they are at present, if the causes which produced them should cease or if their operation should be varied by other circumstances and combinations.[11]

In 1775, Immanuel Kant divided humankind into four races: Hunnic, White, Negro, and Hindu.[12] He reasoned that all races are derived from an original stem genus, and that races had changed in appearance because of environmental and related causes. As with Linnaeus, Kant could not escape his white European background. While he had no evidence on which to base his description of the appearance of original man, he described him as white skinned and brunette. Philosopher and tribesman, Kant and Yaqui, were both trapped by their own ingroup sentiments and ethnocentrisms.

Johann Friedrich Blumenbach, a German physiologist and the founder of modern physical anthropology, divorced cultural and personality traits from physiological classifications. It was Blumenbach who introduced the label Caucasian to refer to white Europeans. He explains his selection of this term thusly,

I have taken the name of this variety from Mount Caucasus, both because its neighborhood, and especially its southern slope, produces the most beautiful race of men, I mean the Georgian; and because all physiological reasons converge to this, that in that region, if anywhere, it seems we ought with the greatest probability to place the autochthones of mankind.[13]

According to Blumenbach, all varieties of humankind issued from the Caucasian stock. Mostly, he suggests the original peoples were in the Caucasus area from which variations "degenerated" with white Europeans to the west, Mongolians to the east, and Ethiopians (Africans) to the south.

He may have been able to set aside the personality traits in his classification, but this in no way divorced him from his own cultural roots and their influence upon his perceived reality of the world. Blumenbach's early classification of 1775 became the most widely-accepted of the racial taxonomies of Homo sapiens proposed until Georges Cuvier's taxonomy of three main races. (See Blumenbach's Taxonomy below.)

Blumenbach's Taxonomy[14]

Race	Skin Color	Head Shape	Hair
Caucasian	white, rose cheeks	oval	brown, chestnut
Mongolian	yellow	square	black
Ethiopian	black	narrow	wooly black
Malay	tawny	narrow	black, soft
American	copper	narrow (varies)	black, stiff

In 1817, Cuvier suggested three distinct racial groups, Caucasian, Mongolian, and Negro. Cuvier accepted Blumenbach's notion of the original location of the Caucasian race. His description of this group combined both phenotypes and cultural traits. "The Caucasian . . . is distinguished by the beauty of the oval formed by its head. . . . To this variety, the most highly civilized nations, and those which have generally held all others in subjection, are indebted for their origin."[15] Cuvier subdivided the Caucasians into three branches. The European branch including German, Dutch, English, Danish, and Swedish were described as that branch from which " . . . philosophy, the arts, and the sciences have been carried to the greatest perfection . . . "[16] As for the Mongolian race, Cuvier suggested that they represented a static civilization. The Negro race was described as " . . . approximate to the monkey tribe: the hordes of which it consists have always remained in the most complete state of utter barbarism."[17] Notwithstanding these descriptions, Cuvier's three racial group classification became the popular prototype for racial divisions of humankind to the present day.

Anthropological research during the nineteenth century accepted the theory of the "missing link." The attempt to fill what was believed to be a gap between the anthropoids and modern Homo sapiens sapiens led anthropologists to unwittingly contribute to many popular misconceptions of race that exist to the present. One of the practices of anthropologists was that of ranking humankind into a hierarchical order. The other was that of comparing individual races to contemporary apes for functional purposes. But physical anthropology was still in its infancy. No record of fossil man had been unearthed, and the idea of evolution was slowly being accepted. Furthermore, there was no knowledge of genetics. Racial classifications continued to rely on a limited number of phenotypic differences.

As early as 1866, a Moravian abbot, Gregor Mendel, had reported the results of experiments indicating the effects of heredity, but his findings were largely ignored until the turn of the century. In 1910, Thomas Hunt Morgan initiated research that ultimately postulated the existence of chromosomes. The rediscovery of Mendel's work and the founding of the science of genetics by Morgan set the stage for a new perspective on the nature of racial groups. Concepts such as breeding population, genetic equilibrium, genetic drift, mutation, and the gene frequency method of differentiating populations emerged. The concept of straight line evolution was modified and the idea of the "missing link" discarded.

The discovery of ABO blood groups by Karl Landsteiner in 1901, and the findings of other biochemical traits such as abnormal hemoglobins, haptoglobins, and antigens permitted further refinements in the study of population distributions. Biochemical classifications have not replaced older structural classifications, but, together with genetic theory, new fossil finds, and the application of statistical methods to population analysis, biochemical research has helped to show that racial classifications based upon assumptions of a racial type are primarily pre–Darwinian. Race, from a scientific perspective, is merely a system of biological classification. The results of scientific advancements developed into two types of classifications used in the twentieth century: typological and geographical.

Typological and Geographical Classifications

The identification of human beings as Homo sapiens is based upon Linnaeus's binomial system of classification. Homo designates the genus and sapiens refers to the species. Homo sapiens includes the subspecies, spaelus, neanderthalensis, and sapiens. The Homo sapiens sapiens includes the Cro–Magnon and modern mankind. Technically speaking, we are Homo sapiens sapiens if we wish to differentiate among subspecies. Both typological and geographical classifications of race begin with the fact that all people constitute a single species, *sapiens*. All modern races are interfertile; they can interbreed and produce offspring. However, the species is polytypic; there are many different types or varieties in the same species. Unlike other animals that are restricted in their present distribution

to one of the six biographic realms, humans are found in every kind
of ecological environment. Despite the variations that have developed among humans, these variations have not created different
species. Finally, it is important to note that a species is a closed system and does not permit breeding with other species.

TYPOLOGICAL CLASSIFICATIONS

Typological classification reflects the original emphasis on
morphological classification. Morphology refers to the structure of
the organism, and this type of classification preceded later classification schemes based on biochemistry and genetics. The fact that
there is a considerable concurrence in typological description with
structural and biochemical classification simply reflects the fact
that both methods describe common breeding populations separated by culture and geographic space. While typological classification has abandoned the concept of pure races from which mixed or
composite races are derived, the case for typological classification
still rests upon the statistical delineation of an ideal racial type or
prototype.

Early typological classification assumed the existence of three
major races, Caucasoid, Negroid, and Mongoloid, and the emergence
of variants from these types as a result of hybridization. These variants were referred to as composite or splinter races. The number of
subdivisions depends largely on the individuals engaged in identifying sub–racial groups and the criteria they establish. A typical set
of criteria for typological classification in anthropology texts may be
seen in this example by Ralph L. Beals and Harry Hoijer:

1. Physical features only, or physical characteristics such as
   blood types.
2. Hereditability of structural variations.
3. Multiple criteria; no single trait may be employed.
4. Classifications representative of population sample.
5. Age and sex held constant for comparative purposes.[18]

The superficial observation of a few traits, such as skin color, hair,
and facial appearance, gave way to multiple measurements and indices. For example, the cranial vault was examined in terms of capacity, cephalic index, cranial height, slope and width of forehead,
thickness of cranium bones, size of supraorbital ridges, and position
of foramen magnum. Blood groups and other chemical factors were

tested to determine type of four group system (A, B, AB, O), Diego factor, and Rhesus factor.

A strictly typological approach to racial classification has been largely abandoned by today's anthropologists. Some of the absurdities of the typological approach are apparent when it is recalled that one of the fundamental assumptions of typological classification is the existence of three main races and that other races result from hybridization, or racial interbreeding. Typologists have found it difficult to find a place in their system for such groups as the Australoids and the Veddoids but, at the same time, have not hesitated to explain their origin by hybridization. Of what scientific value is the statement that the Veddoids resemble in some ways the Caucasoids and in some ways the Australoids, but their true origin is unknown? But the typologist then goes on to explain the existence of the darker Caucasoids of India as an intermixture of Mediterraneans with Veddoids.

Perhaps the ultimate absurdity has been the fantasies associated with the Nordic race. The Nordic was allegedly a "pure" European type—longheaded, blue eyed, and light haired. At the same time, pure Nordic parents produced offspring that were assigned to other racial types, such as Mediterranean and Alpine, because the phenotype does not express all the chance variations of genotype.

Another difficulty with typological classification is the need to assume some kind of relationship between all groups of a race, irrespective of their location. This not only raises problems of explaining geographical distribution, as with Negritos, but also cannot take full advantage of genetic theory and resorts to the rationale of race formation from interbreeding. Typological classification still lingers, but in spirit it is both pre-Darwinian and pre-Mendelian in its scientific outlook. For this reason, many anthropologists preferred to employ a system of geographical classification.

GEOGRAPHIC CLASSIFICATIONS

Classification of populations by geographical location does not abandon the concept of race or the idea that there are trait differences among people. Race, as a term, simply implies variety. The substitution of any other term would not remove the semantic difficulty. The geographical approach to trait differences simply makes the assumption that the people of a particular area have certain physical characteristics as a result of common gene frequency, gene flow, and the breeding habits of a population. Geographical classification also agrees with typological classification in recognizing the existence of three major groups—Caucasoid, Negroid, and Mongoloid, which correspond to the three geographic groups of Europe, Asia, and Africa south of the Sahara. It does not try to explain the existence of sub-groups, however, on the basis of mixture of the three primary races. As with typological classes, there is no agreement as to the number of categories to which geographical races may be assigned.

There are three levels of geographical classification, continental, local, and micro. Geographical classification is based on our historical knowledge of race distribution circa 1500. Since that time, two continental groups, European and African, have become widely dispersed. In addition to Europe, people of this stock have become a majority in the Western hemisphere, as well as in Australia and New Zealand. They are dispersed in smaller pockets over the rest of the world. Africans are found in large numbers in the United States and Brazil. Relatively small numbers of Asiatics are found in Europe, Africa, and the Western Hemisphere.

Continental races, as the name implies, were confined by the major barriers to human migration in a pre-industrial world. Mountains, oceans, and deserts prevented gene flow in particular directions. The migration of races within the period of our historical knowledge has led to the emergence of hybrid populations as a result of the interbreeding of populations. It is probable that contemporary races originated in this manner, and that the fixing of certain dominant traits resulted from geographic isolation.

Continental and island classifications correspond in the main to typological classifications as noted below:[19]

Continental	Typological
Africa, south of Sahara	Negroid
Amerind	American Indian Mongoloid
Australian	Australoid
Euro–Mediterranean	Caucasoid
Indian	Mediterranean Caucasoid
North Asiatic	Mongoloid
Southeast Asiatic	Malay–Indonesian
Pacific Island	
Melanesian	Oceanic Negroid
Micronesian	Derived Negroid
Polynesian	Derived Caucasoid

It should be noted that, in presenting these corresponding classifications, typological classifications include both sub-racial stocks
(e.g., Oceanic Negroid) and splinter races (e.g., Australoid).

Within each of the continental groups there is considerable
variation. A continental race therefore is made up of a series of local
races:[20]

Euro–Mediterranean	(African cont.)	*North Asiatic*
Alpine	Sudanese	Siberian–Mongol Asiatic
Iranian	Bantu	Turkic
Lapp	Bushmen	Tibetan
Northeast	Hottentot	North Chinese
European	African Pygmies	*Southeast Asia*
Northwest	Niolotic	South Chinese
European	*Amerind*	Malay
African	Eskimo	*Indian*
West African	North American	Dravidian
and Congo	Central American	Hindu
East African	South American	Vedda

A third level of geographic classification is micro–race. Micro–
races tend to conform to actual breeding populations, because the
members of a group tend to marry exclusively within the group.
This may result from endogamy (the cultural practice which requires a person to marry within group boundaries) or from isolation. In the Southwest, the Hopi traditionally constituted a micro–
race largely due to rules of endogamy, even though a much larger
Navajo population surrounded them for centuries. The Negritos of
the Andaman Island in the Bay of Bengal, on the other hand, com-
pose a micro–race due to geographic isolation. No doubt the Andaman practice of killing people who were shipwrecked on the islands
also contributed to their genetic isolation.

The classification of human populations by geographical races
does not require connecting each group to the three major groups,
European (Caucasoid), Asiatic (Mongoloid), or African (Negroid).
The basic premises of geographic classification are:

1. There are different human populations in the world.
2. These populations have physical traits different from other
   groups.
3. Groups are separated by physical or social barriers.

4. As a result of physical or social separation, there is little or no gene flow between different groups.
5. Consequently, the gene pool of each group differs from the other.
6. Since the gene pool of the various groups represents only part of the total combination of gene pools in the total human population, geographic populations have somewhat different dominant physical traits.[21]

INEXACTNESS OF CLASSIFICATIONS

Regardless of the method used, whether typological or geographical, racial classification is not a simple process. This results from the fact that the physical characteristics of the subspecies *Homo sapiens sapiens* constitute a continuum. Any selection of traits regarded as either representative of a population (typological) or descriptive of the majority of the population (geographical) are abstractions from the total sample of human population. Classification by any scheme is therefore, at best, somewhat arbitrary and relative. Scientists have not yet found a completely logical and satisfactory way to classify variations of humankind into racial groups.

The inexactness of racial classification and the popular notion of race as natural and stable led Ashley Montagu to charge anthropologists with "race–making." Montagu, who pioneered the study of race among modern physical anthropologists, states:

> The process of averaging characteristics of a given group, knocking the individuals together, giving them a good stirring, and then serving the resulting omelette as a "race" is essentially the anthropological process of race–making. It may be good cooking but it is not science, since it serves rather to confuse than to clarify. When an omelette is done it has a fair uniform character, though the ingredients which have gone into its making may have been variable. This is what the anthropological conception of "race" is. It is an omelette which corresponds to nothing in nature. It is an indigestible dish conjured into being by an anthropological chef. . . . The omelette called "race" has no existence outside the statistical frying–pan in which it has been reduced by the heat of the anthropological imagination.[22]

Montagu's comments were originally made in an address at a meeting of the Association of Physical Anthropologists in Chicago on April 7, 1941. Almost a quarter of a century later, Montagu declared that the term race "has outlived any dubious use it may once have had."[23] Notwithstanding his relentless attack on the use of race, his position generally was ignored.

HYBRID RACES

As indicated previously, all humans share a common gene pool, but in the course of human development certain groups became so isolated that they came to constitute separate breeding populations with certain dominant genetic characteristics. While it is impossible to reconstruct the history of gene flow, it is possible, from our knowledge of historical peoples, to indicate the emergence of certain mixed or hybrid populations.

New environmental and cultural conditions have permitted the genetic potential to manifest itself in different ways. Often, when different phenotypes emerge, they are larger and more vigorous. Some of these larger hybrid groups are: Euroamericans in the United States, South America, and Canada; Euroafricans of the United States, South America, and South Africa; and Ladinos of Central and South America and the Caribbean. This hybridization resulted from the migration of European and African populations to the Western Hemisphere, and from European populations to Africa.

Euroamerican is used to designate the fusion of diverse elements of European origin in the Western Hemisphere. The European continental group is composed of several local populations. Transposed to the new world, local populations of the Northwestern, Northeastern, Alpine, and Mediterranean origin were brought into proximity where they could interbreed. As a result, both in North America and South America, populations of European origin are essentially hybrid populations. This is the case except in isolated areas, such as the Appalachians, where physical characteristics of the early Northwestern European settler are still apparent.

The Euroafrican group is a population that results from the interbreeding of European and African stocks. Euroafricans are found primarily in the United States, Brazil, and South Africa. This population in South Africa was given a distinctive legal status as "Cape Coloured." In the United States, except where Euroafricans "pass" as whites, they were legally and socially regarded as Negroes, Blacks, Afro–Americans, African Americans, or whatever the prevailing term currently was in use to describe people of black African descent. As has been noted earlier, most Black Americans have some European ancestry. Furthermore, it might be a rather conservative estimate to state that at least 20 million white Americans in the United States have some African ancestry.

Euroafricans who constitute the majority of Black Americans are genetically different from Africans but are culturally identified with them because of racial discrimination and racist beliefs. The practical effect of a Euroafrican group is to significantly change the gene pool of the African (Black) population in the United States. Here, social barriers, rather than geographic isolation, contribute to continued separation of European and African groups. In Brazil, social class is more important than physical differences in determining whether a Euroafrican is accepted as African or European.

In parts of the Spanish–speaking countries of the Western Hemisphere, there was a dense Amerind population of village agriculturalists. As a result, there have been two types of hybridization: Afroamerinds of hybrid African–Indian populations; Euroamerinds of hybrid European–Indian populations. These local, mixed populations are variously known as Ladino, Chola, or Mestizo. In some places, as in Argentina, the African immigrant population mixed so completely with the Amerind population that there is virtually no discernible trace of an African population. At one time, the number of Africans in Argentina exceeded the number of Europeans. In addition, it should be noted that, if two types of hybridization can be delineated as above, there is certainly a third which includes African, Amerind, and European. And we should not ignore other forms of hybridization consisting of various combinations among African, Afroamerind, Amerind, Euroafrican, Euroamerind, and European.

The largest amount of hybridization occurred between Europeans and Amerinds. In many Spanish–speaking countries, the bulk of the population is hybrid Euroamerind. On the basis of physical characteristics, it is difficult to differentiate this population. Generally, cultural indices are used. If the individual speaks Spanish, wears European dress, identifies with European culture, he or she is normally classified as European. If the individual speaks an Amerind dialect, wears Amerind dress, and identifies himself or herself with Amerind culture, the person is classified as Amerind.

The problem of classification in the hybrid populations of the Americas emphasizes the problem of racial classification throughout the world on the basis of biological characteristics. So often some linguistic or other cultural criterion is used. This practice is the very negation of the principle that racial characteristics are purely biological. An example is the use of the term Hindu, the name of a religion, to identify an Indian local race.

The fiftieth state of the Union, Hawaii, has a hybrid population formed by the crossing of at least three racial stocks—Polynesian, European, and Asiatic that includes a number of local variations. The various hybridizations resulting from these three and perhaps other groups have produced people whose creativity, productiveness, and sense of social responsibility are no less apparent than among European populations on the mainland of the United States. Contrary to racist thought, as we shall see later, any disadvantages, social deviance, or significant differences in achievement and creativity among various groups is primarily a result of social treatment, discrimination and other manifestations of prejudiced attitudes and stereotyping, not a by-product of gene flow.

Awareness of the emergence of historical hybrid populations is important to an understanding of race in several ways. Hybridization demonstrates how new racial groups emerge, as well as the interplay of factors—geographic and social—that influence gene flow. Social beliefs may serve to prevent or inhibit hybridization. In the United States, the belief that racial intermarriage and interbreeding is harmful is an example of how social barriers are erected that interfere with gene flow.

REFLECTIONS ON RACE AND RACIAL CLASSIFICATION

We might briefly summarize some of the salient features of racial classification as follows:

1. Human variability constitutes a continuum. Regardless of the classification system used, whether typological or geographical, there is no agreement as to the taxonomy.
2. Racial designations are merely convenient labels for discussing and comparing physical similarities and differences among populations—race as something more tangible or concrete than an abstract construct is fiction.
3. These classifications do not imply any kind of biological or cultural hierarchy, and are frequently, if not always, arbitrary.

In confronting the issue of race, racism, and hate violence, it is useful, if not necessary, to have a basic knowledge of the facts regarding race. Without this information, one may accept invalid and often racist positions. In 1964, under the auspices of the United Nations Educational, Scientific and Cultural Organization (UNESCO), a group of scientists met to examine and issued a collective statement on the nature of race. This was not the first time that scientists had issued such a statement; it had been done in 1950 and again in 1952. The more recent statement is presented here in much of its entirety because of its significance in understanding the nature of race. Since the statement repeats and emphasizes many of the points made in the preceding sections, it serves as both a summary of these points and as a concluding statement for this section on race.

Biological Aspects of Race[24]

1. All men living today belong to a single species, *Homo sapiens,* and are derived from a common stock. There are differences of opinion regarding how and when different human groups diverged from this common stock.
2. Biological differences between human beings are due to differences in hereditary constitution and to the influence of the environment on this genetic potential. In most cases, those differences are due to the interaction of these two sets of factors.
3. There is great genetic diversity within all human populations. Pure races—in the sense of genetically homogeneous populations—do not exist in the human species.
4. There are obvious physical differences between populations living in different geographic areas of the world, in their average appearance. Many of these differences have a genetic component.
5. ... Since the pattern of geographic variation of the characteristics used in racial classification is a complex one, and since this pattern does not present any major discontinuity, these classifications, whatever they are, cannot claim to classify mankind into clear-cut categories. ... Many anthropologists, while stressing the importance of human variation, believe that the scientific interest in these classifications is limited, and even that they carry the risk of inviting abusive generalizations.

   Differences between individuals within a race or within a population are often greater than the average differences between races or populations.

Some of the variable distinctive traits which are generally chosen as criteria to characterize a race are either independently inherited or show only varying degrees of association between them within each population. Therefore, the combination of these traits in most individuals does not correspond to the typological racial characterization.

6. In man as well as in animals, the genetic composition of each population is subject to the modifying influence of diverse factors: Natural selection, tending towards adaptation to the environment, fortuitous mutations which lead to modifications of the molecules of desoxyribonucleic acid which determine heredity, or random modifications in the frequency of qualitative hereditary characters to an extent dependent on the pattern of mating and size of populations. Certain physical characters have a universal biological value for the survival of the human species, irrespective of the environment. The differences on which racial classifications are based do not affect these characters, and, therefore, it is not possible from the biological point of view to speak in any way whatsoever of a general inferiority or superiority of this or that race.

7. ... On account of the mobility of human populations and of social factors, mating between members of different human groups, which tend to mitigate the differentiations acquired, has played a much more important role in human history than in that of animals. This history of any human population or of any human race, is in rich instances of hybridization and those tend to become more and more numerous. For man the obstacles to interbreeding are geographical as well as social and cultural.

•••

9. It has never been proven that interbreeding has biological disadvantages for mankind as a whole.... The biological consequences of a marriage depend only on the individual genetic make-up of the couple and not on their race. Therefore, no biological justification exits for prohibiting intermarriage between persons of different races, or for advising against it on racial grounds.

•••

12. ... There is no national, religious, geographic, linguistic, or cultural group which constitutes a race *ipso facto;* the concept race is purely biological. However, human beings

who speak the same language and share the same culture have a tendency to intermarry, and often there is as a result a certain degree of coincidence between physical traits on the one hand, and linguistic and cultural traits on the other. But there is no known causal nexus between these and, therefore, it is not justifiable to attribute cultural characteristics to the influence of the genetic inheritance.

13. Most racial classifications of mankind do not include mental traits or attributes as a taxonomic criterion. Heredity may have an influence in the variability shown by individuals within a given population in their responses to the psychological tests currently applied. However, no difference has ever been detected convincingly in the hereditary endowments of human groups in regard to what is measured by these tests. On the other hand, ample evidence attests to the influence of physical, cultural, and social environment on differences in response to these tests.

• • •

Neither in the field of hereditary potentialities concerning the overall intelligence and the capacity for cultural development, nor in that of physical traits, is there any justification for the concept of "inferior" and "superior" races.

CHALLENGES TO THE UNESCO STATEMENT

With some revisions these propositions had been presented periodically from about 1940, and on occasion they have been challenged. In 1944, Henry Pratt Fairchild presented a number of such challenges. For example, regarding the statement that all humans belong to the same species and have a common origin means only that all humans regardless of their "racial classification" can interbreed. It does not, Fairchild points out, permit one to deduce that there is no superior or inferior racial group.

Along this line, Fairchild continues that if one admits the common stock origin and explains differences due to long periods of isolation and limited group interbreeding, these emergent differences may indeed create groups that are superior or inferior to others in certain traits.[25] However, the common origins hypothesis does indicate that all human beings belong to a closed species—an exclusive family, so to speak, and no particular group is sub-human, as some racists will argue.

Fairchild also criticizes the proposition that members of all races are more alike than they are different when this proposition is used to indicate that human differences are meaningless. Here Fairchild makes an analogy between two types of vehicles, noting that a sedan and truck have more in common regarding general traits. "But this does not mean that it makes no difference which you have at hand on a given occasion—and certainly not that one is superior to the other."[26] According to Fairchild, the proposition that people of different races are more alike than they are different is nonsense. "It is upon the minute, subtle, and elusive differences of personality that we choose our friends, our business and marital partners, and our enemies."[27] As for the effects of interbreeding among racial groups and the question of intelligence, Fairchild takes the position that we have very limited research findings to indicate what those effects are. In reference to intelligence testing among American whites and blacks, he notes that many Black Americans have white ancestry. Therefore, he suggests that some or many test scores of people identified as black may actually be white "from a true racial point of view, in a twofold, fourfold, or eightfold proportion."[28]

Fairchild's reaction to what he called anti–racist arguments was designed to strike a balance between the two extremes. Just as he rejected racists' arguments, he was critical of anti-racists, who in his opinion, were overstating their positions.

Race as a scientific, biological concept is neither stable nor well defined. But when all is said and done, we might ask if it makes any difference within a social context. Would we deny a fellow human being her or his basic human rights if such a person did not have the same intelligence as members of other groups? Would we deny her or him the right to seek equal protection or equal status if he or she did not have the same physical ability in speed or strength as someone else?

So what if one person has an intelligence quotient of 102 and another has a score of 122? So what if one is able to learn a list of dates and events in twenty minutes and another learns it in fifty minutes? And so what if someone has more or less melanin than another resulting in a different skin color? But for a very large number of people there is another response than a mere "it means nothing." For these people, race and racial differences may mean everything or, at the very least, something more than most scientists would recommend.

When race becomes a means by which to evaluate the goodness and badness of groups of people, when it is used to create a hierarchy of superior and inferior groups, race takes on a Machiavellian set of meanings. It becomes a popular or social concept and can be used to justify discriminatory treatment and even violence. In the next chapter, we shall identify the foundations of racism and racist beliefs. As we proceed with this topic, it will be good to stop occasionally and reflect upon the nature and development of race as both a scientific and social concept and also reflect upon how easily one can step into the quagmire of racism and racist activities.

CHAPTER 4

RACE AND RACISM

A person of mixed white and Negro blood should be returned as a Negro, no matter how small the percentage of Negro blood.

—Instructions to U.S. Census
Enumerators in 1940

Although physical anthropologists and other scientists may understand the nature of race as a biological concept, its uses and limitations, there is a continuation of the popular social concept of race. People continue to talk—sometimes constructively, sometimes hatefully—about races. In the United States, the government, for example, continues to guarantee equality to people "regardless of race, creed, or color." Most of us continue to behave as though race were a very real, inherently meaningful thing. Yet, what is meaningful is usually a matter of one's perception of reality as opposed to reality itself.

The difference between perceived reality and reality has a tendency to become blurred, especially when it involves a critical social issue or question. Our perception of reality is often assumed to be reality itself; yet the two are not the same. Perceived reality is, to varying degrees, a distortion of reality. However, human behavior, which is a response to perceived reality, takes place in the real world. The imposition of a somewhat distorted, perceived reality upon the real world often unleashes a violent, unwarranted, and dehumanizing effect upon members of the human species.

In spite of the remonstrations of anthropologists, the idea of race refuses to die in the workaday world. As a result, even governments whose creed is based upon the equality of all people have responded to this concept in a way that fits a social racial perspective void of both science and common sense.

What, for example, is an Indian or Native American? The Census Bureau and the Bureau of Indian Affairs have used different definitions. In the census, the racial identification is that used by a person or the community. According to the Bureau of Indian Affairs, an Indian is one whose name is on the roll of a tribe under their jurisdiction. In some Latin American countries an Indian is anyone who dresses, lives, and speaks like an Indian, regardless of her or his genetic background. So, if you were to ask how many Indians there are in the Americas, the correct answer may be 8 million or 80 million, depending upon whose definition you use.

As for determining who is a Black American, legal definitions have differed from state to state and even within the same state depending upon the subject under discussion. During the first half of the twentieth century, the Census Bureau classified anyone with any trace of black ancestry as "Negro." State laws that prohibited miscegenation varied in the amount of ancestry that determined if one were white or non-white. By contrast, in Brazil and Puerto Rico, the situation was somewhat reversed. There, people were classified as white if they had mixed black and white ancestry.

What it comes down to, then, is that each person, institution, and society gives the word race an individual meaning and interpretation. The word *race* is difficult enough for anthropologists to deal with when it is used as a scientific term. It becomes almost unintelligible when we attempt to make sense out of the social applications of race.

Origins of the Popular Social Concept of Race

The popular or social concept of race probably originated in feelings toward ingroup and outgroup associations. Conquest, slavery, and cultural differences also accentuated the perception that racial differences included more than merely physical appearance.

Within some societies the presence of different groups as the result of conquest or related subjugation created superordinate–subordinate relationships. When these respective groups differed in physical traits, social and class differences became identified with appearance. In addition, scientific explanations of race preceding the discovery of genetics also tended to reinforce rather than to modify popular conceptions of race.

Cultural Development and Conquest

Many populations of the world have displayed, at different periods in their history, different stages of cultural development. The

Achaeans and Dorians who invaded Greece beginning in the twelfth century B.C., destroyed the Bronze Age culture of Mycenaean Greece and ushered in a "dark age" from which it took centuries to recover. These invaders, founders of classic Hellas, were regarded as boorish compared to the civilizations of the Near East and Egypt that were already thousands of years old. When these Greeks finally became civilized and developed a flourishing culture, they looked upon others as inferior and barbaric—indeed, the term barbarian referred to one who did not speak Greek.

Fifteen hundred years later another wave of invaders, antecedents of modern Europeans, overran and destroyed the Roman world. It took another fifteen hundred years for Europe to regain the level of cultural development and the amenities which a citizen of Rome enjoyed. Yet, as with the Greeks, these later Europeans came to regard themselves as inherently superior to the rest of humankind.

This ethnocentrism became more marked after the 1500s. In this century, population growth and technological development permitted the European to begin a dynamic period of colonization and trade. For a period of four centuries, various European states came to dominate much of the world. Every inhabitable continent felt the terrible swift sword of European exploration and conquest.

Prior to the industrial revolution in the West, the technologies of Europe, Asia, and Africa were not markedly different. Industrialization and technological development, however, permitted Europeans to conquer most other cultures throughout the world. Is not conquest, so the argument goes, conclusive proof of superiority? As conquerors of other cultures had done before, the European looked at the world from a egocentric and ethnocentric position, claiming the right of manifest superiority.

SLAVERY

Slavery had been a social, political, and economic institution among cultures throughout the world. Among some nations, the taking of slaves eventually served to fill human vacancies within the society. For example, a slave might be assigned to care for a family whose male head had been killed in battle. After some time, the slave might even be given membership status within the culture. Women slaves often were accepted as wives and their offspring were granted ingroup status. In some cases, political aspects of slavery involved little more than maintaining control over a conquered people, subjugated to serve the needs of the conquerors. In some tures, slaves actually became members of the armed forces and took part in future conflicts.

A common form of slavery included having individuals serve the economic interests of their masters and mistresses. In most of these forms of slavery, the bond person was viewed as a human being with basic needs, wants, and, in many cases, rights. In the Near East and Africa, slaves were often freed after a fixed number of years of servitude. In Greece, it was not unknown for free Greeks to sell themselves into slavery in order to pay off debts such as home mortgages. During the Middle Ages in Europe, a quasi–form of slavery existed in the form of serfdom. The concept of chattel slavery, in which a human was regarded as an object of property much like a tool or other artifact, scarcely existed in post–Roman Europe until the conquest of African kingdoms. Demands for cheap and permanent labor in the newly conquered Western Hemisphere invited the use of chattel slavery.

The establishment of the African slave trade with the British colonies began a traffic in human flesh that led to the depopulation and cultural destruction of large areas of Africa, leaving a bitter legacy that haunts the United States to this very day. One of the very unfortunate by-products of the so-called New World slavery was the development of racist attitudes. The African was different from his European overseer—he or she had dark skin. The association between the inferior status of slaves and dark skin was made and has persisted to this day. Many arguments were advanced to justify the holding of Africans as slaves. These included the charge that Africans had no culture and were little better than animals, Aristotle's concept on the nature of some peoples as innately inferior (see chapter 3), and some individual interpretations of the Old Testament.

The main motive for slavery was economic, not only in the area of cheap labor, but also providing a profitable industry in the slave trade. The latter became a major element in the economics of Europe, and monarchs contended for *asiento,* the right to supply Africans to Spanish dominions in the Americas.

By 1800, the economic worth of slavery in the United States had declined, and there were more free blacks in the fledgling state than slaves. Many thought that slavery would die as an inefficient means of economic production. Technological change, however, fixed the "peculiar institution" on the United States for another half-century. The invention of the cotton gin in 1792 provided the South an alternative plantation crop to the rice and indigo which were no longer subsidized by the British.

As intense friction mounted among abolitionist, pro–free soiler, and pro-slave factions, slavery already had become an integral part of the social system of the South. The conflict over slavery was no longer a matter of economics; it also was political and social.[1] By the time the first blast of cannon shot exploded over the parade ground at Fort Sumter on Friday morning, April 12, 1861, the Federal and Confederate States had become inextricably deadlocked in a cultural conflict.

The status of the Black American in the United States mirrors the long agony of the United States over this question, and the struggle of a people to attain respect and equality in the face of racial discrimination and hatreds. But these acts and feelings of racial bigotry are not merely the by–product of the economic institution of slavery and its history. Perhaps the most embedded and reprehensible effect was the development of racist thought.

SOCIAL DARWINISM

Social thought in the nineteenth century accentuated the trend toward attributing cultural differences to differences in racial abilities. One of the dominant theories was Social Darwinism, a misapplication of a biological concept to social groups. Notwithstanding the label Social Darwinism, it was the philosopher–social scientist Herbert Spencer who applied the concepts of evolution and natural selection to the development of human cultures.

Contrary to the impressions of many, it was Spencer, not Charles Darwin, who coined the expression, "survival of the fittest."[2] Spencer had already conceived of the idea that people and cultures evolve prior to the publications of Darwin, but it was Darwin's later influence upon him that led Spencer to accept the theory of natural selection. Spencer reasoned that cultures, like people, evolve and develop through natural selection, and that this evolution leaves in its wake a continuum of cultures from the most primitive and inferior to the most sophisticated and superior.

In this way, he explained the existence of so–called primitive races. Their development had been permanently arrested at an early evolutionary stage, and the minds of their people were as limited as the minds of children. Little or nothing could be done to improve their civilization. For Spencer, the "primitive" society and its people were locked in a fixed stage of social evolution. As for natural selection and survival of the fittest, those social groups that succeed in their struggles against others do so because they are indeed the superior—innately, biologically, and culturally.

On Evolution. Concerning evolution, Spencer believed that the evolutionary process could be progressive or regressive. In addition, Spencer notes that evolution only occurs when there is an imbalance or lack of equilibrium between internal and external forces. A particular living organism or aggregate may merely remain unchanged, as when the environment is stable. It is this latter condition that is most common; therefore, there is little probability that a "primitive" society can do much to improve.[3]

The principle that stronger, more evolved societies will dominate less evolved societies also connects with his regression hypothesis. "The conquest by superior societies results in a decrease of size, or decay of structure or both for the vanquished." Spencer explains:

> Direct evidence forces this conclusion upon us. Lapse from higher civilization to lower civilization, made familiar during school–days, is further exemplified as our knowledge widens. Egyptians, Babylonians, Assyrians, Phoenicians, Persians, Jews, Greeks, Romans—it needs but to name these to be reminded that many large and highly–evolved societies have either disappeared, or have dwindled to barbarous hordes, or have been long passing through slow decay.[4]

ON "PRIMITIVE MAN"

Spencer's specifications regarding his notion of "primitive man" parallels the beliefs of a number of his contemporaries as well as many of today's racists. The concept of "Primitive man" seems to include virtually any non-European, as Spencer draws examples from every other continent, including islanders. It also includes ancient peoples.

In terms of physical development and strength, "primitive man" is definitely weaker and less developed, with a few exceptions such as superior sense of sight, stature, and muscular development. As for stamina, the "uncivilized" are inferior, being unable to exert sudden energy and maintain it for very long.[5] The rapid maturation among Spencer's "primitives" is explained as a result of limited brain capacity as compared to "civilized man."[6]

In two succeeding chapters of his *The Principles of Sociology,* Spencer describes the emotional and intellectual states of "primitive man." His conception of "primitive man's" emotional state involves being overly submissive, overly aggressive, childlike in extremes of temperament, and incapable of delaying gratification. On the question of intellectual ability, Spencer is quite specific. "Primitive man" is depicted as limited in his ability to comprehend the sequence of historical events or causal relationships over time since he lacks a recorded history.[7] This absence of the concept of causation leads to an absence of rational surprise. Things just happen, and there is no reflection or thought of any consequence. With absence of surprise, Spencer suggests that a lack of curiosity is a correlate.[8] And without curiosity there can be no creativity or innovation. "Primitive man" also is unable to develop a flexibility of mind due to limited experiences and cannot make probable estimates based upon a collection of experiences. The ability to deal with abstraction is clearly out of the question. Spencer's "uncivilized" creatures are unable to conceptualize beyond the most tangible of objects.

It is hardly a positive note, but Spencer does consider "partially–civilized races" to have the ability to imitate, "Everyone has heard of the ways in which Negroes, when they have opportunities, dress and swagger in grotesque mimicry of whites."[9] Synthesizing these deficiencies, the esteemed British social philosopher identifies the "lack of constructive imagination." This lack naturally goes along with a life of simple perception, of imitativeness, of concrete ideas, and of incapacity for abstract ideas.[10] Finally, Spencer points out that "the savage" lacks the ability to maintain an attention span. "The mind of the child, as well as that of the savage, soon wanders from sheer exhaustion when generalities and involved propositions have to be dealt with."[11]

Herbert Spencer's perceptions and analyses of what he variously referred to as the savage, primitive, or uncivilized were not the machinations of some lunatic. He based his generalizations upon the writings (diaries, letters, articles, and books) of those who had visited and lived in various "strange and exotic" lands. These included explorers, traders, missionaries, and military personnel, as well as others. What he describes is in many respects not so much a picture of Native Americans, black Africans, Papuans, Indonesians, Indians, Arabs, and Australian aborigines, but rather the perceptions of these and other groups as seen from the politically dominant white European.

THE INFLUENCE AND LEGACY

Spencer's impact upon scholars and educators was exceedingly powerful. Social Darwinism and its offshoot, geographic determinism that promoted the notion of environmental influences in the development of superior and inferior groups, cropped up in various areas, including education. Amory Bradford, writing in *The Educational Review* (later known as *School and Society,* the journal of the Association for the Advancement of Education), stated:

> Moral, physical, and intellectual characteristics are transmitted from parents to children, or by atavism, skipping one or more generations... Heredity is constantly modified by the environment... A dweller in the lowlands of South Africa is indolent; life calls for no struggle; he is little better than the swine and his descendants are like himself.[12]

In the United States, William Graham Sumner and other scholars initially accepted the Social Darwinist line of thought, but Sumner's later writings showed signs of rejecting it. The influence of Social Darwinism also penetrated the thinking of the Supreme Court in *Plessey v. Ferguson* in 1896. The court reasoned that separate but equal public facilities for blacks and whites did not violate the political equality of blacks before the law which is guaranteed in the Fourteenth Amendment. The Constitution, the court argued, had no power to place blacks on the same social plane as whites when, in fact, they were not. This could only be accomplished by the natural social evolution.[13]

Spencer's theory of natural selection and the conception of survival of the fittest provided the basis for strong pro-laissez-faire economics. In a later case, *Lochner v. New York, 1905,* the Supreme Court reversed a New York Court of Appeals ruling that upheld a state law restricting the required hours an employee was required to work to 10 hours per day or no more than 60 hours per week. Justice Oliver Wendell Holmes lamented in his dissent, "The 14th Amendment does not enact Mr. Herbert Spencer's *Social Statics.* . . . Some of these laws embody convictions or prejudices which judges are likely to share. . . . But a Constitution is not intended to embody a particular economic theory, whether of paternalism and the organic relation of the citizen to the state or of laissez faire."[14]

The legacy of Social Darwinism never totally vanished from public or scholarly circles. It appears to have taken new root during the sixties and to have obtained notoriety in a somewhat more refined state in the mid–seventies under the label of sociobiology. According to one of its leading proponents, Pierre L. van den Berghe:

Human sociobiologists merely insist that human language and culture themselves evolved biologically, and hence are under some genetic influence, however remote, indirect, and flexible that influence might be. They only reject the extreme environmentalism holding that humans are equally extremely likely to learn anything with equal facility, and that cultural evolution is entirely unrelated to biological evolution.[15]

Van den Berghe describes sociobiology as neo–Darwinism and stresses that the major difference between this new theoretical approach and earlier renditions is that sociobiologists emphasize individual selection as opposed to group selection. But there can be little doubt about the concern of associating sociobiology with earlier racist thought as noted in the work of Carl Degler. Degler presents the thesis that sociobiologists are not ideologues of the racism found among earlier Social Darwinists. Rather, like van den Berghe, Degler suggests that they are merely attempting to bridge the gap between strict social environmental determinists and biology.[16]

Furthermore, Donald Campbell notes that modern attempts to examine the interaction between genetics and environment can be respectably void of "pseudo–scientific rationalizations for racist political ideologies."[17] To illustrate this, he notes studies regarding the effects of culture on genetics—e.g., the effect of the use of tools on the evolution of bipedal locomotion and on changes in cranial size. Nevertheless, there are those such as Seymour Itzkoff whose written works make it difficult to find even a modicum of difference between Social Darwinists of yesteryear and the neo-Darwinists.[18]

ANTHROPOLOGICAL PRACTICES

In addition to the rise of Social Darwinism, anthropologists in the nineteenth century also contributed to popular stereotypes about race. One act of what is now regarded as ludicrous was the search for the "missing link"—the connecting organism between people and apes. Added to this were comparisons between racial groups and primates. While Social Darwinist theories may have provided a somewhat intellectual foundation for racist thought, the search for the "missing link" and the comparisons between racial groups and primates added the mental pictures necessary to illustrate ideology.

The concoction of the "missing link" became part of the popular view that nature had an hierarchal order with humankind at the top. Between the anthropoids and Homo sapiens was a "missing link." As a result, various groups of aborigines were studied at various times to see if they would fill the gap. Since the gap was above ape but below humans—and since anthropologists were European and white—the white man was placed at the apex of the hierarchy. The "missing link" persisted as a popular concept long into the twentieth century and is still used by hard–core racists to prove that blacks are not only inferior, but are akin to apes.

Notwithstanding that today physical anthropologists, on the basis of fossil finds, now infer that ape and Homo sapiens are descended from independent species, the comparison of racial groups to apes became a standard among physical anthropologists. These comparisons appeared in college textbooks through the 1950s, and more often than not, it was the black who was depicted as most similar to the ape.

The fact that both blacks and whites share some common features with the ape did little to dispel the black–to–ape association. The perceived appearance of the apes as being black, having thick-lips, and being found in Africa certainly reinforced the association of black people with apes. The fact that apes have straight hair, ash–white skin (once the hair is removed), and have very thin lips (it is the jaw that protrudes) is not readily noticeable, since most people are not intimate with apes.

Social Darwinism was not limited to physical anthropologists. Cultural anthropologists reflected the Social Darwinist spirit as well. One of the early principles of ethnography was the principle of linear social evolution. Early descriptions of particular groups of people tended to fit perceived schemes of stages of cultural development, neglecting evidence showing the patterning and divergence of cultural forms.

One result was to take certain cultural stereotypes found in association with certain groups and to explain the lack of cultural development, by European standards, on the basis of race. Since much of the language of ethnography was tinged with derogatory terms—such as savage, tribe, barbarous, primitive—the result was that early anthropologists unwittingly helped produce a scientific rationale for racism. Today, anthropologists are more precise and less value–oriented in their terminology, in order to prevent the development of such misconceptions.

From Race to Racism: A Product of Synthesis

The popular concept of race developed as a synthesis of a multitude of factors. These included early scientific developments, contact with alien cultures through conquest and exploration, the rise of Social Darwinism, and a host of other social, economic, and political developments.

This misapplication of science defines the essence and meaning of racism in its truest form. *Racism is the belief that certain groups of people are innately, biologically, socially, and morally superior to other groups, based upon what is attributed to be their racial composition.* As an antecedent to social action, racist thought almost always dictates that 1) the mixing of superior and inferior groups lead to degeneration of the superior, and 2) that inferior groups deserve a role of being subordinated by the superior group.

Racist thought usually but not always includes the belief that race establishes a group's potential level of development. In addition, it should be noted that not all people who hold racist thoughts are overt hatemongers. In fact, the most insidious form of racist behavior comes from those who harbor racist beliefs but allow others to commit acts of violence.

The Cornerstone of Modern Racism

Joseph Arthur Gobineau, Comte de Gobineau, has been called the father of racist ideology, as the title of Michael Denis Biddiss's book *Father of Racist Ideology: The Social and Political Thought of Count Gobineau* suggests. Gobineau's *Essay on the Inequality of Races* first appeared in 1853, with additional volumes being published in 1855. His views regarding the inferiority and superiority of races were welcomed by many Europeans as well as by Americans who maintained that blacks indeed were inferior and could never function in a civilized society.

According to Gobineau, the decline of civilizations was not due to poor government, religious fanaticism, immorality, materialism, or the decline of religion. Rather, nations fell due to the disease of degeneration. This degeneration occurred when racially superior nations permitted their people to interbreed with members of inferior racial stocks. In his analysis, Gobineau pointed out that this degeneration can only occur among civilized nations. Some societies remain in an embryonic state, unable to achieve the level of a civilized nation.[19]

Those that remained in an embryonic state included "pure-blooded yellow and black races," and any attempt to civilize such groups would meet with failure. Uncivilized societies could not survive the complexities of civilization.[20] Furthermore, except in the case of interbreeding, races do not change. Not unlike others of his day, Gobineau held to the belief that racial groups were physically, mentally, and morally different. In his chapter on "Characteristics of Human Races," Gobineau, a friend and colleague of Alexis de Tocqueville, sets forth descriptions of the black, yellow and white races. Some of these traits of the "yellow" and "black" races are presented below:

> Black: "The animal character, that appears in the shape of the pelvis, is stamped on the negro from birth, and foreshadows his destiny.... mental faculties are dull or even nonexistent... has an intensity of desire... taste and smell are developed to an extent unknown to the other two races. He kills willingly, for the sake of killing... "[21]
>
> Yellow: "little physical energy and inclined to apathy... desires are feeble, will–power obstinate... tends to mediocrity in everything... he understands easily enough anything not too deep or sublime. He has a love for utility and a respect for order... He is practical, in narrowest sense of the word.... does not dream or theorize;... invents little. His whole desire is to live in the easiest and most comfortable way possible."[22]

It should not come as a surprise that Gobineau's description of the white race is of a superior type in beauty, intelligence, and strength. But Gobineau laments that over time, due to race mixing, "hybrids were created, which were beautiful without strength, strong without intelligence, or, if intelligent, both weak and ugly."[23]

Finally, Gobineau determines that all civilizations were and are created from one primary source, the white race.[24] Furthermore, only ten civilizations have ever emerged throughout the history of humankind. These included the Indian ("It arose from a branch of a white people, the Aryans"), Egyptians (" ... created by an Aryan colony from India ... "), Assyrians ("with whom may be classed the Jews ... They owe their civilizing to the great white invasions ... "), Greeks ("who came from an Aryan stock as well as modified by Semitic elements."), Chinese (from an "Aryan colony from India ... "), Romans ("mixture of Celts, Iberians, Aryans, and Semites."), Germanic races ("These were Aryans."), the American Alleghanian, Mexican, and Peruvian.

He ends by noting that only when the Aryan (the original and purest of which is the Germanic people) branch is present has there been any true European civilization. As for the fact that he lists no black civilization, Gobineau remarks, " ... no negro race is seen as the initiator of a civilization. Only when it is mixed with some other can it even be initiated into one."[25] As for the remainder of European civilizations, Gobineau concluded that they could only survive so long as Aryan blood was not exhausted.

Despite the fact that Gobineau provided a doctrine for racist thought that would become popular among Germany's Nazis, post World War II neo–Nazis, and other racists near the end of the twentieth century, he was no more vicious in these early writings than others including Spencer. His writings did seem to influence Stewart Houston Chamberlain, who would also be lauded by twentieth century white supremacists and anti-Semites. Indeed, Hitler referred to Chamberlain as a prophet.

Racist literature and acts of violence spread like a prairie fire both in Europe and the United States during the latter half of the nineteenth century and well into the twentieth. Chamberlain's work was heavily anti-Semitic and reflected a long history of Jew-baiting in Europe. In the United States, the Ku Klux Klan and other groups produced their own brands of racism directed against Asians, Blacks, Hispanics, Catholics, and Jews. In some cases, these outbursts of hate were directed at groups across the United States in general. In other cases, they were restricted to specific geographical locations.

RACISM AND ANTI-SEMITISM IN EUROPE

In Europe, racist thought was largely directed at Jews. For centuries, Jew-baiting was common in virtually every state on the continent. Jews have been ghettoized, plundered, expelled, and murdered at various times. It has been generally accepted that early anti-Semitism was not racially motivated, but rather was the result of religious anti-Judaism including the refusal of these people to embrace Christianity.

However, Jerome Friedman argues that anti-Semitism was transformed from the religious issue to a racial one during the sixteenth century.[26] According to Friedman, the courts of the Spanish Inquisition introduced the racial factor in attempting to determine who was a Jew and who was not. Their "pure blood laws" defined a Jew as anyone with a Jewish ancestry. Such a person might be a *converso* but could not be regarded as a true Christian. The fact that Jesus and his earlier followers were Jewish led the courts to reexamine the amount of Jewish ancestry needed to be a Jew—

"1/16, 1/32, or 1/64." Friedman concludes his findings by arguing that racial anti-Semitism of the sixteenth century laid the foundation for racism against Jews in the nineteenth.[27]

Notwithstanding, Friedman's position regarding the racist aspect of early anti-Semitism, it more generally has been accepted that among the main sources of anti-Semitism were: the belief that Jews were a "deicidal and perfidious race,"[28] the Jews' refusal to accept Christianity, and the belief that Jews were the offspring of Satan—the Antichrist.

The Devil's Seed. During the middle ages the myth of Jews as descendants of Satan began to spread throughout Christian Europe. After all, were these not the killers of Christ? Certainly, it would follow that only those akin to the Devil could commit such a nefarious and putrid crime. Tales were spread that Jews had been commissioned by their Satanic father to bring havoc and destruction to Christian nations. They were accused of poisoning wells, murdering Christian children for their blood, and using Satanic magic to confound and gain supremacy over innocent Christians.[29] The goal of the Satanic Jew was world domination. Once the Jew had gained control of the world, the Antichrist, the Devil, would then appear and Christians would be enslaved by Satan and his seed.

Notwithstanding their apparent evil, some Church leaders often opposed such views and instead sought to have Jews accept Christianity. For there were those who believed that the second coming of Christ was contingent upon his acceptance by the Jews. In addition, there were those Church leaders that, from time to time, condemned Judanhass (Jew hating) and noted that Jesus and his disciples were Jews. Nevertheless, the Jew remained the major target of hate throughout the history of Christendom.

The Martyrs of York. Just how hazardous it was to be a Jew during the medieval period can be illustrated by the events in England in the twelfth century. As in other states of Europe, Jews were expected to show homage to the ruling personage. In Rome, it was the Pope; in England, obeisance was to the monarch.

On September 3, 1189, a Jewish delegation appeared at the coronation of Richard the Lion–Hearted in London. The Archbishop of Canterbury urged Richard not to accept the delegation and they were turned away, insulted and beaten. Londoners, seeing this, immediately turned upon the Jewish community in London, vandalizing and burning their homes, offering them the choice between baptism or death. The fury spread to the city of York. There Jews fled to the citadel and, after they warded off a number of assaults, the mob began to show signs of waning. A monk appeared to reignite the hatred. The siege continued until March 17, 1190.

Faced with capture or starvation, the Jewish community of York had arrived at a decision: " . . . the besiegers, noting the absence of the usual signs of resistance, broke into the citadel. When they reached the tower, they stood facing five hundred corpses. The men, after slaying their wives and children, had slain each other."[30] To this day, when Jews fast and lament the destruction of the Temple on the 9th of Av (usually occurring in late July or early August), they also offer an elegy for the martyrs of York: "O Awe–inspiring One! thy servants stood for judgment, fathers to be slaughtered with their children . . . "[31]

The Love-Hate Relationship. The Church–State relationship with the Jews of Europe was strange and often bizarre. On one hand, the Jews were the most despised of humans—to be humiliated and destroyed, but on the other hand, they were to be saved if only they would embrace Christianity. In *From Prejudice to Destruction,* Jacob Katz summarizes Johann Andreas Eisenmenger's goal for the latter's 2,120 page anti-Semitic work entitled *Entdectes Judentum,* published in 1700:

> Eisenmenger's declared purpose, as explained in his book, is to help the Jews recognize their error and acknowledge the truth of Christianity. In order to divert the Jews from their religion, Eisenmenger suggests several concrete steps: restricting of their economic freedom, limiting their rights, prohibiting them from writing against Christianity, and proscribing the synagogues and law courts . . . Above all, . . . to point out to the Jews the folly and blasphemy of the beliefs and opinions expressed in their writings and the immorality of their laws . . . "[32]

Eisenmenger's work set the foundation for August Rohling's *Talmudjude* published in 1874.

Rohling, a professor of theology at the University of Prague, borrowed heavily from Eisenmenger, and it was the former's publication that spread throughout Europe. Rohling also engaged in charging Jews with using Christian blood in their religious ceremonies. The ancient blood libel had been used earlier against Jews and before that time, by Romans against Christians. In 1879, Wilhelm Marr introduced the term anti-Semitism in his publication, *Der Sieg es Judentums uber das Germanentum,* that replaced the more common Judeophobia. According to Marr, the Jews were taking

Belmont University Library

control of Germany and seeking world domination.[33] Marr formed the League of Anti-Semites and was joined by a number of professors who further popularized the notion that Jewish blood was mixing with the German Aryan, creating the degeneration of the latter race.

Against this insanity, there were educated Christians who sought to combat the anti–Semitism sweeping over central Europe. In 1891, they formed an organization to combat anti-Semitism as cases of blood libel and raw violence were erupting against various Jewish communities in Germany, Austria, Hungary, and Poland. In France, anti-Semitism resulted in the Dreyfus Affair in 1894. This period from 1879 may be regarded as the beginning of modern anti-Semitism.

The Protocols of the Elders of Zion. No review of modern anti-Semitism can be complete without addressing the infamous forgery of the *Protocols of the Elders of Zion.* The *Protocols* made its first official appearance in 1905 in Russia, being revealed by one Sergey Nilus, but it represented a collection of various anti-Semitic works stemming back to the first half of the nineteenth century. The *Protocols* is alleged to be a collection of minutes from the meetings of Jew leaders. These minutes tell of a Jewish conspiracy to take over the world. To bring about this new world order, the Elders of Zion plotted to overthrown Christian governments. They had already succeeded in France by spreading the slogans of "Liberty, Equality, and Fraternity."

> The heads of the Goyim [non-Jews] are fuddled by spirituous liquors, and their young men have been rendered dull by classicism and early licentiousness, into which they have been enticed by our agents—tutors, lackeys, governesses in rich families, shop–assistants and others . . . [Intuitive Education has as] its chief task . . . transforming the non-Jews into a herd of mentally indolent, obedient, animals, who are unable to understand a thing until they are shown a picture . . . [34]

The *Protocols* discusses how the economic and political systems are to be controlled by Jews and the role of Jewish control of literature and newspapers. At the end of the first publication of the *Protocols,* Sergey Nilus states that "There is no room for doubt. With all the might and terror of Satan, the reign of triumphant King of Israel is approaching our unregenerate world; the King born of the blood of Zion—the Antichrist—is near to the throne of universal power."[35]

The *Protocols of the Elders of Zion* was eventually published in virtually every state in Europe and in the United States. The reaction was astounding. At first, the *Protocols* was accepted as fact and reported in newspapers. That it was a forgery was not revealed until a year after it had been publicized in England and the United States. To this day, the *Protocols,* in one form or another, is made available by racist organizations throughout the United States and elsewhere.

The Enlightenment brought Jews out of their ghettoes and into the mainstream of western civilization. The rise of scientific racism, as epitomized in the works of Spencer, Gobineau, and others, combined well with the anti-Semitism of almost 2,000 years and with the hundreds of anti–Semitic publications declarations between 1800 and 1933. Jews could now be identified as a sub-human race or species. The foundation for anti-Jewish racism had been laid for the advent of Nazi Germany.

By the mid-1930s, German school children were being given lessons on how to recognize the Jew as expressed in the *Stuermer Book for Young and Old:*

> "It is almost noon," he said, "now we want to summarize what we have learned in this lesson. What did we discuss?"
> All the children raise their hands. The teacher calls on Karl Scholz, a little boy on the first bench. "We talked about how to recognize a Jew."
> "Good! Now tell us about it."
> . . . .
> "One usually recognizes a Jew by his nose. The Jewish nose is crooked at the end. It looks like the figure 6. Therefore, it is called the "Jewish Six." Many non–Jews have a crooked nose, too. But their noses are bent, not at the end but further up. Such a nose is called a hook nose or eagle's beak. It has nothing to do with a Jewish nose."
> "Right!" says the teacher. "But the Jew is recognized not only by his nose . . . " The boy continues. "The Jew is also recognized by his lips. His lips are usually thick. Often the lower lip hangs down. That is called sloppy. And the Jew is also recognized by his eyes. His eyelids are usually thicker and more fleshy than ours. The look of the Jew is lurking and sharp."
> . . . The children recite it in a chorus:
>
> From a Jew's countenance—the evil devil talks to us. The devil, who in every land—is known as evil plague. If we shall be free of Jews—and again will be happy and glad. Then the youth must struggle with us—to subdue the Jew devil."[36]

The continuation of anti-Semitism in Europe culminated in the destruction of six million Jews during World War II. That is approximately 3,000 men, women, and children each day—seven days a week, for six years. When we consider the violent racial hatred of the past 120 years in the United States and the results of an approximate 5,000 lynchings, we might ask how much hatred did it take to kill the six million?

It was not until after the rise of fascism and the horrors of Nazism in Europe that efforts to counter racism became a popular concern of various groups, including UNESCO. In 1950, the United Nations Educational Scientific and Cultural Organization was directed "to study and collect scientific materials concerning questions of race; to give wide diffusion to the scientific information collected; [and] to prepare an educational campaign based on this information."[37] As a result some dozen or so booklets were published under the series, "The Race Question in Modern Science." But even in these booklets, one may find ethnocentrism and misinformation. The case of Juan Comas, for instance, illustrates just how embedded racial and ethnic prejudices are in the human psyche.

THE EMBEDDEDNESS OF RACISM

Juan Comas, Professor of Anthropology at the Mexican School of Anthropology, authored the UNESCO publication, *Racial Myths,* first published in 1958 and continually through at least 1965. Comas begins his treatment of racial prejudices and myths with reference to Western religions, Judaism, Christianity, and Islam. There can be little doubt that Comas refers to Judaism in the following passage:

> In the Old Testament we already find the belief that the physical and mental differences between individuals and groups alike are congenital, hereditary, and unchangeable. The Book of Genesis contains passages apparently assuming the inferiority of certain groups to others: "Cursed be Canaan; a servant of servants shall he be unto his brethren," while some sort of superiority is implied in . . . a compact with *Abraham and his "seed."*[38]

Having set the tone that Judaism is inherently racist, Comas proceeds to argue that, "the majority of religions disregard individual physical differences and regard all men as brothers and equal in the sight of God." He explains how Christianity has been "anti-racist from the beginning." Comas notes that one of the Magi was a "Negro" and there are Saints who are "yellow men and Negroes." He refers to the anti-racist position of Pope Pious XI and stresses that the "12 apostles themselves were Semitic as was Mary, mother of Jesus Christ."

In the next one–line paragraph, Comas summarizes Islam with "Similarly, Mohammedans [sic] have never displayed racial intransigence or intolerance to other peoples so long as those peoples adopted the Faith."

The interpretations given by Comas in no way reflect Jewish Talmudic thought, the source of understanding the pentateuch in Judaism. Notwithstanding their strong ethnocentrism, Jews never rejected converts based upon racial or physical characteristics.

At a more general level, we might speculate on the reason that a professor of anthropology finds it necessary to delve into religious writings as if they were empirical facts. Quite often, we find empirical minds selecting information from the same source that contains information they reject. It is doubtful that Comas would accept every event described in the so-called *"Old Testament"* as actual.

Against his glowing picture of Christian tolerance, Comas ignores the Church's edict requiring Jews to live in ghettos, the edict requiring them to wear the "badge of shame;" the requirement of Pope Paul II in 1468 that Jews run in the Corso races—"to run nude, wearing only a loin cloth;"[39] the forced conversions of Jewish children; and the public burning of the Jewish Talmud and of Jews themselves. He also ignores the condemnations of Martin Luther, whose writings are still used by modern racists to show Jews as seeds of the devil.

As for Comas' view of Moslem tolerance, history is replete with atrocities committed in the name of Allah against the infidel Christians and Jews. In more recent years, non-Moslems in predominantly Islamic countries have been exposed to restricted liberties and even genocidal acts. Coptic Christians in Egypt have been the targets of religiously and politically motivated violence. In Iran and Egypt, Baha'is have been targeted for religious persecution. To this day, citizenship in Saudi Arabia is denied to non-Moslems.

The case of Juan Comas illustrates just how difficult it is for one to shed ethnocentric and prejudiced attitudes. Here we find a man, a social scientist, writing about the myth of race and, at the same time, exposing his own biases. To add to this, we find an organization, UNESCO, attempting to educate against racism and prejudiced attitudes, publishing these biases. In later years, UNESCO would endorse the political position that Zionism, Jewish nationalism, is racist, while ignoring all other forms of nationalism found among virtually all national groups. There is no doubt that the study of racism and racial prejudice is a difficult road to follow. It is composed of twists and turns that lead us to understand how the simplistic presentation of history found in textbooks belie the complex nature of human thought and interaction.

Racism in America

During the time European Jewry was being converted into a racial stock and being driven to the precipice of the Holocaust, racism in the United States was achieving a new stranglehold on the morality and social conscience of the Land of Freedom and Equality. The major targets of racism were Blacks, Native Americans, Asians, and immigrants from southern and eastern Europe.

ANTI–BLACK RACISM

The rise of modern racism in America was developing in parallel fashion with racism in Europe. In reference to blacks, its beginnings predated the War of Rebellion and even the antebellum period when abolitionists and anti-abolitionists were at each other's throats. From the earliest times, the black slave was viewed as a creature something less than human.

Rise of the Klan. After the War of Rebellion, six former Confederate veterans met in Pulaski, Tennessee in the winter of 1865. Within two weeks they had formed a secret society; they ascribed fantasy titles to the roles of members—Cyclops, Grand Turk, Grand Magi, Grand Scribe—and eventually decided on the Greek word for circle, kuklos, for their group's name. To this, clan was added, and, after further consideration, they came up with the name, Ku Klux Klan. The group's main activities centered on pranks such as dressing in a white sheet, riding up to a black family's home, and demanding water.

> When the well bucket was offered, the Klansman would gulp it down and demand more, having actually poured the water through a rubber tube that flowed into a leather bottle concealed beneath his robe. After draining several buckets, the rider would exclaim that he had not had a drink since he died on the battlefield at Shiloh, and gallop into the night.[40]

Eventually other groups, such as the Knights of the White Camelia and the White Brotherhood formed, and, along with various Klan dens (local organizations), were committing nothing short of deadly terrorism. Under the leadership of former Confederate General Nathan Bedford Forrest, the Klan's membership was over half a million in 1868.[41] But Forrest had little or no control over the various Klan dens. He was probably little more than a figurehead. The violence and murder perpetrated against Northern whites, many of them teachers who headed south to assist blacks, and especially rural blacks was too much for even Forrest. Although known for having butchered black, Union soldiers during the rebellion, Forrest could not stomach Klan terrorism. He called upon all Klan members to destroy their "masks and costumes" and to desist from unwarranted violence.[42] The effect of this General Order of 1869 seems to have had a nominal effect.

By 1870, the situation was so out of hand that Congress began passing "Force Acts" that prohibited the use of force or intimidation designed to interfere with the voting rights of citizens. On April 20, 1871, Congress passed the Ku Klux Klan bill that permitted citizens to sue in federal court any person or group who acted to deprive them of those rights guaranteed under the Constitution. It also gave the President the authority to use military force to put down civil disturbances that were designed to deprive people of those rights.[43]

The use of Federal troops to stem the Klan tide of terror and the revulsion of Klan atrocities resulted in mass arrests and seems to have been a major stumbling block for the Klan. In another legislative attempt to insure the rights of all citizens, Congress passed the Civil Rights Act of 1875. This law prohibited discrimination in employment and public accommodations to all citizens regardless of race. For the most part the Civil Rights Act of 1875 marked the last major attempt to combat discrimination and racist violence in the South. As Democrats regained congressional seats and hardline Republicans began to die off, the remaining years of the nineteenth century witnessed a turn of events in the area of race relations.

In 1883, the Civil Rights Act of 1875 was declared unconstitutional by the Supreme Court. Then in 1896, racial segregation of American society was buttressed by the Supreme Court decision in *Plessey versus Ferguson*. De facto segregation became de jure segregation. During this same period, a wave of anti–Catholicism hit in the form of the American Protective Association. Though the organization lasted but three years, it helped lay the foundation for a new enemy. In addition, anti–Semitism increased during the early twentieth century as large numbers of immigrants from Eastern and Southern Europe reached the shores of the United States.

Although racial tensions between whites and blacks continued to erupt periodically, the Klan seemed to fade from national view during the final years of the nineteenth century. It did not re-emerge as a viable force until after 1915. This re-emergence seems to be closely associated with the film *Birth of a Nation.*

Birth of a Nation made its debut in the January of 1915. The film portrayed the Klan as the protector of white women and civilization. Blacks were depicted as brutal savages. Within a short time, the American image of the Ku Klux Klan seemed to have changed from bands of vicious terrorists to modern day saints. But as Wyn Craig Wade illustrates in *The Fiery Cross: The Ku Klux Klan in America,* the foundation of such heroic perceptions had already been set down in the works of historians. It was a perception that would continue to be for the next two to four generations. The basic message of these histories was that the Klan attempted to bring law and order to an area of the country that was in chaos. Further, the Klan attempted to combat overly harsh and ven-geance–seeking radical Republicans whose only motivation was to punish the former member states of the Confederacy. According to Wade:

> This is what Americans would be taught about Reconstruction and the Ku–Klux–Klan for the next sixty years of the twentieth century. . . . the distortion of history would be a critical factor in reviving the Klan . . . [and] the impact of historians would be magnified a hundredfold by a misguided genius who made the Reconstruction Ku–Klux–Klan the subject of the first motion-picture box–office smash.[44]

Notwithstanding the biases of historians and the popularity of the film—that incidentally introduced the concept of the fiery cross, racial and ethnic fears and hatreds were already in the minds and hearts of Americans. It was only a matter of time before these would be unleashed. Unfortunately, those who should have known better were also among the xenophobes and ethnocentrists.

Politicians and Scholars. A stage for the appearance of racist thought directed at blacks could not have been better prepared in these final decades of the nineteenth century. In 1890, Alabama Senator John T. Morgan presented the view that God had arranged black and white people to be different and that the two races could not live side by side as equals. He compared the civilization of white Europeans with the "barbarism of Central Africa," claiming that blacks were a servile multitude by nature and their physical appearance dictated an aversion to any mixing between blacks and other races.[45] He also held that "slave laws" were necessary to keep blacks within the norms of civilization: "slave laws held the negro to his daily work; made him temperate; enforced subordination; repressed crime and misdemeanor; and made him a safe and harmless neighbor."[46]

The popular white view of Black Americans by the turn of the century was of semi-savages who could not survive in a civilized world without strict supervision. By 1910, the impact of scientific racism was well underway. The question of black intellectual capacity became a topic of discussion and research. One popular line of thought was the attempt to correlate brain size with intelligence. Findings that black brain size was somewhat less than white brain size led to the speculation that blacks had a lesser capacity for learning that whites.

Historian Hubert Howe Bancroft's 1912 perception of the Black American illustrates a not uncommon view of the times:

> The slaver found the object of his pursuit, as a rule, an enslaved cannibal in the hands of cannibals, to be sold or else to be killed and eaten. . . . It was from such atrocities as these that the southern planter rescued him, gave him work, and made him happy.
>
> • • •
>
> He is a failure here, for effective work is not to be obtained from him except under compulsion. As an American citizen he is a monstrosity. . . .
>
> . . . the negro is good for nothing as a working man, or for anything else, except on the southern plantation, and he is not all that he might be there.
>
> The African is lazy and licentious. . . . It is kismet . . . The animal in him overbalances the mental.
>
> He is by nature and habit a servant, not alone because of his long period of enslavement, but because of his mental inferiority.[47]

By the time of the race wars in the teens and twenties, the second rise of the Klan, and numerous lynchings, the Black American was viewed not only as subhuman, but as a threat to whites—especially to white women. Race mixing emerged as a major racist concern. As with all forms of racism, these views combined various strands of fiction. Some of these fictions were exposed by anthropologists and sociologists in studies during the thirties and forties. The studies by John Dollard (*Caste and Class in a Southern Town*), Hortence Powdermaker (*After Freedom: A Cultural Study of the Deep South*), and Allison Davis, Burleigh B. Gardner, and Mary R. Gardner (*Deep South*), show yet another bizarre relationship between superordinate and subordinate castes. Perhaps the most elucidating work on this strange relationship is to be found in Lillian Smith's *Killers of the Dream*. She notes: "However the white man may have enslaved the Negro's body he did not enslave his soma—his inner stamina, his functions were kept free; and this audacious fact is one of the causes of some white men's envy and fury."[48]

OTHER TARGETS OF RACISM IN AMERICA

During the period from 1870 to the outbreak of World War II, racist thought manifested itself in the attitudes and actions of Americans toward virtually every minority group in a given area. Chinese were viewed as ugly, criminal, sly, and a cursed race. The beliefs and treatment of Chinese in the United States, particularly in California, were a reflection of blind hate and fear—especially economic fear. In his 1876 testimony before the Congressional Joint Special Committee on the question of Chinese immigration, Frank M. Pixley, representing the city government of San Francisco, expressed the following:

> The Chinese are inferior to any race God ever made. . . . there are none so low. . . . Their people have got the perfection of crimes of 4,000 years. . . . The Divine Wisdom has said that He would divide this country and the world as a heritage of five great families; . . . Asia He would give to the Yellow races. . . . the White Race is to have the inheritance of Europe and America and that the Yellow races are to be confined to what the Almighty originally gave them; . . . *they are not to be permitted to steal from us what we have robbed the American savage of.* . . . I believe the Chinese have no souls to save, and if they have, they are not worth saving.[49]

The committee's report, summarized by Mary Roberts Coolidge, described the Chinese in San Francisco as:

> living in "filthy dwellings, on poor food, crowded together, disregarding fire and health ordinances, corrupting the young; they did not assimilate . . . there was no European race which was not su-

perior to them; and that there was not sufficient brain capacity in the Chinese race to furnish motive power for self–government; that they did not desire to become citizens . . . they bought their women; were cruel to the sick, and made their way in California as they had in islands of the sea, not by superior force of industry or virtue, but by revolting characteristics.[50]

By 1882, the Chinese were excluded from entering the United States. In 1888, this exclusion was modified to include Chinese who had been in the United States prior to 1882, had left and sought to return. The following year, the Supreme Court upheld the constitutionality of the Act of 1888. In its decision, the Court held that "they [the Chinese] remained strangers in the land, residing apart by themselves, and adhering to the customs and usages of their own country. It seems impossible for them to assimilate . . . "[51]

Initially, in the last decades of the 1800s, Japanese immigrants were saved from the violence and hatreds that were focused upon Chinese. But by 1910, they too had become targets of racist minds, as illustrated in the following excerpts from an article in the *Sacramento Bee* published in 1913:

Florin, CAL., May 1.—Florin, California is a town of Japs. . . . Less than one–fourth of its population of 500 are white; the rest are Japs. . . . The school, built for children of white men, is now almost half Japanese. . . .

John Reese is the only white man who owns a store in Florin. "Eight years ago," he said, "Florin was a flourishing town. . . . Then the Japs came. Before we had cheap Chinese labor—'bout seven dollars a week, a Chink would work for—but the Skippies [Japanese] took the same jobs for 75 cents a day, and pig tails had to go."

"Now the Jap is a wily an' a crafty individual—more so than the Chink. The Japs realize that the whites do not like to live next to them, so they try to scatter their holdings. They try to buy in the neighborhoods where there are nothin' but white folks. Then its just like when you throw a rock in the river. Mr. Jap is the rock and when he splashes into the midst of . . . white folks he starts a wave of migration. . . . "

"The Jap will always be an undesirable. They are lower in the scale o' civilization than the whites and will never become our equals. They have no morals. Why I have seen one Jap woman sleepin' with half a dozen Jap men. . . . If the state legislature don't enact an anti–alien law that keeps Japs from ownin' land in California, the farmers WILL PASS ONE."[52]

On May 3, 1913, the state of California legislature passed the Alien Land Law. The object of the law was to prevent "aliens"—Japanese and Chinese—from purchasing or inheriting land. Although parts of the law were declared unconstitutional, it would not be repealed in toto until 1956. According to Eldon R. Penrose, the Alien Land Acts of 1913 and 1920 were initiated and created by "yellow journalism, labor unions, party politics, cheap politicians, and job seekers."[53] But underlying all of these forces was the binding fiber of racism and hate prejudice.

Native Americans also were the object of late 19th century racism, but with a twist—they could be civilized. This was unlike the popular conception of blacks as innately and permanently limited in their ability to become totally civilized and intellectually developed.

In 1882, Commissioner of Indian Affairs, Hiram Price, stated the following in his October 10 report:

> If we expect to stop sun dances, snake worship, and other debasing forms of superstition and idolatry among Indians, we must teach them some better way. This, with liberal appropriations by the government for the establishment of industrial schools, where the thousands of Indian children now roaming wild shall be taught to speak the English language and earn their own living, will accomplish what is so much desired, to wit, the conversion of the wild, roving Indian into an industrious, peaceable, and law–abiding citizen.[54]

The conceptions of some of these early officials were relatively positive compared to the views of some scholars. At least in their reports, the commissioners conceded that civilizing these "savages" was a possibility. Daniel G. Brinton, a physician and professor at the University of Pennsylvania, resorted to using cranial vault capacity to argue that Native Americans were innately and permanently inferior to whites.[55] In the Eastern United States, Native Americans had a combined image of the "noble savage" and "savage." West of the Mississippi, the mentality was more of a "Good Indian is a Dead One."

Certainly, there are more cases and episodes that can describe this period of history, a period that may rightfully be called the age of savage superiority. For what can be more savage than to view others as such in the name of civilized superiority? In America, Blacks, Chinese, Italians, and others suffered from lynchings and mob attacks. In Europe, Jews and Gypsies supplied the fodder for ethnic hate and violence. And much of this was reinforced, if not predicated upon the notion of racial and cultural superiority. Again, against this dismal background, it must be pointed out that there were those on every continent and in every country who opposed this wave of ethnocentrism, but their voices could not diminish the brutal cruelty.

Racist Thought: From Past to Present

Gobineau and others reflected a line of thinking that would eventually manifest itself in some of the most savage acts ever committed by nations. If there are those among us who believe that the expressed thoughts of people can do no harm, let them trace the concept of racial thought from the writings of a Gobineau to the ovens of an Auschwitz, to the smoldering lynch victims in the United States.

Gobineau certainly held a classical racist view, but today's racists hold not only to an intellectual form of racism, they represent a total attitude: racist beliefs, hate prejudice, and a predisposition to hate violently. Furthermore, they are not all extremist crackpots babbling to themselves on park benches. They come in all walks of life: teachers, preachers, professors, engineers, the old, the young, the white and the black.

In chapter eight, we shall survey both groups and individuals who have made racism their religion, their vocation, their hobby— their source of inspiration. However, before this encounter with hate groups and individual haters, the following three chapters may prove useful. These chapters on prejudiced attitudes, stereotyping, and discrimination and aggression will provide us with a framework by which to examine the nature of hate groups and individuals bent on hate.

CHAPTER 5

PREJUDICE AND ATTITUDES

Prejudice, if not acted out, if kept to oneself, does no great social harm. It merely stultifies the mind that possesses it.

—Gordon W. Allport

Unlike acts of violence and discrimination, prejudice is an attitude and cannot be directly observed. Nevertheless, attitudes by their nature provide the basis for social action, and those attitudes of ethnic and racial prejudices form the wellspring from which violence flows. In this chapter, we shall explore the nature of attitudes and their relationship to prejudice.

Since prejudice is an example of attitude, the problem arose as how to address the relationship between prejudice and attitude. Should attitude be explained and discussed first and then prejudice, or should we commence with a discussion on prejudice and lead to attitude? Indeed, a number of definitions describe prejudice as an attitude within the former's definition. In these instances, the utility of the definitions seems to be inadequate unless one has a grasp of what the authors mean by attitude. On the other hand, it may be of value to stipulate a definition of prejudice at the outset, address attitude, and return to prejudice at some later time. This sequence would provide an anchor for the main concept, prejudice, and permit us to explore attitude within the context of prejudice.

Prejudice

A Definition of Prejudice

For most people, prejudice assumes a meaning of prejudging some person, group, or thing. Although prejudices do contain an element of prejudgment, the two concepts are not synonymous. In addition, prejudice, from a social psychological perspective, includes a more complex set of attributes. In this chapter and throughout the book, we shall define ethnic or racial prejudice as *a readiness to act, stemming from a negative feeling, often predicated upon a fixed overgeneralization or totally false belief and directed toward a group or individual members of that group.*

Prejudice can be conceived as positive as well as negative. One example of a positive prejudice might be when an individual prejudges a situation in favor of someone he or she loves. However, prejudice generally has negative connotations in the area of race and ethnic relations. The issue of treating prejudice as solely negative will be more fully addressed later in this chapter. Furthermore, it should be noted that there is no definitive definition of prejudice, but there is almost universal agreement that prejudice is an attitude. The definition provided above is designed to include the essential attributes of attitude as treated in this chapter.

OVERGENERALIZATIONS

An overgeneralization is a belief about all members of a group that is not actually true of all members. For instance, the belief that Japanese are shrewd, sly, and treacherous may be true about some Japanese, as it would be of some members of any other ethnic or racial group. But it is preposterous to apply it to all members of a group. Nevertheless, one holding such a belief may feel uneasy about trusting, dealing with, or associating with Japanese people.

An overgeneralization may be based upon cultural norms, individual experiences, and psychological processes, or a combination of these. Ethnocentric beliefs and certain xenophobias are often indicative of cultural norms. Personal experiences and an individual's psychological make–up may also determine how one perceives other groups and the extent of his/her tendency to over generalize. More often than not, these cultural and personal aspects are interwoven.

ETHNOCENTRIC BELIEFS

An ethnocentric belief is one that judges other cultures and groups as inferior or innately evil as compared to one's own. Blind patriotism that results in notions of "my country, right or wrong" tends to reflect ethnocentric beliefs. Terms such as chauvinism and jingoism have been used to describe extreme nationalist convictions.

Most religious groups tend to exhibit some degree of ethnocentrism. The Protestant denominations, Catholicism, Islam, and Judaism all maintain that their individual belief system reflects the "Truth." Therefore, it follows that anyone who is not in accord with a particular dogma must be in error. Ethnocentric beliefs are not always overgeneralizations. What they do is to create a perspective that encourages negative beliefs that may be only partially true or totally false.

Xenophobia, or the fear of strangers (racially and culturally different people), also may be a cause for negative overgeneralizations and feelings. It is closely linked to ethnocentrism and reinforces it by maintaining social contact distance. So long as groups are separated, members of each group may associate and presume the existence of all sorts of objectionable traits of the other. Xenophobia will be treated more extensively in the following chapter on stereotyping.

FALSEHOOD

Most definitions of prejudice that use the concept overgeneralization fail to mention totally false belief. An overgeneralization usually implies that a statement is true in some but not all cases to which it has been applied. Therefore, I have added the alternate attribute of totally false belief.

A totally false belief requires no introduction. It is simply a blatant lie. One such belief is that black people are capable of reproducing offspring by mating with apes. This belief has been used to justify the feeling that blacks are innately disgusting objects, subhuman, and should not be permitted to "mix" with whites.

While I have added the attribute of "totally false belief" to the definition of prejudice, it should be noted that all overgeneralizations are false. They are false by nature of the fact that they are applied to all members of a group when they are not true about all members of the group. For example, the statement, "all white southerners are bigots," is a falsehood, even if it is true about some southern whites. Why, then, is it necessary to dwell on the notion and add the concept of totally false belief? The answer is a matter of stressing the other dimension of an overgeneralization. Some may think that an overgeneralization necessitates that it must be true for at least one, if not a few, members of the target group. In this dimension of the concept, the individual often ignores the fact that the statement is entirely false.

OTHER DEFINITIONS OF PREJUDICE

At this juncture, one may ask why prejudice simply cannot be regarded as a negative feeling stemming from a negative belief. Indeed, Wolfgang Stroebe and Chester A. Insko define prejudice as "an attitude [consisting of a belief, feeling, and behavior] toward members of some outgroup and in which the evaluative tendencies are predominantly negative."[1] They are quick to emphasize that their definition is not limited to "a dislike based upon irrational beliefs." Accordingly, they state, "While outgroup rejection may often seem unjustified, there are other instances when it is justifiable and legitimate (e.g., the rejection by American blacks of the KKK, . . . "[2]

It appears that Stroebe and Insko would have us regard any dislike or negative feeling toward members of any outgroup as a prejudice. Literally of course, this is nonsense, since a person of one group may have a legitimate reason for hating a person who happens to be a member of another group. Therefore, let us proceed with the notion that Stroebe and Insko mean a dislike *because* of the person's membership in an outgroup. But even in this case, one may contest their definition.

One might argue that a dislike, feeling of contempt, or hatred is not a prejudice if it is "justifiable and legitimate." If we were to accept this contraposition, it undoubtedly would place us in the role of Stephen Crane's wayfarer who, seeking the pathway to truth, found it overgrown with weeds and "each weed was a singular knife."[3] For we are struck immediately with the problem of how one determines what is justifiable and legitimate. But to pursue this issue at length may take us off course. Let it suffice at this time to respond so. Justifiable and legitimate are determined by empirical, observable evidence, the facts, if you will, and by application of what in legal circles has come to be known as the mind of the reasonable person. Further, let the judgment of justifiable and legitimate be regarded as tentative and subject to change as new facts are brought to bear on the particular issue. This may not offer much, but it is somewhat more than the wayfarer, who upon noting that each weed was a blade of steel, mumbled, "Doubtless there are other roads."[4]

If we were to accept the Stroebe and Insko definition and regard any negative feeling toward any outgroup including its members as a prejudice, then we would be inclined to regard blacks who have contempt for the KKK and Jews who regard Nazis with disdain as prejudiced. Furthermore, in the education of children, if teachers include in their mission the reduction of prejudice, how should we expect the teacher to handle these prejudices? One can imagine the outcry from parents and others if a teacher were to suggest that it is wrong for black children to regard the KKK as "bad" or "evil."

On the other hand, it may seem appropriate to teach that what Klan and Nazi members believe is wrong or evil, but one should not despise them. This closely approaches the principle of rejecting what one does or believes without rejecting the individual. This may seem theoretically sound, but it may be very difficult to actualize. It becomes a problem of whether one can regard the snake as venomous in toto or regard merely its venom glands as poisonous. Answering the question of whether it is a prejudice to dislike members of a group that threaten one's own life (to use an extreme example) is not an easy task. It certainly falls into the category of shades of gray.

There is nothing sacrosanct about either Stroebe and Insko's definition or the definition proposed for this work. As Thomas F. Pettigrew noted, "Definitions of prejudice abound."[5] The definition proposed in this work is a slight modification of the meaning expressed by Gordon Allport in his work, *The Nature of Prejudice*.

Allport defines ethnic prejudice as "an antipathy based upon a faulty and inflexible generalization. It may be felt or expressed. It may be directed toward a group as a whole, or toward an individual because he is a member of that group."[6] Although a prejudgment is implied in both definitions, Allport explains that not all prejudgments are necessarily elements of prejudice. They become "prejudices only if they are not reversible when exposed to new knowledge."[7] Similarly, in their text, *Racial and Cultural Minorities: An Analysis of Prejudice and Discrimination*, George E. Simpson and J. Milton Yinger define prejudice as "an emotional, rigid attitude (a predisposition to respond to a certain stimulus in a certain way) toward a group of people."[8] Adding to their definition, Simpson and Yinger stress the element of irreversibility in their statement: "When a preexisting attitude is so strong and inflexible that it seriously distorts perception and judgment, one has a prejudice."[9]

Other authors and researchers have chosen to define prejudice in more general terms. Walter G. Stephan makes a point of presenting a more ambiguous definition—"Prejudice consists of negative attitudes toward social groups."[10] Stephan claims that, "If there is a controversial aspect of this definition, it is in the omission of a moral rejection of prejudice as unjustified and wrong."[11] However,

Stephan's definition seems to have eliminated more than a value judgment. Without some understanding of what he means by attitude, his definition of prejudice tells us little. Since prejudice belongs to the more general class of attitude, definitions such as Stephan's are more relational than stipulative. They identify the more general class to which the concept belongs rather than the criterial attributes or properties of the concept. If social scientists had some universally accepted definition of attitude, these relational definitions would not be difficult to understand. Unfortunately, such has not been the case.

Attitude

William J. McGuire notes that numerous definitions of attitude have been reported since 1935 when Allport identified sixteen, and that, in a 1972 review, Ajzen and Fishbein reported finding "500 different operational definitions of attitude."[12] Despite this large number of definitions, McGuire fails to mention the degree of overlap among them. In this section, we shall examine one generally accepted or partially accepted definition of attitude and a model of attitude components that has been used to describe the meaning of attitude. During this examination, we shall attempt to cull those aspects of attitude that may provide us with a more operational understanding of prejudice.

Allport's Meaning of Attitude

In a seminal 1935 work entitled, "Attitudes," Gordon Allport defined attitude as a "mental and neural state of readiness to respond, organized through experience, exerting a directive or dynamic influence upon the individual's response to all objects and situations with which it is related."[13] The key elements of this definition include: (a) mental and neural, (b) readiness to respond, (c) organized through experience, and (d) a directive or dynamic influence on behavior. How each of these elements has a direct bearing upon the nature of prejudice as an attitude will be seen.

MENTAL AND NEURAL STATE

The conception of a mental and neural state suggests that an attitude involves a complex interaction among mind, emotion, and physiology. As such, we can expect an attitude to encompass the entire dynamic structural makeup of the personality. In other words, attitudes are neither passive nor quiescent. In addition, the mental and neural state denotes that attitudes have both a cognitive and affective component.[14]

ORGANIZED THROUGH EXPERIENCE

When the attribute of a mental and neural state is viewed along with the notion that attitudes are organized through experience, it becomes apparent that Allport perceives attitudes as learned. Although there is strong agreement to this effect, Robyn M. Dawes and Tom L. Smith take issue with the idea that all attitudes are learned. Accordingly, they state, "We don't understand the insistence of attitude theorists that all attitudes are learned. There is no evidence mandating learning as a mechanism."[15] But in this case, Dawes and Smith are referring to attitudes in general. When Dawes was asked about racial and ethnic prejudiced attitudes, he immediately refuted the notion that such attitudes were hereditary.[16]

McGuire addresses the role of genetics in attitude formation, but he relies heavily on non-human subjects in his research.[17] There is no reason to reject the hypothesis that genetics may play a role in certain aspects of attitude formation and the expression of certain attitudes. However, there is currently no evidence that heredity is a major factor in those attitudes reflecting racial or ethnic prejudices.

The stipulation that attitudes are organized indicates that they exist within a cognitive structure or schema.[18] This may imply that strong prejudiced attitudes are not merely bits of misinformation that can be corrected by simply supplying isolated pieces of counter information. Although prejudgments based upon misinformation or misconceptions are more readily changed among those maintaining flexibility of mind, this does not necessarily indicate a reduction or change in prejudice. As Allport and others noted, the prejudgments of an open–minded individual are not prejudices. On this point, we might question whether prejudice reduction treatments used in educational settings are effecting changes in prejudiced attitudes or merely correcting misconceptions of basically non–prejudiced individuals.

READINESS TO RESPOND

The most salient attribute of Allport's definition is a readiness to respond. The issue of whether an attitude is a readiness to respond or an actual response has been the subject of debate for over half a century among social scientists. But it appears to make more sense to accept the readiness to respond for attitude and to describe actual responses in terms of how the attitude is manifest in overt behavior. For example, a prejudice may be a readiness to respond, while scapegoating or discrimination are best described as particular actions stemming from prejudices.

In his treatment of the readiness to respond, Allport distinguishes between attitude and other forms of readiness. Some of these distinctions may be of value in attempting to better understand the nature of prejudice. For if prejudice is an attitude, it is distinct from the other forms of readiness. Allport differentiates between attitude and habit by noting that habits "are not accompanied by a customary feeling of favor or disfavor; they are more automatic and less partisan."[19] In his comparison of attitude and instincts, Allport provides four essential differences: (a) attitudes are almost always learned; (b) they are "highly individualized . . . and not universal;" (c) attitudes are "directive" as opposed to "driving"—meaning that one chooses when, where, how, and to what extent the attitude will be expressed as compared to an almost involuntary compulsive attitudinal response; and (d) attitudes have a greater cognitive foundation.

In contrasting attitudes and opinions, Allport presents two views. He states that Thurstone regards an opinion as the expression of an attitude. In other words, an individual's opinion makes his or her attitude known. From another perspective, Allport quotes Robert Ezra Park, who holds that opinions are one's "explanations and justification of his attitudes, rather than his actual tendencies to act."[20] From these two views, the critical difference between attitude and opinion is that an opinion is an overt expression either indicating the nature of the attitude or one's rationalization for it. A person may very well refrain from expressing her/his true attitude either consciously or unconsciously in a given situation.[21] This may be especially true when one is asked to express an attitude regarding a highly sensitive topic such as beliefs and feelings toward racial and ethnic groups.

In his comparison between attitude and trait, Allport describes a trait as "a form or manner of behaving" and an attitude as a "directed tendency." Accordingly, he states: "One may have an attitude of fear *toward* objects, persons, . . . or classes of ideas, but one *is* in one's very nature yielding, shy, submissive, retiring, or bashful."[22] Here Allport has distinguished between actual behavior and a predisposition to act.

Directive and Dynamic Influence

Allport suggests that attitudes have a directive or dynamic influence on behavior. Actually, he should have stated that attitudes have a directive *and* dynamic influence.[23] Direction identifies the nature of the attitude as being either positive or negative. What Allport identifies as a dynamic influence seems to be the intensity or the amount of energy with which one holds a given attitude. These two features of attitude provide the basis of how often, where, and to what extent an attitude may be expressed.

Although Allport's definition stipulates that an attitude sets the stage for action, both social and psychological forces may curtail the acting out of a given attitude. Indeed, it has been suggested that these influences may actually create three somewhat distinct attitudes when viewed from the conative (readiness to act) attribute of attitude.

During the mid-seventies, a study among high school juniors and seniors revealed that individuals may be said to hold three levels of attitude toward the same attitude object. These were labelled as intergroup, intragroup, and mental. The researchers defined the intergroup level as attitudes expressed by members of one group (A) toward members of another group (B) in the presence of the other group—when groups A and B were mixed. The intragroup level was defined as attitudes expressed about a different group when the latter was not present—what members of group A expressed about group B when group A members were amongst themselves. Finally, the mental level referred to an individual's (e.g., group A member) thoughts about another group (e.g., group B), which were not shared, even with her or his own group.[24]

The results of the study showed that at the intergroup level, attitudes expressed were more tolerant, and at the intragroup level, attitudes expressed were less tolerant. When individuals were asked what they thought about the other group when alone, rather than in either of the former settings, the responses were most negative. The study indicates that prejudiced attitudes can be and are controlled under various conditions. On the other hand, these attitudes may be so ingrained that, if push comes to shove in a conflict or perceived conflict situation, the predisposition to act on a set of prejudiced attitudes may emerge in violent behavior.

This review of the nature of attitudes is by no means exhaustive. Theories of attitude formation, structure, and change have been at the center of attention among social psychologists for over fifty years. But in this highly select treatment, we can begin to appreciate its complexities and its implications when attempting to examine the concept prejudice.

In addition to the above treatment of attitude, there are two topics that beg our attention. These are the notion of the influence of attitudes on perception and the concept of the prejudiced or authoritarian personality. Regarding the former, Allport noted that, just as an attitude contains a readiness to respond, it also includes a readiness to receive. In other words, our attitude toward some object, place, event, or person will influence how and what we perceive as reality.

Readiness to Receive

The emphasis of the discussion on the readiness to respond has been limited to a readiness to act outwardly on the part of the owner of the attitude. However, we should be cognizant of the fact that attitudes determine what and how information and experiences are received and evaluated by the same individual. Allport states:

> Without guiding attitudes the individual is confused and baffled. Some kind of preparation is essential before he can make a satisfactory observation, pass suitable judgment, or make any but the most primitive reflex type of response. Attitudes determine for each individual what he will see and hear, what he will think and what he will do.[25]

From this, we might infer that, not only are attitudes the preparatory mechanisms for acting, but they also are preparatory mechanisms for receiving. As such, ethnic or racial prejudices will serve to influence the perceptual processes of an individual at various stages of perception. A prejudiced attitude may serve to determine what is selected in perceiving and how it is to be interpreted. We select those aspects of an experience upon which to focus our attention, and we ignore other aspects. This selection process structures our perceptions of reality.

PREJUDICE AND SELECTIVE PERCEPTION

The selection process can be positive or negative. On one hand, it prevents cluttering up the mind with irrelevant minutiae that can result in a world of a "jumble of experiences."[26] On the other hand, selectivity may result in overlooking and thereby rejecting important details and facts, leading to a distortion of reality. Prejudices that are well embedded in the cognitive structure of an individual will influence what is selected and, if it is selected, how it is handled in at least four ways.

First, the individual may ignore conflicting information or experiences through selective exposure. The safest mechanism of ignoring something is to avoid it altogether. When a person receives a negative impression of another either through an initial encounter or secondhand, he or she may resist obtaining further knowledge about the individual. There is little doubt that avoidance can lead to a distorted perception of the individual's true character. In the case of a prejudice, avoidance serves to maintain the original structure and stability of the prejudice. Albert Hastorf, et al. suggest that we tend to avoid people who, after initial contact, remain puzzling to us. "No wonder the behavior of most people we 'know' makes sense."[27]

Repression is another form of ignoring something that involves filtering out portions of an experience. Through repression, an individual may alter aspects of reality. Repression is a useful technique, albeit often unconscious, in avoiding aspects of reality that are unpleasant, fearful, painful, or disagreeable. A strong prejudice in conflict with a contradictory experience may contain all or some of these aspects. This is especially true if the prejudice serves as the foundation for a person's status, self–esteem, or understanding of reality.

Second, he or she may misinterpret or reinterpret the new experience in order to fit the prejudiced attitude. This may or may not involve some aspects of repression. Misinterpretation may occur when a person perceives some positive fact or statement about another person or group as a criticism of her or his own group. Misinterpretations also may result from erroneous associations. The story is told of a new office manager assigned to a federal installation. Upon his initial tour of the work area, he commented that the government was niggardly—referring to its allocations for equipment. A number of black employees present in the area were immediately offended by the remark—having associated the term niggardly with the pejorative term, nigger.

Reinterpretation is the process of changing the facts surrounding a situation in order to accommodate one's attitudes towards individuals or groups involved in the situation. For example, individuals and hate groups have attempted to deny the destruction of European Jewry by constructing a revisionist version of the

Holocaust. According to one revisionist position taught to high school students, the Jews died of a disease only acquired by Jews. Another aspect of reinterpretation might be illustrated when one is exposed to a positive fact about some group or its members, but finds a way of interpreting it as a criticism. Pettigrew identifies four ways in which this may be expressed:

> 1) an exceptional case ("She is certainly bright and energetic—not like other Chicanas."); 2) luck or special advantage ("He either made it through dumb luck or affirmative action—he could never have done it on his own."); 3) unusually high motivation and effort ("Jewish students make better grades just because they study so hard."); 4) manipulable situational context ("What could the cheap Scot do but pay the whole check after the waiter handed it to him and we all looked at him in silence?").[28]

A third conflicting experience may be rationalized through bifurcation, as implied in Pettigrew's notion of the exceptional case. Allport refers to this as "rationalization by making exceptions."[29] He explains bifurcation as a tool that permits one to acknowledge exceptions to a prejudiced attitude without modifying the attitude.

> If one makes a few exceptions, then one can justify holding the remaining portion of the category intact. . . . If one has good friends within a group, then one's adverse opinion of the remainder of the group cannot possibly be due to prejudice. It appears to be a carefully considered and discriminated judgment. The device usually fools both speaker and listener. But the fact is that the phrase, "Some of my best friends are. . . . " is almost invariably a cover–up to protect the remainder of the prejudiced category intact.[30]

A fourth way by which one's prejudices can influence what or how something is received is by rejection. This may take the form of outright refusal to accept the conflicting experience. Here the individual may respond that "This is not what it seems—it's fake; it's just not true." Rejection also may manifest itself in the individual's presentation of information or beliefs that attempt to discredit the conflicting experience. Indeed, selective exposure resulting from a prejudice may include "seeking out information that confirms one's preconceptions and avoiding information that is discrepant with one's initial belief, thus minimizing the introduction of inconsistencies into one's belief system."[31]

The interaction between attitudes—especially prejudices—and perceptual processes should indicate the need for communication and interpersonal relations skills among trainers and teachers who wish to engage effectively in prejudice reduction education. It also indicates a need for such educators to have a strong knowledge base in the areas of racial and ethnic relations. It has been said that good communication is the lifeline to good human relations. To this we might add that good communication skills are necessary to deal effectively with educating about racial and ethnic prejudice.

Personality and Prejudice

Following World War II, Theodore W. Adorno and his associates attempted to determine the relationship between attitudes of hate prejudice and personality. In 1950, following extensive research, Adorno and his team introduced the concept of the authoritarian personality. The researchers described the authoritarian personality as the result of one's traits developed during their upbringing. They state:

> Thus, a basically hierarchical, authoritarian, exploitive parent–child relationship is apt to carry over into a power–oriented, exploitively dependent attitude toward one's sex partner and one's God, and may well culminate in a political philosophy and social outlook which has no room for anything but a desperate clinging to what appears to be strong and a disdainful rejection of whatever is relegated to the bottom. . . . Conventionality, rigidity, repressive denial, and the ensuing break-through of one's weakness, fear and dependency are but other aspects of the same fundamental personality pattern, and they can be observed in personal life as well as in attitudes toward religion and social issues.[32]

In their attempt to measure authoritarianism, Adorno and his fellow researchers identified nine variables that led to the development of what was labelled the F–scale (Fascist scale). These variables and their definitions are presented below. They describe the attributes of what Adorno, et al., regard as the authoritarian personality:

a. Conventionalism. Rigid adherence to conventional, middle–class values.
b. Authoritarian submission. Submissive, uncritical attitude toward idealized moral authorities of the ingroup.
c. Authoritarian aggression. Tendency to be on the lookout for, and to condemn, reject, and punish people who violate conventional values.

    d. Anti-intraception. Opposition to the subjective, the imaginative, and the tenderminded.

    e. Superstition and stereotypy. The belief in mystical determinants of the individual's fate; the disposition to think in rigid categories.

    f. Power and "toughness." Preoccupation with the dominance–submission, strong–weak, leader–follower dimension; identification with power figures; overemphasis upon the conventionalized attributes of the ego; exaggerated assertion of strength and toughness.

    g. Destructiveness and cynicism. Generalized hostility, vilification of the human.

    h. Projectivity. The disposition to believe that wild and dangerous things go on in the world; the projection outwards of unconscious emotional impulses.

    i. Sex. Exaggerated concern with sexual "goings–on."[33]

From these descriptions, it appears that the authoritarian personality occurs in an individual who has acquired strong hostile traits resulting from childhood. There is no reason to believe, however, that this personality may not develop in later years based upon adult experiences. The latter might include such cases as an abused spouse or individual belonging to a organization where her/his role is one of a child in a child–parent transactional relationship as described by Eric Berne in his *Games People Play.*[34]

For Adorno and company, the authoritarian personality seems to be a case of victimized child turned adult victimizer. In the role of victimizer, this person seeks to identify with a power figure, symbol, or ideology and to act out aggressively toward susceptible targets, as in the case of ethnic or racial minorities. This aggression might be explained as an attempt to seek empowerment over others. This is much like the individual's perceived aggression employed against her/him during an earlier period of her/his life. It might even be interpreted as a role–modelling effect combining a love–hate ambivalence with fear and aggression.

A barrage of criticism that has emerged regarding the research of Adorno and his colleagues, ranging from weaknesses in their research method to charges that the study was innately biased because it was sponsored by the American Jewish Committee. However, "more than 1,200 studies on the authoritarian personality have been reported . . . " since 1950.[35]

The authoritarian personality has been loosely referred to as a highly prejudiced personality. Research regarding authoritarian personality traits may help explain the relationship between prejudiced attitudes and other constructs such as moral judgment and ethnocentrism. One such study, carried out in the mid–eighties, attempted to determine the relationship between these constructs and three of the nine traits of the authoritarian personality. This study, by Marinus H. van Ijzendoorn, selected conventionalism, submission, and aggression to compare with ethnocentrism and moral judgment.[36]

AUTHORITARIANISM AND MORAL DEVELOPMENT

Van Ijzendoorn hypothesized that authoritarianism might be a dysfunction of moral development. Van Ijzendoorn found that "First, higher levels of moral judgment were related to a less authoritarian attitude. Second, a less authoritarian attitude was related to a less ethnocentric attitude. . . . Third, a less ethnocentric attitude was found to be related to higher levels of moral judgment."[37] These findings led van Ijzendoorn to conclude, "that cognitive–development theory of morality could add some specific insights to the theory of the authoritarian personality."[38] Finally, van Ijzendoorn suggests that the authoritarian personality may be more of a matter of "stagnation in moral development" than the psychodynamic explanations offered by the earlier researchers. Van Ijzendoorn's findings and suggestions may provide insights into the development of the Skinhead movements in the United States and elsewhere. The authoritarian personality concept in addition to van Ijzendoorn's suggestion may explain the attitudes held by a large number of highly prejudiced individuals, as well as others. In addition, it may help explain the formation of hate groups and the psychology of their members—especially among adolescents and young adults.

The definition of attitude provided by Allport paved the way for social psychologists for over fifty years. His definition has been at the center of discussions and debates in every major compendium on research and theory of social psychology since 1935. While there is no universal agreement as to the nature of attitudes and the sources of prejudice, what has been offered may merit serious consideration. However, there is yet one more model of the structure of attitude that may be useful in examining the nature of prejudice.

This model considers three components of attitude, the affective, cognitive, and conative.

Prejudice and the Components of Attitude

Having examined attitude from Allport's perspective and in relation to the concept of prejudice, we shall follow with a brief examination of the three-component model of attitude. These components already have been mentioned. The model defines an attitude as consisting of a cognitive, an affective, and a conative component. As in the case of the stipulated definition of attitude, we shall attempt to find linkages between this model of attitude and the concept of prejudice.

AFFECTIVE COMPONENT

The affective component of an attitude refers to one's feeling toward the attitude object, the person or thing toward which an individual's attitude is directed. The affective component of an attitude expressed in the above definition of prejudice is the "negative feeling."

Many students and teachers, as well as others, have asked why a prejudice cannot be positive. Three standard explanations have been offered from time to time.

The first is that prejudice within the study of ethnic and race relations is always negative by stipulation. In other words, it is negative because we say it is. The second response is quite similar to the first but more apologetic. Prejudice used in the context of ethnic and race relations is always negative, and perhaps it would be more accurate to use the label ethnic or racial prejudice.

The third response acknowledges the existence of love prejudice but rationalizes that its flip side is negative. Notwithstanding that "love prejudice" may exist, when it involves a comparison to another individual or group, the results will tend to be a negative evaluation of the latter. How often do we notice that, when a person criticizes another's spouse or child, it creates an almost instant and aggressive reaction in defense of the "loved one" being criticized? Although none of these explanations may be satisfactory in all instances or for all inquirers, we shall refer to prejudice in this work as consisting of a negative feeling.

The affective component of attitude includes three dimensions which can assist in understanding levels of prejudices that may result in behaviors ranging from mildly negative and non-violent to acts of mass murder. These dimensions include direction, degree, and intensity. The *direction* of an attitude, as noted earlier, merely refers to whether one's feeling is positive or negative. In the case of prejudice, we have stipulated that a prejudice includes a negative feeling.

Degree of feeling of an attitude identifies the extent to which an individual feels or perceives the attitude object as positive or negative. For example, suppose a group of people were asked to respond to the question: "How do you feel about marriages between people of different racial groups?" Furthermore, they are instructed to indicate their responses by selecting one of the following choices:

> very good, good [x] wrong, very wrong

Assuming the respondents answered honestly, we would be able to determine both the direction and degree of their attitudes on this topic. The "x" indicates a point of departure for direction. If an individual indicates a feeling to the left of the "x", we can identify this as a positive feeling. If the response is to right of the "x", we would identify this as a negative feeling. However, if one individual responded with the choice of "wrong" and another individual selected "very wrong," we might conclude that the person selecting "very wrong" has a greater negative degree of feeling than the former individual. Anyone attempting to deal with prejudice reduction programs should realize instantly the importance of having some indication of both the direction and degree of her/his clients' attitudes toward ethnic and racial groups.

Intensity of an attitude is the amount of emotional energy associated with one's feeling about the attitude object. In their text, *Social Psychology: The Study of Human Interaction,* Newcomb, Turner, and Converse, acknowledge that "Sometimes a distinction is drawn between the degree of attitude and the intensity with which that attitude is held."[39] On the other hand, since some studies indicate that intensity is highly correlated with degree, the authors conclude that "For most purposes, then, we can afford to ignore such a distinction."[40]

William A. Scott approaches the relationship between degree and intensity more cautiously. Scott states, "Whether or not one regards this as a tautology depends upon one's ability to conceptualize the two attributes in ways that are sufficiently distinct to generate distinguishable sets of measures."[41]

The notion expressed by Newcomb, Turner, and Converse was challenged in a study by Kleg, Borgeld, and Sullivan. Their research indicated no meaningful or significant correlation between degree and intensity.[42] Nor did they find a meaningful or significant correlation between degree and frequency (how often the attitude is expressed). However, the researchers did report a significant and somewhat meaningful correlation between intensity and frequency. These findings lead them to suggest the following:

> Knowing that a negative attitude exists and the extent [degree] of the attitude is one thing; knowing whether or not the attitude involves disdain *with* or *without* vigor and the number of times this attitude is presented is something else. The skilled teacher of ethnic relations must be equipped to analyze a situation in such a manner that he will be able to identify a viable and appropriate treatment for his subjects.[43]

A number of prejudice reduction programs have emphasized the affective component of attitude. Yet, rarely do they address the structure of attitude in relation to the nature of prejudice. As a consequence, the results of such treatments may have been relatively superficial.

COGNITIVE COMPONENT

The cognitive component of attitude refers to the beliefs or knowledge one has about some person, place, event, or object. These beliefs or knowledge may be accurate, partially accurate, or totally fictitious.

The cognitive or belief component of prejudice is found in the phrase "often based upon a fixed overgeneralization or totally false belief." A generalization is a true statement about all cases or instances to which the generalization is applied. An overgeneralization is a statement that is applied to all cases but is not true in all cases, as noted earlier. By their very nature, all overgeneralizations are false since they are applied to all members of a group when the statement is not true about all members of the group. In addition, there are beliefs that are totally false.

The cognitive component of ethnic and racial prejudices is intrinsically tied to the concept, stereotype. Stereotypes are usually described as fixed mental pictures that often are applied to all members of a group. This concept is so salient in the development of prejudiced attitudes that we shall treat stereotypes and stereotyping as the major focus in the following chapter. For the moment we shall confine our examination of the cognitive component of attitude and prejudice to three other properties of attitude: centrality, embeddedness, and ambivalence.

Centrality is the term used to describe the extent to which an individual remains attentive to an attitude object. The concept, salience, also appears to be used to describe the same condition.[44] The compulsive hater of other groups may spend much of her/his time thinking and discussing the danger of such groups. For this individual, we might conclude that her/his prejudices toward the group have high centrality. Another person who may hold similar negative beliefs and feelings toward a group, but who does not give these prejudices much thought may be said to have a lower centrality of attitude as compared to the compulsive hater. An awareness of the degree of centrality of a person's ethnic or racial attitudes can be a useful tool in analyzing how to deal with another's prejudices.

The individual whose prejudiced attitude involves a very high level of centrality will not be readily influenced by mild, reflective activities. Furthermore, there is a high probability that such an individual will "know" more about the attitude object—particular group, than one whose level of centrality is relatively low. The former individual can be expected to pose more challenges, more false or partially false information, and to resist change to a greater extent than those with lower levels of centrality. The appearance of a high level of centrality may indicate a strong degree of embeddedness.

When an individual's beliefs about an attitude object are preeminently intertwined within her/his cognitive structure, the attitude may be said to be embedded. The degree to which the attitude is interrelated with other beliefs and intellectual schema is known as the degree of *embeddedness*.[45] When the attitude is not highly integrated into the cognitive structure of an individual, it may be regarded as "isolated."[46] A strong degree of embeddedness may exist for the individual who seems continually to find some way to introduce or express her/his prejudiced beliefs about some group regardless of the topic of discussion.

A third attribute of the cognitive component of attitude is *ambivalence*. Ambivalence results from a mixture of positive and negative beliefs about the attitude object. It also can refer to mixed feelings and therefore be regarded as both a cognitive and affective attribute. A person who holds only negative or only positive beliefs about a group will tend to have less ambivalence than one who has mixed beliefs. The more one holds ambivalent beliefs, the more likely this individual can be expected to be flexible in changing her/ his overall attitude toward a group. This change can be in either a more positive or more negative direction.

CONATIVE COMPONENT

The conative component may be described as either behavior or a readiness to behave—a predisposition to act in a certain manner. In the case of prejudice this component is expressed in the above definition by the phrase "readiness to act." The extent to which one will act on a given attitude depends upon both personal psychological and social forces. Social expectations, social conventions, conformity, and psychological needs and impulses usually will determine the degree of actually acting out a prejudiced attitude.

The greater the degree, intensity, and centrality of an attitude, the more likely it will be expressed in some active form. Once an attitude is expressed through overt action, we can begin to evaluate and infer the nature of one's attitude. However, it must be emphasized that inferences are subject to error and revision.

The Components of Attitude and Educational Programs

Before leaving the topic of the three components of attitude, it may be beneficial to examine the types of educational and training designs that reflect one or more of the three components of attitude. The most common educational treatments or programs for reducing prejudice have emphasized the cognitive, affective, or both cognitive and affective components of attitude. Usually, this is not a matter of conscious choice by the curriculum or instructional designers. More often, it is a matter of emphasizing what their gut feeling tells them needs to be done. We might refer to this as the good citizen approach. This contrasts with the analytic approach in which the designer attempts to develop a program to address all or some of the components of attitude and attitude change situations.

Cognitive Centered Approach

Instructional materials emphasizing a cognitive approach stress factual information and tend to be less controversial. Consequently, the approach will be more acceptable for teachers, parents, and others who may influence what will be used in a classroom setting. In addition, factually based information can be legitimately integrated into an existing curriculum without charges of "wasting time on feely, touchy activities."

Affective Centered Approach

Affectively centered educational treatments or supplementary units are more subject to criticism. As can be expected, they are designed to create positive feelings which in turn may create discomfort and resistance among those receiving the instruction or treatment. Prejudiced attitudes are not readily subject to change. Often, an individual's affective component of attitude is more consciously an integral part of one's self-concept than the cognitive component. In other words, it is much easier to say, "Oh, I didn't know that (as a matter of fact)," rather than to admit one's feelings about something or some persons are wrong.

Cognitive–Affective Approach

The cognitive–affective approach includes a treatment whereby the instruction presents factual information and also attempts to have subjects reexamine both their beliefs and feelings. In this scenario the individual may be asked to examine her or his feelings in light of the new knowledge obtained.

The cognitive–affective approach may use a variety of activities designed to have subjects apply new information and to evaluate the consequences of actions stemming from prejudices. The use of metaphors and analogies, quality films, literary works, and guest speakers or resource persons can be of significant use in a cognitive–affective based program.

Conative Centered Approach

A conatively focused program or situation may have either negative or positive effects. A program or treatment designed along conative lines stresses intergroup activities. Subjects are provided with the opportunity to work with members of different groups in a cooperative manner. When the focus is on behavior, there may be a tendency to ignore the cognitive component and, to a lesser degree, the affective. The conatively focused treatment has a greater degree of success in controlled situations that will last for a long duration.

Summary

Ethnic and racial prejudices are more than preferences or predilections. As attitudes, they consist of rather stable beliefs and feelings that create a predisposition to behave toward some group or person because he or she is a member of that group. Furthermore, these prejudices are not isolated from the self. They serve to explain and give substance to the relationship between an individual and his or her external environment. The individual does not regard his or her prejudices as being based upon falsehoods or overgeneralizations. People consider their feelings of disdain to be predicated upon valid generalizations.

One's perceived reality should not be underestimated. It is the foundation of an individual's world and her or his role within that world. By analogy, it is a window through which one sees the world and, at the same time, his or her reflection. To expect an individual to suddenly and eagerly replace or redesign one's perceived reality is quite unreasonable in most cases. In the following chapter, we shall probe more deeply into the perceived reality of people as we explore the construct of stereotyping and its relationship to prejudiced attitudes.

CHAPTER 6

STEREOTYPING

Yet even the eyewitness does not bring back a naive picture of the scene. For experience seems to show that he himself brings something to the scene which he later takes away from it . . .

—Walter Lippmann

Just as prejudice forms the wellspring for acts of ethnic and racial violence and discrimination, stereotypes may be regarded as a wellspring for prejudiced attitudes. The term *stereotype* as it is applied to the perceptions of people, was coined by Walter Lippmann in his book, *Public Opinion,* published in 1922. For about sixty years following its publication, social scientists did little more than acknowledge Lippmann's introduction of the concept, along with making a few isolated references. These references include attributing Lippmann with the definition of a stereotype as a "picture in the head" and the notion that stereotypes were fixed and rigid.

According to Carl Friedrich Graumann and Margret Wintermantel, "It has often been stated about stereotypes, mainly of the national, ethnic, or racial kind, that they are relatively stable, even rigid. This permanence is at the core of the original concept of stereotype as introduced into social science by Lippmann (1922)."[1] But as we shall soon learn, Lippmann's concept of stereotype was much more than a picture in the head, and it was not necessarily fixed or rigid.

With a resurgence of interest in cognitive psychology beginning in the mid–to–late sixties, more attention was given to Lippmann's work. This was especially true between 1975 and 1985. In some cases what Lippmann stated was ignored, and the same concept was attributed to others. Stroebe and Insko refer to Henri Tajfel's "Cognitive Aspects of Prejudice" published in 1969 as "the watershed . . . in which he formulated what were to become the basic postulates of the 'cognitive approach' to stereotypes and prejudice. . . .

The biases and exaggerations characteristic of stereotypes were seen as the result of limitations of the human capacity for processing information."[2] It is difficult to find this very novel when in fact Lippmann, almost half a century earlier, stated:

> For the real environment is altogether too big, too complex, and too fleeting for direct acquaintance. We are not equipped to deal with so much subtlety, so much variety, so many permutations and combinations. And although we have to act in that environment, we have to reconstruct it on a simpler model before we can manage with it.[3]

If we are to appreciate fully an understanding of stereotype and its relationship to prejudice and hate violence, we might begin with Lippmann and his introduction of the concept, and then proceed to its development by social scientists.

The Origin of Stereotyping as a Social Concept

Lippmann did not explicitly define stereotype as it applies to intergroup relations. His main concern was to describe how people perceive and interpret reality. During the time of his writing, he was no doubt acquainted with the term as it pertained to the production of books and newspapers. A stereotype was the commonly used printing plate that was set on the presses to produce copies of printed material. The stereotype produced the same image without variation, time and again. According to a number of social psychologists who followed Lippmann, the stereotype concept, as it applied to people, indicated a fixed or rigid belief. But for Lippmann this was not necessarily true.

A WORLD TOO COMPLEX

Since the world is too complex for one to fully and totally perceive, Lippmann suggests that people receive some bits of the total picture of an object, place, event, person or group. The missing information is filled in by imagination or by what the perceiver expects it to be. Lippmann notes,

> Man is no Aristotelian god contemplating all existence at one glance. . . . Yet, this same creature has invented ways of seeing what no naked eye could see, of hearing what no ear could hear. . . . He is learning to see with his mind vast portions of the world that

he could never see, touch, smell, hear, or remember. Gradually he makes for himself a trustworthy picture inside his head of the world beyond his reach. . . . The pictures inside the head of these human beings, the pictures of themselves, of others, of their needs, purposes, and relationship, are their public opinions.[4]

Walter Lippmann had no idea that, within two paragraphs after the above excerpt, he would be introducing a concept that was to puzzle, intrigue, and challenge social scientists in future generations. It was a concept that in and of itself would lead others to carry out extensive research and formulate theories centered upon it. In describing the remaining structure of his book, the author, who would eventually be awarded the Pulitzer Prize on two occasions, relates:

The analysis then turns from these more or less external limitations [in the acquisition of information] to the question of how this trickle of messages from the outside is affected by the stored up images, the preconceptions, and prejudices which interpret, fill them out, and in their turn powerfully direct the play of our attention, and our vision itself. From this it proceeds to examine how in the individual person the limited messages from the outside, formed into a pattern of *stereotypes,* are identified with his own interests as he feels and conceives them.[5]

For Lippmann, "The subtlest and most pervasive of all influences are those which create and maintain the repertory of stereotypes. . . . We imagine most things before we experience them. And those preconceptions, unless education has made us acutely aware, govern deeply the whole process of perception."[6]

STEREOTYPE AS PERCEIVED REALITY

Lippmann regards stereotypes as an individual's perceived reality. This perceived reality is formed by a combination of information obtained from the real world and personal ideations constructed from one's cultural values, experiences, and desires. The rather simplistic notion that he regards a stereotype as a "picture in the head," is an understandable inference, but it is incomplete. While the stereotype may consist of "a picture in the head," the fact is that it stamps itself upon reality and transforms reality to fit the stereotype. The projection of preconceptions ("pictures in the head") upon reality is analogous to the print plate stereotype as it strikes the paper. This analogy, however, is not perfect. The stereotype of the mind may be modified or may be rigid; whereas, the printing plate stereotype always is fixed.

Uses of Stereotypes

In describing stereotypes and stereotyping as a natural process of human perception and thought, Lippmann explains that stereotypes serve an economic function, "For the attempt to see all things freshly and in detail, rather than as types and generalities, is exhausting . . . "[7] Lippmann's view of stereotypes is that they are a natural necessity, and it is the character of the stereotype that determines its positive or negative value. If a stereotype is held in a rigid manner and based upon one's own philosophy, the stereotype has greater negative implications than in those who "hold them lightly, to modify them gladly."[8]

At this point, we might note the relationship between stereotyping and the concept of prejudice as treated by Allport and others in the previous chapter. Lippmann's view of stereotype coincides with Allport's suggestion that prejudgments are not prejudices if they are readily changed upon the reception of new information. The concept of a rigidly held stereotype relates to both Allport's notion of prejudice as well as that of Simpson and Yinger. Allport describes a prejudice as an "inflexible generalization," and Simpson and Yinger state that prejudice is an inflexible attitude that "seriously distorts perception and judgment." It is also interesting to note that Lippmann, in the case of rigid stereotypes, and Allport and Simpson and Yinger, in their discussions of prejudice, intimate the negative consequences of each.

Finally, according to Lippmann, stereotyped beliefs serve to defend one's place and status in society and are grounded in one's moral values. Near the end of his treatment on stereotypes, Lippmann explains,

> I am arguing that the pattern of stereotypes at the center of our [moral] codes largely determine what group of facts we shall see, and in what light we shall see them. And since my moral system rests on my accepted version of the facts, he who denies either my moral judgments or my version of the facts, is to me perverse, alien, dangerous.[9]

The connection between stereotypes and moral codes indicates that stereotypes are not limited to an individual's superficial impressions of the world around him/her. Stereotypes may be intrinsically embedded within an individual's total conception of reality and his/her place within that reality. Furthermore, Lippmann implies that a threat to one's stereotypes may be perceived as a threat to one's self-concept and security. These connections between stereotypes and prejudices should be considered when attempting to work at changing prejudiced attitudes.

PRECURSOR TO SOCIAL PSYCHOLOGICAL ORIENTATIONS

Notwithstanding that Lippmann's treatment of stereotype was accurately described by Allport as "loose on theory,"[10] he did touch upon the precursor of three orientations in the study of stereotypes as outlined by Richard D. Ashmore and Francis K. Del Boca in 1981.[11] Lippmann suggested that stereotyping was part and parcel of one's cognitive structuring in his discussion of how reality is transformed into a mental construct. Later, this would be labelled the cognitive orientation. He also suggested a relationship between culture and stereotyping that connects closely with the sociocultural orientation.

In his treatment of stereotypes as defense mechanisms to rationalize and protect "our position in society," Lippmann touched upon what Ashmore and Del Boca refer to as the psychodynamic orientation.[12] In his discussion of the stereotype as defense, Lippmann points out that stereotypes are not neutral. He further states:

> It is not merely a way of substituting order for the great blooming, buzzing confusion of reality. It is all these things and something more. It is the guarantee of our self-respect; it is the projection upon the world of our own sense of our own value, our own position and our own rights. The stereotypes are, therefore, highly charged with the feelings that are attached to them. They are the fortress of our tradition, and behind its defenses we can continue to feel ourselves safe in the position we occupy.[13]

It is within the context of this discussion that Lippmann posits the probable reactions of one who experiences a contradiction of his or her stereotypes. In the following description of these reactions, it is interesting to note Lippmann's distinction between one who maintains stereotypes as flexible and subject to change and one who maintains a rigid stereotype. He states:

If the man is no longer plastic, or if some powerful interest makes it highly inconvenient to rearrange his stereotypes, he pooh–poohs the contradiction as an exception that proves the rule, discredits the witness, finds flaw somewhere, and manages to forget it. But if he is still curious and open–minded, the novelty is taken into the picture, and allowed to modify it.[14]

FIVE CONSIDERATIONS FROM LIPPMANN'S DISCOURSE

In addition to having set the stage for future theories and research on the nature of stereotyping, there are five points stemming from Lippmann's discourse that we might consider. First, we should not expect stereotyping to be some sort of aberration residing only in the minds of socially ill and bigoted people. All of us have our stereotypes.

Second, stereotypes are in essence the perceived reality of an individual. It is this perceived reality to which a person responds and not reality itself. Therefore, in order to change a person's behavior, we might consider the need to change his or her perception of reality.

Third, much of education, and especially the instruction in social studies, history, and geography, provides only a superficial treatment of subject matter, leaving it to the imagination of the student to fill in the details. This filling in process may form highly distorted images of what is or was real. In turn these distorted "pictures in the head" may lead to further distortions when stereotypes are used to fill in future bits of information.

Fourth, the influence of stereotypes on concept learning may result in faulty prototypes that are used to develop a schema of one's world. Indeed, the entire description of a stereotype by Lippmann seems to suggest that stereotypes may be what cognitive psychologists and educational researchers regard as concept prototypes. The concept prototype theory maintains that the learner develops a prototype or ideal, mental picture that is associated with what is outside. This prototype is used to determine whether a novel object belongs to the same category as the prototype. Peter H. Martorella's review of concept instruction indicates that researchers have, for the most part, failed to address the relationship between stereotypes as exaggerated truths and concept learning.[15] This may not be a major problem if one is employing the use of prototypes to develop a concept of bird or chair, but it certainly can be a serious matter in the study of national, ethnic, and racial groups.

Fifth, stereotypes are closely connected to an individual's self–image and his or her values and moral code. As such, any direct assault on a person's stereotyped beliefs may be resisted. This resistance may be in the form of closing off communication, refusing to receive new information or by causing the individual to selectively seek support for stereotyped beliefs. In these instances, diplomacy and tact combined with experiential learning activities may prove more valuable in changing strong, negative stereotypes than by using a direct and aggressive approach.

Ethnic and racial stereotypes are learned as a result of direct personal contact with other group members or as a result of what one has read, seen, or heard about them. In some cases within a particular culture, a label may conjure up a prototype of a particular alien group. It is the stereotype that often is conjured up when one is asked why he or she finds a particular group offensive, inferior, or deserving of contempt. In the following section, we shall examine selectively how social psychologists have dealt with the stereotype construct since Lippmann's introduction of the term.

A Social Psychology of Stereotype

The term stereotype as applied to racial and ethnic groups refers to a generalized mental picture that an individual applies to all members of a particular group. In 1954, Allport defined a stereotype, either favorable or unfavorable, as "an exaggerated belief associated with a category. Its function is to justify (rationalize) our conduct in relation to that category."[16] Allport criticized Lippmann for confusing stereotype with a category or concept.

According to Allport, the stereotype is merely a "mark upon a category." He illustrates this by stating: "If I say, 'All lawyers are crooked,' I am expressing a stereotyped generalization about a category. The stereotype is not in itself the core of the concept. It operates, however, in such a way as to prevent differentiated thinking about the concept."[17]

If we accept Allport's position, then the effects of stereotyping take place after the perceived object or person has been categorized. For example, most Americans conceptualize a Black American as having dark skin, wide nasal index, and wooly hair. Upon seeing a person with these attributes, the perceived individual is categorized as a Black American. If the individual has a stereotype of blacks being lazy, dishonest, and stupid, these attributes would then be associated with the individual prior to learning whether nor not they actually apply to this particular person.

The problem with Allport's perspective on the nature of stereotypes is that he ignores the influence of stereotyped beliefs when the initial act of perceiving is made. For instance, let us say that we are listening to someone describe an attempted attack on a young woman. He says, "This young, oh about 24-year-old, woman was almost raped by a guy she describes as about 18, with a knife, and who she says was about six feet tall and dark." The final descriptor, "dark" may elicit the picture of a black man; especially if one associates black males as being potential rapists of women. In actuality, dark could have described a white, Asian, Mexican, Indian, or member of any number of groups, ethnic or racial. In other words, while Allport's definition may be seen as a more social scientific explanation of stereotype, the fact is that Lippmann maintained that stereotypes impose themselves on reality at the onset of perception— the stereotype transforms reality to the set of expectations of the perceiver. An individual may have some but not all the physical traits of a group and still be perceived and categorized as a member of that particular group.

Thomas F. Pettigrew, a protege of Allport, maintains that Allport was among the first to counter the prevailing view that stereotypes or "cognitive distortions" were some sort of aberration of a sick mind.[18] Notwithstanding that Lippmann had maintained that stereotyping was a normal product of perception, during the post World War II period, a number of theorists and researchers treated prejudice and stereotyping as indicative of personality maladies.

In the late sixties, it became popular to trace human violence and hatreds to primordial beginnings of mankind. Two publications instantly became the focus of attention throughout academia and the nation. In 1966, playwright and pop-anthropologist Robert Ardrey produced *The Territorial Imperative* and the following year Desmond Morris's *The Naked Ape: A Zoologist's Study of the Human Animal* was published. In 1968, Henri Tajfel received the first annual Gordon Allport Intergroup Relations Prize for his essay, "Cognitive Aspects of Prejudice." The paper was eventually published in the *Journal of Social Issues* one year later. Social scientists have lauded Tajfel's essay as the watershed in the study of the nature of stereotyping. Tajfel referred to such popular ideations expressed in the works of Ardrey and Morris as a "blood and guts model" for seeking to understand social phenomena.

> In this new blood and guts romanticism so fashionable at present in some science and semi-science, man's attitudes and beliefs con-

cerning the social environment are seen mainly as a byproduct of tendencies that are buried deeply in his evolutionary past or just as deeply in his unconscious.[19]

Tajfel is credited with refocusing the study of prejudice and especially stereotyping on the cognitive processes. Not unlike Allport and Lippmann, Tajfel acknowledged the role of stereotypes in simplifying reality and the effects of culture and its traditions. The problem of stereotyping, Tajfel suggested, was that members of human groups vary or are what he called continuous in variation. Stereotypes create limited categories in which the variations of individuals assigned to a category are ignored.

He also stressed three observations regarding "social categorizations." First, Tajfel noted that social characteristics assigned to people usually are made upon a comparison basis. The extent to which one is regarded as intelligent or lazy is relative to others. Second, the dimensions of comparative judgments are ascribed to groups and their members. Therefore, if being slovenly is ascribed to a given group, the trait will also be ascribed to its individual members—"as long as we have little specific knowledge about the individual . . . "[20]

Tajfel's third observation was that given a continuous dimension of a group of objects or people, the greatest perceived differences will be between those objects or items that are assigned to different categories. In other words, when people are categorized into groups, members of different groups will be perceived as being more sharply different than members within groups, even if the categorization is superficial and all members of the combined two groups are equally different. Categorization creates greater perceived differences between groups than is actually the case.

Notwithstanding that Tajfel's main thrust was to stress the importance of three cognitive processes, categorization, assimilation, and conceptual coherence, in relation to prejudiced attitudes, his treatment of stereotyping seems to have directed the attention of researchers toward examining the cognitive component of prejudice and the influence of stereotyping on this component.

THREE ORIENTATIONS IN STUDYING STEREOTYPES

During the seventies and extending to the end of the eighties, social psychologists continued to theorize and research the influence of stereotyping on prejudice. Richard D. Ashmore and Frances

K. Del Boca identified three traditions or, as they call them, "orientations" in the study of stereotypes. These are sociocultural, psychodynamic, and cognitive.[21]

Socio–cultural Orientation. In their discussion of the socio–cultural orientation of the study of stereotypes, Ashmore and Del Boca credited Lippmann for introducing the concept that societies and cultures maintain stereotypes of alien groups and of themselves. They also cite the work of Daniel Katz and Kenneth Braly with its initial development among social psychologists.

In the thirties, Katz and Braly noted that previous studies dealing with racial and ethnic group attitudes showed a consistency across the United States. This "uniformity in the pattern of social prejudice" led them to conclude that,

> Attitudes toward racial and national groups are in good part attitudes toward race names. They are stereotypes of our cultural pattern and are not based upon animosity toward a member of a proscribed group because of any genuine qualities that inhere in him. We have conditioned responses of varying degrees of aversion or acceptance toward racial labels and where these tags can be readily applied to individuals, as they can in the case of the Negro because of his skin color, we respond toward him not as a human being but as a personification of the symbol we have learned to despise.[22]

In their review of previous studies, Katz and Braly hypothesized that two sets of attitudes may explain ethnic and racial prejudices. They identified these as private and public attitudes. In order to test the hypotheses that public attitudes (or what we may refer to as sociocultural) did exist, Katz and Braly presented 100 college students with a list of 84 traits, such as intelligent, sly, kind, cruel, loud, progressive, etc.. They asked their subjects to assign those traits that were characteristic of ten groups—Germans, Italians, Negroes, Irish, English, Jews, Americans, Chinese, Japanese, and Turks.

The following identifies the degree of agreement among the 100 subjects regarding each group for the top five traits:

Germans: Scientifically-minded, Industrious (65),
               Stolid (44), Intelligent (32), Methodical (31).
Italians: Artistic (53), Impulsive (44), Passionate (37),
               Quick-tempered (35), Musical (32).

Negroes:	Superstitious (84), Lazy (75), Happy-go-lucky (38), Ignorant (38), Musical (26).
Jews:	Shrewd (79), Mercenary (49), Industrious (48), Grasping (34), Intelligent (29).
Americans:	Industrious (48), Intelligent (47), Materialistic (33), Ambitious (33), Progressive (27).
English:	Sportsmanlike (53), Intelligent (46), Conventional (34), Tradition–loving (31), Conservative (30).
Irish:	Pugnacious (45), Quick-tempered (39), Witty (38), Honest (32), Very religious (29).
Chinese:	Superstitious (35), Sly (29), Conservative (29), Tradition–loving (26), Loyal to family ties (22).
Japanese:	Intelligent (47), Industrious (45), Progressive (25), Shrewd (23), Sly (21).
Turks:	Cruel (54), Very religious (29), Treacherous (24), Sensual (23), Ignorant (17).

Katz and Braly concluded that "the degree of agreement among students in assigning characteristics from a list of 84 adjectives to different races seems too great to be the sole result of the students' contacts with members of these races."[23] In the discussion of their findings, the authors note if an individual stereotypes a German as one who is scientifically-minded, the individual will confirm this by interpreting select behaviors as such. In the event that one meets an individual whose behavior totally violates the stereotype, Katz and Braly suggest that such an individual will be categorized as an exception such as a "white Jew" as opposed to a Jew. Twenty-five years later, Allport will refer to this category of exceptional cases as bifurcation—a defense mechanism by which one can sustain his or her stereotype and negative feeling toward the group in general by admitting the existence of exceptions. "Bifurcators still believe that there is an evil Negro or Jewish or Catholic 'essence,' even if this essence permeates only part of the group."[24]

Ashmore and Del Boca identify two perspectives regarding the sociocultural stereotype orientation. These are the structuralist–functionalist and conflict perspectives. Both, accept the postulates that (1) as members of a society, individuals "internalize social values and norms;" and (2) in their desire to be accepted by the greater society, they are motivated to conform to the prevailing values and norms. A major difference between the two perspectives is that one, the structuralist-functionalist, views members of society as conforming to the norms and values of the mass culture; whereas, "the conflict theorists assume that individuals incorporate the belief system of their particular sub-group."[25] The sociocultural orientation of stereotypes helps explain how stereotypes support the existing status–quo in society and allow individuals to justify their role relationships with others in society. It is from this orientation that studies of the effects of stereotyping in the education of children might be profitably studied.

Psychodynamic Orientation. The psychodynamic orientation is most concerned with the relationship between stereotypes and prejudice. One perspective within this orientation focuses upon the concept of the prejudiced personality. The stereotypes are perceived as projections upon outgroups and their members in order to justify feelings of hate and acts of violence. These stereotypes are used to blame others for the evils in society. The concept of the authoritarian personality, discussed earlier, illustrates this perspective within the psychodynamic orientation.

Cognitive Orientation. According to Ashmore and Del Boca, the cognitive orientation views stereotypes as mental constructs, either as categories or generalizations associated with categories. Those maintaining the cognitive perspective regard stereotyping as a basic function of cognitive structuring. They consider the processes of stereotyping as a natural result of attempting to perceive and understand reality in a stable, meaningful, and manageable fashion. Research in this arena of the study of stereotypes has abounded. The findings of researchers not only convey the complexity involved in what might be regarded as the psychology of stereotyping, these also may provide a greater understanding of how stereotypes influence the perceptions and behavior of people.

Stereotypes and Cognition

The cognitive orientation of the study of stereotypes has resulted in a number of new concepts related to stereotyping with some rather meaningful implications for intergroup relations and the study of prejudice. In this section we shall touch upon some of the more recent findings as well as some not so recent.

As previously mentioned, Tajfel reported that the mere categorization of objects into separate groups resulted in exaggerated differences between groups. This suggests when people are viewed as belonging to different groups, there will be a tendency to perceive them as being more different from non–group members. They also will appear to be more homogeneous among other members of a group to which they are assigned.

The process of categorizing people into groups creates a mind set on the part of the perceiver. This mind set leads the perceiver to select and interpret traits that members of the group seem to have in common. In some cases, this may include the creation of traits that reside only in the mind of the perceiver. This, in turn, often leads to behaviors among both, the perceiver and categorized members, consistent with the perception. If one perceives a group of people as having a certain trait or patterns of traits, he or she will treat them accordingly. In turn, this external treatment may result in behavior among the members of the group in accordance with the external treatment.

CATEGORIZATION EFFECTS ON BEHAVIOR

When, based upon race, religion, or ethnicity, people are categorized into we–groups and they–groups or, more commonly, ingroups and outgroups, there is a tendency to judge individuals in terms of group membership. Shelly Taylor cites numerous studies indicating "that once people are categorized into ingroup and outgroup, ingroup favoritism and outgroup discrimination often result . . . "[26]

Ingroup–Outgroup Education. This finding should not come as a surprise. The development of positive ingroup attitudes is basic to the socialization of people in any society. Notwithstanding that Americans eschew the concept of indoctrination, that is exactly what social education in any society is designed to do. Indeed, American history traditionally was taught at grades five, eight, and eleven (or twelve), in order to insure that all students received a knowledge of the cultural heritage of the United States. This was deemed essential since many students dropped out of school after the fifth and eighth years—especially during the depression years.

In interviews with twelve-year-old school children in 1931, Rose Zeligs found the same results as indicated by researchers years later. When asked why they preferred Americans, one typical response was illustrated by "C.W.B. (Girl)" who stated, "The American nationality is naturally my favorite because it is my own and one must be patriotic." Two years later, the same child responded, "Americans are very progressive in every way. They are educated and they try to improve themselves. They are very friendly, clean, and make a good appearance." Finally, in 1937, she answered the same question with, "The Americans show no hatred to other countries but are very patriotic to be America [sic]."[27]

In a multiethnic and multiracial society, these favorable and unfavorable attitudes are displayed at both national and sub–national levels. It is not uncommon for individuals within a state to view other nationalities with greater favor than more immediate sub-groups within their own society. This is especially true when the other nationalities appear to be (are stereotyped as being) more similar to one's own sub-group than other sub-groups within the general national or state society.

Zeligs's report of three interviews in 1931, 1933, and 1937 with the aforementioned child, further illustrates this tendency:

> 1931. I like the English because they speak the same language we do.
>
> 1933. I like the English because they are like Americans in customs, dress, actions, and speech.
>
> 1937. I like the English race because they are so much like myself in customs and manners.[28]

When the student was asked why she rated "Negroes" low on a Friendliness Towards Various Peoples scale, the child responded:

> 1931. The Negro isn't of my race of people. Most of the time white people don't associate with Negroes. They are not clean. Some of the girls are rough and not careful when they play.
>
> 1933. I don't like the Negro race. I know the ones in our school are awful wild. They are an unclean, unpleasant race to have around.
>
> 1937. In some respects I dislike the Negro intensely because of their unclean ways of living, and yet, I pity them because people are so prejudiced against them.[29]

SINGLE TRAIT STEREOTYPING

It has also been suggested that the categorization of people may be based upon one trait when stereotyping is involved. The name Goldberg may immediately classify a person as Jewish and bring to bear all of the stereotypic traits associated with a Jew in the mind of the perceiver. It most probably would not conjure up a picture of actress/comedian Whoopi Goldberg. Just how easily a single cue combined with one's motivation can initiate a stereotype is exemplified by a job search for a professor at the University of Colorado in Denver. A certain Mr. B., whose name did not elicit any particular stereotype, was invited for an interview partially on the basis that most search committee members thought him to be black. Their cue was that he had a publication in the *Journal of Negro Education*. As it turned out, he was white.

THE SALIENT STEREOTYPE FACTOR

Another aspect of research according to Taylor and other cognitive oriented psychologists and sociologists deals with stereotype as the salient factor. The more salient a trait of an individual within a group, the more likely the individual will be categorized as such. A black person will be more readily seen as being black if he or she is in a group that is predominantly white.[30]

Furthermore, it has been found that the extent to which an individual has a greater knowledge of members of a particular group, the more that individual will perceive variations. Conversely, the stereotype of that group will be less generalized and possibly less rigid. An individual not acquainted with the diversity among Native Americans might picture all traditional Native Americans as Plains Indians. A person well acquainted with various Native American cultures will more likely discriminate among Navajo, Hopi, Chinook, Lakota, and other groups. Another example of this is the common occurrence for white people to confuse individual blacks upon initial contact. Here the color of race seems to cloud the individuality of group members. However, the same has occurred with those who initially encounter bearded males among the Amish and Hasidic Jews. The categorization at more general levels tends to support valuations that all members of a group are the same.[31]

ILLUSORY CORRELATION

What has been labelled the illusory correlation is somewhat related to the processes that occur when one is not very knowledgeable about a particular group. An illusory correlation may be said to exist when one perceives a trait or behavior in a member of a particular group and exaggerates its occurrences among members of the group as a whole. David Hamilton provides an impressive commentary on the research literature related to this topic.[32] What may prove to be a key point related to illusory correlations in intergroup relations is Hamilton's suggestion that it will be prevalent among perceivers who are not well acquainted with the group whose member or members are being perceived. If, for instance, one has little or no knowledge about Cambodians and reads or hears about a gang shooting involving Cambodians across town, the individual may exaggerate this incident to the point of believing or picturing Cambodians as a culture of "hatchet men."

COGNITIVE BOLSTERING AND BEHAVIORAL CONFIRMATION

In his article, "On the Self-Perpetuating Nature of Stereotypes," Mark Snyder addresses the issues of cognitive bolstering and behavioral confirmation of stereotypes. Snyder maintains that once an individual assigns a person or target to a group for which the former holds a stereotype, the individual will, "(1) remember and interpret past events in the target's life history in ways that bolster and support these current stereotyped beliefs; and (2) will act upon these current stereotyped beliefs in ways that cause the actual behavior of the target to confirm and validate the individual's stereotyped beliefs about the target."[33]

These postulates found some support in a series of experiments by Snyder and Uranowitz. They designed an experiment to examine how people reinterpret targeted individuals after eliciting a stereotype about the target. The researchers provided a life case study of an individual referred to as Betty K. to three groups. One week after the subjects had read the life history, one group was informed that Betty K. was now living a lesbian lifestyle. Another group was told that she was living with her husband—a heterosexual lifestyle, and the third group was told nothing more about Betty K.'s life. Following this additional information, a multiple choice test on the life of Betty K. was given to each group. Each group answered the test items in a manner that suggested Betty K. was either heterosexual or lesbian depending upon what they had been told at a later date. The subjects in the study reconstructed her life history to fit one of these two lifestyles.

Later, Snyder and Uranowitz refined their experiment by having new groups of subjects exposed to the same treatment. The dependent variable was in the form of an essay that members of each group were to write about Betty K.'s life. Then Snyder and Uranowitz had judges rate the essays. The judges were able to "substantially and reliably" classify those essays that were written by subjects who had been told Betty K. was living a lesbian lifestyle. The judges could not distinguish between those subjects that were told Betty K. was heterosexual or were told nothing regarding her sexual preference. Snyder and Uranowitz were unable to detect what it was in the essays that made some "lesbian biographies."[34]

These and other studies carried out and reported by Snyder led him to conclude: "In the face of current stereotyped interpretations, people both remember and 'write' all the history that fits and reinterpret and 'rewrite' all the history that seems not to fit. Accordingly, the purpose of reconstructing the past may create cognitively, for the individual, a world in which even erroneous stereotyped inferences about other people may perpetuate themselves."[35]

It seems almost haunting that these findings fit so nicely with what Lippmann had suggested a half century earlier, that stereotypes are used to modify and fit one's understanding of what is. Snyder suggests that such reconstructions serve to reinforce existing stereotypes. In essence, the cognitive structuring or schemata of an individual becomes laden with greater support for the original stereotype—thereby confirming it. This process easily leads to Snyder's second proposition related to the target's behavioral confirmation of the stereotype.

The confirmation of the stereotype involves an interaction between the perceiver and target (individual being perceived). If the perceiver stereotypes the target as having certain personality traits, the interaction with the target will result in these traits being displayed by the target.[36] The concept, confirmation of stereotype, may be somewhat synonymous with what has been called the self-fulfilling prophecy.[37] The self-fulfilling prophecy refers to the extent that a person's behavior is dependent upon how he or she is viewed and treated. If we treat someone based upon the stereotype or belief that the individual is stupid and incapable of performing a task, the individual exhibits behavior that fits the treatment and stereotype.

Consider the case where an employer does not believe his staff of workers to be capable of handling decision–making tasks in their work. The employer cautions his staff, "Your job is to do, not to think." This attitude may well elicit a reaction among the staff epitomized by the thought, "Ok, you want me to be a robot, then I'll be a robot." Later, the employer complains to a friend, "These people can't do anything on their own. They have no initiative or common sense." In this case, not only does the self-fulfilling prophecy come into play, but it also may result in a vicious circle.[38]

THE VICIOUS CIRCLE THEORY

A vicious circle theory was proposed by Gunnar Myrdal and his associates in their seminal study of race relations in the United States. Based on the stereotype that Black Americans were lazy, undependable, stupid, and slovenly (as well as other negative qualities), blacks were denied educational and employment opportunities that were made more readily available to whites. As a result, many blacks lived in poverty, and those who could afford to live in better neighborhoods were denied access to them. Using these dilapidated neighborhoods as an example, whites could be quick to point out that blacks were indeed slovenly, undependable, lazy, and stupid—"after all, look how they live. They can't even take care of their own neighborhood."

During the earlier nineties, a number of sports commentators, athletes, and enthusiasts took note of the fact that certain professional sports, basketball, football, and baseball, had a large number of black players, but few or no black coaches or managers. If one views a particular group as having certain positive qualities, such as physical strength and agility, but lacking in organizational and management skills, then we might expect that one's treatment of a member of that group will elicit behaviors that confirm the stereotype. In this case, the fact that few, if any, black athletes were hired for coaching or managerial positions may have led a number of people to confirm their stereotype regarding black athletes. While acknowledging their ability to play well, the stereotype questioned their intellectual and organizational skills to direct a team. It is quite possible that if and when a black coach were hired, observers might unwittingly employ other cognitive processes mentioned earlier to confirm their stereotype. It is not inconceivable that this in turn may come back to haunt the coach or manager and actually create behaviors that result in incompetent management. On the other hand, such stereotypes, combined with prejudices, may result in some players not performing as well as they should and projecting their failures upon the coach or manager.

Bigotry, Xenophobia, and Social Distance

Three concepts that have a direct bearing upon the nature of prejudice and stereotyping and that we have not addressed are bigotry, xenophobia, and social distance. Bigotry and xenophobia are not used much, if at all, in prejudice research, but they are useful in describing and illustrating levels of prejudiced attitudes. Social distance, on the other hand, has been a major concept related to the study and measurement of prejudiced attitudes and of stereotyping.

BIGOTRY

Bigotry describes the intolerance of one who cannot or refuses to accept others who are different in appearance, belief, or some other trait that conflicts with the person's own strongly held beliefs. The term bigot might be useful to describe those people who are members of extremist groups such as the White Aryan Resistance or the Aryan Nations. Their hatreds for other racial and ethnic groups are manifest in their beliefs about these groups. Quite often the bigoted zealot's stereotype of select groups includes a combination of hate and fear, which brings us to the problem of xenophobia.

XENOPHOBIA

Xenophobia is a fear of strangers. This fear is not unnatural. Young children may exhibit fear of people who look or dress differently. Others may find strangeness interesting and somewhat appealing. There is not much interest at the present regarding the study of xenophobia as a social relations concept. However, it may serve as a useful tool in explaining that people will tend to have some degree of fear of others who seem strange or different. This fear among adults or older children may stem from the fact that a person who appears strange or different may be perceived as a threat to one's need for stability and predictability. Since seeking a stable and predictable world appears to be a basic social need or desire, it is not difficult to see how some person or group can create a threat by virtue of their being different in the eyes of the beholder.

Although xenophobia has not been a major interest among social science researchers, it may account, at least in part, for the process of cultural shock. Cultural shock is a condition where an individual who has been exposed to another culture finds the situation exceedingly uncomfortable. If the individual is living within an alien culture, he or she may become somewhat dysfunctional in a number of social aspects. Xenophobia may be latent or active. When active, xenophobia may result in an immediate negative reaction or attitude. The latent effects of xenophobia may be illustrated by the processes of cultural shock.

One process of cultural shock includes stages. Initially, the new arrival into an alien culture finds the folkways of the culture interesting, exotic, or even refreshing. The second stage may occur between two and six months after arrival. During this stage, the individual begins to find certain aspects of the culture strange, odd, or even distasteful. It is in this time frame that our visitor or immigrant begins to critically and emotionally question the society. The third stage involves the development of hostile attitudes—the people of the culture are viewed as inferior to one's own group in many ways. At about this point, the visitor may seek to leave or the immigrant may become depressed and think more fondly of his or her native land. Usually, if the individual does not leave and overcomes her/his depression, she/he may acculturate and adjust to the new society. Or with others the individual may form a cultural pocket and remain somewhat isolated from others. Xenophobia may explain why researchers have found groups totally unknown to subjects to be least desirable in terms of social distance. It may also explain why people may find it difficult to maintain long associations with culturally different people within their own native environment.

SOCIAL DISTANCE

The interaction or lack of interaction between peoples of different cultures often is described in terms of social distance. Since Bogardus began measuring social distance in the mid-twenties, there has been a consistent pattern among subjects to maintain a greater degree of social distance than one might consider warranted. Social distance was defined by Robert Ezar Park as "the grades and degrees of understanding and intimacy which characterize personal and social relations generally."[39]

The most common measure of this construct has been the Social Distance Scale, developed by Emory S. Bogardus.[40] Along a continuum of seven categories ranging from "close kinship by marriage" to "would exclude from my country," subjects are asked to respond to various groups (Armenian, Germans, etc.). He found, for example, that although his subjects had little or no knowledge about Serbo–Croatians, they were listed among the least desirable groups.

In addition to measuring what he called social contact distance, Bogardus reported what he called social contact range. This he stated, " . . . does not indicate merit or traits of the respective races, but rather something of the extent of the social contacts open to each race."[41] If we correlate the average social distance or social contact distances, as Bogardus calls it, with average number of types of social contacts by groups in his early studies, we shall note a rather significant and meaningful correlation. This correlation may indicate not only a tendency of people to limit the number of different types of social contacts with those they dislike, but also those about whom they know little or nothing. As Bogardus notes:

> That is to say, the Canadian immigrant is doubly fortunate, and the Turkish immigrant is doubly unfortunate, for the Canadian immigrant is not only admitted to a large range of group contacts, but he is admitted to the most intimate groups; the Turk, on the other hand, is admitted only to a small range of contacts and these are of the most remote and least intimate types.[42]

•••

The effects of stereotyping lie at the base of prejudice. Stereotypic beliefs form the rationale for feelings of disdain and disparagement. When tied to prejudiced attitudes, stereotypes help create a number of behaviors ranging from avoidance to violence. Our review of stereotypes indicates that one's perceived reality is not reality itself, but is a mixture of fact and fiction, if not total fiction. Yet when people act upon these stereotypes, the actions are carried out in the real world, not in their stereotypic world. Furthermore, not only do stereotypes shape how and what we perceive, they also influence the behavior of those for whom we hold the stereotype.

The nature of prejudice represents one of the most complex systems in the study of Homo–sapiens sapiens. The sources of prejudice are varied. But regardless of how and why prejudices form, the fact remains that, like seeds, prejudice takes root, grows, and blossoms into what may become violent hate. In turn, this hatred, like flowers, goes to seed and is scattered by the winds of xenophobia, ethnocentrism, and stereotyping.

Ethnic and racial prejudices are attitudes found among both, members of the minority and majority groups. Furthermore, it is essential to comprehend that prejudice and stereotyping are not limited to extremists and bigots. Nor are they necessarily indications of a corrupt and sick mind. They are manifestations of information processing and cognitive structuring, as well as other experiences encountered in the social world of humankind.

In this chapter, we explored the concept of stereotyping and its relationship to prejudice and related salient concepts. With a knowledge of these concepts, along with an understanding of attitude from the previous chapter, we should be able to begin to understand their complexities and influences upon individuals in society.

CHAPTER 7

DISCRIMINATION, AGGRESSION, AND SCAPEGOATING

The theme of my discussion was "You Owe Me"—three little words that can mean just anything when the orator happens to be black. . . . I said that white America, which supported black civil rights, voting rights, academic rights and human rights, now must grant the black middle class the right to succeed or fail on its own. And it must give the underclass the authority to remain poor if it so wishes. I made the point that—despicable as it may be—poverty, too, is guaranteed under the Constitution.

—Ken Hamblin, 1991

When ethnic or racial prejudices are acted out, they usually consist of some form of aggression. These forms may range from avoidance to acts of violence. In an earlier work, Gordon W. Allport described acts of prejudice as falling into one of two categories, discrimination or scapegoating. He also presented a continuum that was designed to illustrate a range of attitudes or behaviors from friendly to hostile. This continuum first appeared in his *ABC's of Scapegoating* published in 1950:[1]

Cooperation—Respect—Tolerance—Predilection—Prejudice—Discrimination—Scapegoating

Figure 1. Allport's Continuum of Social Relationships.

Allport differentiated between discrimination and scapegoating by suggesting that discrimination involves a lesser amount of aggression.[2] Furthermore, he also acknowledged that in some cases discrimination may be an expression of scapegoating.[3] He referred to these cases as borderline cases. The key attribute distinguishing between these is the degree of hostility directed toward the attitude target.

In his later, seminal work, *The Nature of Prejudice*, published in 1954, Allport listed discrimination as the third in a five point scale describing the acting–out of prejudice. These included acts that he regarded as forms of scapegoating in the earlier work: "1. Antilocution . . . 2. Avoidance . . . 3. Discrimination . . . 4. Physical Attack . . . 5. Extermination."[4] Allport seems to have disregarded the earlier continuum that dichotomized acts of discrimination and acts of scapegoating. Allport seemed to suggest that discrimination was a more aggressive form of hostility than were acts previously classified as scapegoating (e.g., anti-locution and avoidance). Nevertheless, the original continuum, as illustrated above, was still being used in "A World of Difference", possibly the largest prejudice reduction, education program in the United States during the late eighties and early nineties.[5]

The fact is that prejudice may be acted out either in the form of discrimination or some other form of aggression. Moreover, Allport's concept of scapegoating may not be the most appropriate term for describing the all non-discriminatory forms of prejudiced acts of hostility and violence. Not all forms of aggression stemming from prejudice consist of blaming, and certainly, they do not all involve transference or projection. Therefore, I have suggested the expression AGGRESSION to describe the acting–out prejudice that may lead to discrimination and scapegoating or other forms of hostility.

In addition, some authors and researchers have concluded that not all forms of discrimination are manifestations of prejudiced attitudes.[6] Carl Friedrich Graumann and Margret Wintermantel illustrate this by noting the refusal of property owners to sell or lease homes and apartments out of fear of what neighbors may do.[7] But this and other similar studies fail to conclusively establish that prejudice is not involved in the act of discrimination.

On the other hand, there is more evidence that prejudiced attitudes do not always result in discrimination. Individuals may hold strong prejudices against certain groups at a universal or general plane, but when confronted with face-to-face social situations, they may restrain their hostile feelings and not discriminate.[8] With these issues and conditions in mind, the following illustrates the model used in this chapter; but again, it is only one of a number of ways to examine the issue of overt acts of hate prejudice.

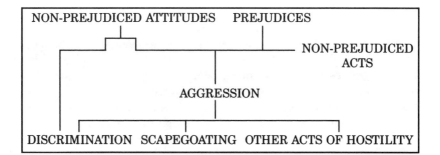

Figure 2. Sources of Discrimination, Scapegoating, and Other Acts of Hostility.

In order to understand the nature of hate prejudice as it is expressed in society, it is necessary to explore the nature of both discrimination and other overt acts of aggression, including scapegoating. These concepts describe the ways in which ethnic and racial prejudices are exhibited in social relationships.

Discrimination

A variety of definitions have been offered for discrimination. Most of these definitions resemble those offered either by Thomas F. Pettigrew or George M. Frederickson and Dale T. Knobel. Discrimination is defined by Pettigrew as "an institutional process of exclusion against an outgroup, racial or cultural, based simply on who they are rather than on their abilities."[9] With the exception of the concept of an "institutional process," Pettigrew's definition is quite similar to the one offered by Allport in 1954[10] and accepted by Stroebe and Insko in 1989.[11]

Frederickson and Knobel define discrimination as "actions that serve to limit the social, political, or economic opportunities of particular groups."[12] Although some differences may be perceived in these two definitions, one key element they share is that discrimination denies equal treatment of people because of ethnic or group membership, unrelated to the person's individual or personal characteristics. The working definition proposed below shares the basic intendment.

Discrimination may be defined as unequal and unfavorable treatment directed toward a target group or its members. At a general level, the group or individuals capable of exercising treatment are those who hold political, economic, or social power. Traditionally, in the United States, these powers were perceived as being in the hands of a white dominant population. This perception led to the overgeneralized belief among some that the United States was a racist society. Although racism in the form of discrimination and other hostilities has been a part of the American scene since its inception, the fact is that not all white Americans are racists. Nor are all American institutions designed to maintain superordinate and subordinate relationships between groups.

With the exception of legalized, national discriminatory policies, discrimination takes place in situations at the local level. Consequently, the ability to discriminate is situational. It is effectuated by those who have the power to do so in a given place and at a particular time. This means that, regardless of what group maintains power at the general societal level, there may be occasions when a member or members of the group lacking power at the general societal or national level may be able to discriminate against those belonging to the outgroup. Since the nature of discrimination is negative, it may preclude the target group and its members from receiving treatment on an equal par with the group in power. It is this concept of discrimination that determines which group is the majority and which is the minority.

Minority and Majority

Contrary to popular beliefs, the concept of minority and majority in intergroup relations is not determined by group size, as is the case with the political concepts of the same label. The group in power and holding sway over others is referred to as the majority. In some cases, social scientists have used the term sociological majority. The target group or those subject to discriminatory behavior is called the minority or sociological minority. Finally, when a member of the general majority group in society is discriminated against, the expression 'reverse discrimination' has been used.

Another construction to explain these group concepts is offered by R. A. Schermerhorn. Schermerhorn suggests the concepts of dominant groups and subordinate groups.[13] The dominant group is that group holding power. If the dominant group is in also the numerical majority, it is simply called the majority. A group possessing power but numerically a minority is referred to as an elite. Among subordinate groups, that group lacking power and fewer in numbers is referred to as the minority. If they are numerically superior but lack power, the term mass subjects may be used. Notwithstanding the merit in Schermerhorn's preference for dominant and subordinate, the terms majority and minority will be used in this work. It is these terms that seem most widely used, and although they often are perceived as being correlated with size, they have been used to identify those groups in superordinate and subordinate positions. Nevertheless, Schermerhorn's concepts may have utility when it is necessary to delineate groups by both power and size.

Predilection and Avoidance

Discrimination may be expressed by acts of denial or acts of avoidance. Avoidance discrimination usually occurs at personal social levels of intergroup relations. Refusing to associate with someone because of his or her race or ethnicity would illustrate this form of discrimination. Avoidance discrimination may or may not be regarded as an expression of aggression. Yet, even when it is not a consequence of aggression, avoidance discrimination involves more than a preference or predilection. In the case of predilection, a person may choose to associate with people based on commonality of interests and shared beliefs.

PREDILECTION

A predilection is a preference and does not necessarily entail a prejudiced attitude. For example, an individual may find it more desirable to associate with someone who shares a common interest in mountain climbing than with non–mountain climbers. Another individual may find that he or she prefers to associate with others who work in the same profession rather than people working in unrelated fields. While these preferences may limit one's associations, they are not necessarily predicated upon avoiding others. Quite often, it has been noted that black and white college students tend to segregate themselves into social groups that result in all-black and all-white gatherings. If these groupings are not based upon a desire to avoid members of other racial or ethnic groups but are the result of some common interests, then we do not have a case of avoidance discrimination.

Just as isolation breeds strangeness regarding those with whom we do not associate, so predilections may result in feelings of strangeness and may in turn lead to prejudices and discrimination. When individuals begin avoiding others because of prejudices or feelings of strangeness, this avoidance may be considered a form of discrimination. Because avoidance discrimination is often a private matter, it does not receive major attention from civil rights activists and others concerned with seeking an end to discrimination in the arena of economics and politics. Yet, it is this form of discrimination that may account for the lack of integration or the development of positive feelings among groups in desegregated schools.

AVOIDANCE DISCRIMINATION

Avoidance discrimination manifests many of the hostilities and misunderstandings among members of different groups. In his discussion of discrimination, Pettigrew tends to view this behavior as a form of passive aggression and cites Joel Kovel's concepts of "aversive racism" and "dominative racism."[14] In the case of "aversive racism," one avoids members of racial groups because of racist beliefs and prejudices. Dominative racism, on the other hand, is an overt, proactive attempt to coerce members of a racial outgroup to assume or remain at a subordinate social level. However, the concept of "aversion racism" explicitly refers to enmity as the cause of the avoidance.

Regardless of whether the act of avoidance results in discrimination predicated upon hate or not, its effects are similar. It tends to keep people socially segregated at interpersonal levels. It does not permit one to alter his or her conception of outgroup members. Indeed, avoidance discrimination plays a major role in distinguishing between integration and desegregation.

Integration v. Desegregation. In an integrated society, members of different groups have developed positive intergroup relations at the personal level. While quite aware of racial or ethnic differences, they choose to treat one another as equals and as fellow humans. Integration involves goodwill among members of different groups. Desegregation is merely the removal of physical barriers between groups. When the United States Supreme Court ruled that schools must desegregate, its ruling initiated the removal of such barriers; schools became desegregated, but not integrated. Integration, then, requires a social psychological change among people—a willingness to accept each other. What the desegregation of schools accomplished was to proscribe an act of discrimination by denial; it did not and reasonably could not force an end to discrimination by avoidance.

Discrimination by avoidance differs from discrimination by denial to the extent that the former does not require the target group or individual member to be actively seeking some desired, equal treatment. When members of Group A intentionally avoid associating with members of Group B, this may constitute discrimination by avoidance. It is not necessary for the Group B members to seek the association or even be aware of the discriminatory behavior on the part of Group A. As has been noted, this form of discrimination has prevented groups and their members from reducing social barriers and modifying stereotypes and prejudiced attitudes. It is this type of discrimination that is ignored by the definition that discrimination "comes about only when we deny to individuals or groups of people equality of treatment which they may wish.[15] By contrast, discrimination by denial is that form of discrimination that has been the main focus of attention and has been at the center of various rights movements in the United States.

Discrimination by Denial

Discrimination by denial is the most popular and widely recognized form of discrimination. It permeates the three basic systems, social, political, and economic, within a society. Discrimination by denial is the process by which groups are denied the same privileges, rights, and opportunities enjoyed by the majority group. This form of discrimination may be expressed in law, mores, and customs. A long history of legalized discrimination based upon the notion of white superiority provided the basis for the concept of institutional racism in the United States.

INSTITUTIONAL RACISM

Institutional racism was a term coined by Stokely Carmichael and Charles V. Hamilton in 1967, and has become widely used by civil rights activists, academics, politicians, and journalists. According to Carmichael and Hamilton, institutional racism is an "active and pervasive operation of anti-black attitudes and practices. A sense of superior group position prevails: whites are "better" than blacks; therefore blacks should be subordinate to whites. . . . it permeates the society, on both the individual and the institutional level, covertly and overtly."[16] Responding to this concept, Michael Banton states,

Such a formulation has great advantages for polemical purposes. It rolls into one ball cultural assumptions, motives, institutions, attitudes and beliefs about superiority. For purposes of social policy and remedial action these various components need to be distinguished and analysed separately. Since white society had been slow to respond to the results of such analyses, it was very understandable that black activists should feel impatient with what to the victims of prejudice and discrimination is apt to feel like hair–splitting and an excuse for procrastination.[17]

Regardless of how one wishes to view the idea of institutional racism, it does present the problem of prejudice and discrimination as part and parcel of the norms and traditions found in society. One of the roots of cultural prejudices and acts of discrimination is ethnocentrism.

ETHNOCENTRISM AND DISCRIMINATION

In the chapter on prejudice and attitudes, the concept of ethnocentrism was addressed briefly. Here we shall examine the nature of ethnocentrism as a force behind discrimination within the context of cultural prejudices. Cultural prejudices include ethnocentric beliefs found in virtually all cultures. Ethnocentrism is generally regarded as a love and feeling of superiority for one's ingroup and a feeling of disdain for and inferiority of outgroups. While this simple and direct description may suffice in many situations, it ignores the function and influence of ethnocentrism in society.

Ethnocentrism was coined by William Graham Sumner in 1906 and used to describe how group loyalty and social order are maintained by fear and hatred of outsiders.[18] He notes that the greater the degree of intensity of conflict between ingroup and outgroup, the greater the ingroup ties. As for the meaning of ethnocentrism, Sumner states:

Ethnocentrism is the technical name for this view of things in which one's own group is the center of everything, and all others are scaled and rated with reference to it. Folkways correspond to it to cover both the inner and the outer relation. Each group nourishes its own pride and vanity, boasts itself superior, exalts its own divinities, and looks with contempt on outsiders. Each group thinks its own folkways the only right ones, and if it observes that other groups have other folkways, these excite its scorn. . . . For our present purpose the most important fact is that ethnocentrism leads a people to exaggerate and intensify everything in their own folkways which is peculiar and which differentiates them from others. It therefore strengthens the folkways.[19]

If ethnocentrism is a foundation of social cohesiveness and source of ingroup–outgroup hostility as suggested by Sumner, then it certainly must have a major function in intergroup relations. This especially should be true for those societies that are multicultural and multiracial.

When one examines the nature of ethnocentrism, it frequently is viewed as a matter of ingroup–outgroup relations at the national or state level. Political jingoism and chauvinism often are cited as exemplars of ethnocentrism. However, in the context of ethnic and race relations within a multicultural–multiracial society, the concept is seldom applied. The question arises as to how such a society can maintain a sense of cohesiveness and at the same time be accepting of ethnic and racial diversity. If the events of interethnic conflict in Eastern Europe and the former Soviet Union tell us anything, it is that some ethnic groups maintained feelings of loathing for each other and, when given the opportunity, expressed these hostilities after years of repression.

In the United States, as elsewhere, ethnocentric attitudes serve a dual function. First, they maintain ingroup cohesiveness and reinforce positive ethnic and racial identities. Second, the enhancement of these identities is made possible by the ethnocentrisms that establish a group's identity as superior to others. As an eventuality, ethnocentric beliefs and feelings may permeate ethnic and racial groups at organizational and individual levels of intergroup relations.

So long as members of ethnic and racial groups maintain ethnocentric attitudes, there can be little doubt that ethnocentrism will play a role in discriminating against outgroup members in the social, economic, and political life of society. Those who advocate a multicultural–multiracial society, in which all peoples maintain their rights to live according to their ethnic heritages and still be accepted as equals within a larger social context, overlook the role of ethnocentrism as a divisive influence within the mass society.

Ethnocentrism by its very nature divides the world into we and they, good and bad, superior and inferior. At the same time, it serves as the hallmark of maintaining group cohesiveness. Therefore, how can one speak of a multicultural society that is tolerant and in which members of various groups will not be prone to discriminate?

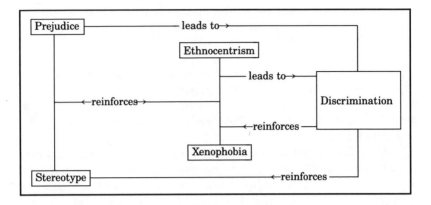

Figure 3. Some Interactive Influences of Ethnocentrism, etc.

It is a complex situation. Of course, one may argue that people of various groups must learn to inhibit their ethnocentrisms. Under many conditions ethnocentrism can be inhibited, but there are points at which ethnocentric attitudes may not permit social cohesion and integration with those viewed as outside the group.

Since ethnocentrism tends to be both a dividing and cohesive influence for groups, it lends itself nicely to the concept of xenophobia. That xenophobia may be regarded as a source of discrimination should not be surprising. Surely one does not employ, live near, or desire to associate with people whom he or she fears or who seem strange and different in the eye of the beholder. But xenophobia, like ethnocentrism, has an involved relationship with the processes of stereotyping and prejudice, as well as discrimination. Both xenophobia and ethnocentrism create barriers that prevent social familiarity. This, in turn, leaves the perceptions of ingroup members with stereotypes and prejudices that are constantly reinforced by the restructuring of reality, as noted by Lippmann and in our discussion on selective perception in chapter 6. The following illustrates some of the interactive influences among ethnocentrism, xenophobia, prejudice, stereotyping, and discrimination.

THE LIFE FORM OF DISCRIMINATION

Discrimination is rooted in the history of the United States. These roots reflect the history of Western civilization, the development of racist and ethnocentric beliefs, and behaviors that emerged during the past several hundred or so years. Some may contest that this is a history of brutality and savagery when considering the treatment of those culturally and racially different. There can be little doubt that such criticisms are warranted and can be well documented.

However, there must also be recognition of the flip side of this history, the development of an awareness of the rights of all people, regardless of nationality, race, religion, and creed. In the area of intergroup relations, the twentieth century represents a period in which this awareness clashed with the historical precedents set forth in previous eras. It has been a troublesome clash, and it will probably continue well into the twenty–first century.

In the area of intergroup relations, the major problem remains one of finding a viable solution to the problem of racial and ethnic discrimination. For generations, discrimination based upon one's race or ethnicity had been accepted as the natural order of things. It had taken on a life form of its own. Minority groups had their place in society; the members of the majority had their place. The former was subordinated to the latter. Separate neighborhoods, schools, restaurants, medical facilities, and theaters seemed to be a natural state for those in the privileged caste.

Yet, many Americans did not see themselves as part of a caste system. After all, one could move up or down the socio–economic class. There was no thought about the fact that Black Americans and other racial minorities were locked into a closed class system. On occasion, this "natural state" would be shattered momentarily by civil unrest. Then came a more protracted movement of civil rights activists. Eventually, there was government action in the form of Supreme Court decisions, executive orders, and Congressional laws—designed to set things right. It was not until the sixties that the mass American society began to shed the life form of discrimination. It was no longer a natural life form.

Civil Rights Legislation. The Civil Rights Act of 1964 prohibited discrimination against blacks and other minorities in matters regarding voting, employment, or use of public accommodations. The Fair Housing Act of 1968 prohibited real estate companies from discriminating when seeking buyers for houses. By way of a number of executive orders, the government even went so far as to introduce a policy of affirmative action. This policy sought to insure that minorities be adequately and fairly represented in the work place.

Affirmative Action Against Discrimination. At the federal level, Executive Order 8002, issued by President Roosevelt, was the first in a series of actions that prohibited racial discrimination by companies having federal contracts. Under the Kennedy administration, Executive Order 10925 set forth the requirement of contractors to seek a policy of affirmative action, and it provided penalties for those who did not comply. President Johnson's Executive Order 11246 and Title VII of the Civil Rights Act of 1964 supplied additional impetus to the policy of affirmative action. The Equal Employment Act of 1972 extended the requirement of affirmative action to include both contractors and subcontractors. In addition to these and other federal–level actions, states began to require affirmative action policies. Combined with state commissions on human rights designed to handle complaints, federal and state governments pursued an end to discrimination by legal means.

For some, if not most, white Americans, affirmative action appeared to be an unfair process of reverse discrimination. The feeling associated with such beliefs seemed to be suppressed beneath the surface for almost twenty years. Then, in the late eighties and early nineties, more and more individuals began to express their fears and frustrations over the affirmative action mandates. This was especially true among civil service job applicants, such as those seeking employment in law enforcement. On the other hand, large businesses did not oppose affirmative action and, in fact, often defended it.

In 1988, Herbert Hammerman, the first chief of the reports unit of the Equal Employment Opportunity Commission, explained that big business supported affirmative action because it was based upon goals rather than quotas. "And goals, unlike court–ordered quotas, do not have to be met—provided that the employer has made a good faith effort."[20]

In drafting the affirmative action report forms, Hammerman additionally admits that he identified only a limited number of ethnic and racial groups, based upon the degree to which they were victims of discrimination. In doing this he intentionally instructed employers to avoid "scientific definitions of anthropological origin." This was done, he explains, in order to discourage employers from requiring employees to identify their racial or ethnic membership. However, he readily acknowledges that this conflicts with the listing of specific groups such as "Indians, Pakistanis, and Pacific Islanders." How one was to determine which of these groups, under the general category of Asian, was to be applied to a particular individual seems to be anybody's guess.

Reflecting on affirmative action after twenty years, Hammerman readily notes its weaknesses, but concludes that it is still a necessity:

> There remains the question: Is it desirable that the labor force reflect demographic features? Is it even feasible, in view of different interests, educational levels, seniority, and various other considerations? Probably not. Affirmative action is designed to attack pervasive forms of discrimination not remediable by fine tuning. And yet, in spite of affirmative action faults, I do not believe we are ready to dispense with it. Although we should not indefinitely continue labor–force percentages in the way we do now, the time for the change has not arrived. And at least for now, the nation's largest firms support the policy.[21]

What is interesting about Hammerman's perspective is his admission that the affirmative process is flawed at its very foundation— the use of percentages in determining whether one has met the goals of affirmative action. Furthermore, one can question whether there is a practical difference between quotas and goals when it comes to the individual. Hammerman's statements seem to reflect a greater concern for the support of the heads of large businesses than for the attitudes and frustrations of those to be excluded from employment due to affirmative action.

Near the end of 1991, a number of black scholars began to question whether affirmative action policies and racial quotas were viable. The positions expressed by these individuals ranged from determining whether a given situation actually requires an affirmative action policy to the position espoused by economist Walter E. Williams. Williams holds that preferential treatment based upon race, numerical goals, and set–asides, causes blacks to doubt their own ability, their own sense of self–reliance, and at the same time cultivates the notion among whites that blacks cannot succeed without special consideration.

Asian Americans also have felt the effects of racial reverse discrimination in the area of higher education. A study by Dana Y. Takagi found that Asian Americans were being systematically discriminated against in their attempts to gain entrance into Harvard, Yale, the University of California at Berkeley, the University of California at Los Angeles (UCLA), Princeton, and Stanford.[22] In this case, the problem was that Asian Americans had excelled in the traditional requirements for entrance to major universities.

Therefore, there is evidence to indicate that a systematic and overt effort was made to exclude a number of Asian American students by establishing other admission criteria. The history of these cases of discrimination covered a period of seven years. During this time, some of the universities in the study attempted to rationalize their policies by shifting the question of discrimination to the issue of diversity—seeking other activities besides scholarship when considering applicants. At Berkeley, the issue became politicized and attached to affirmative action policies. Eventually, the controversy seemed to be resolved, or at least put to rest, but it demonstrates the complexities and growing conflicts over the concepts of affirmative action, ethnic and racial goals and quotas.

The Civil Rights Acts were designed to prohibit discrimination. Affirmative action policies were designed to halt discrimination and correct the imbalance created by discriminatory practices. After twenty or so years, these acts and policies appear to have made a major impact upon the problem of discrimination for many members of minority groups, including women. But it also must be conceded that affirmative action has done little to assist those in the grips of abject poverty. It will take more than affirmative action to address these individuals.

Affirmative action also has created highly politicized controversies and may be the source of resentment and disdain among those who either have been the victims of reverse discrimination or who perceive that they have been. Furthermore, there has been a rise of opposition to affirmative action based upon the premise that it is no longer necessary. During the next decade or so, the problem of discrimination and legal means of combatting it may very well come to a head. Just what will happen is simply a matter of conjecture.

EFFECTS OF DISCRIMINATION

The effects of extreme and long–term discrimination are well known. Discrimination has contributed to poverty, ignorance, crime, disease, mental illness, increased infant mortality, and a shortened life expectancy. It is difficult for many white Americans to accept this. After all, they claim, look at the Italians, Poles, Jews, Irish. They too faced discrimination and prejudiced attitudes, but they pulled themselves up. These white Americans forget the slums and poverty in which these immigrants lived. They may not know of the violence that also permeated the ghetto conditions of long–ago immigrants. But what each and every one of us must know is that the treatment of Black Americans cannot be regarded as comparable to any group in the United States—not Irish, Italian, Japanese, Chinese, Jewish, or Native American.

Each case of minority-majority relationships must be evaluated and judged with the context of the particular minority group's experience. The black experience was horrendous. This is not to say that other groups did not experience dreadful effects of discrimination and hate violence. They did. But their experiences and treatments were not the same.

The social psychological effects of and reactions to ethnic and racial discrimination vary among groups and is dependent upon the personal experiences of individuals. For many Jews, the effects and reactions included the development of self-hate and group denial or distancing. Self-hate has also been found among other minority groups even where denial was not feasible.

Self-hate refers to the condition whereby an individual attempts to blame her or his group for those problems encountered by acts of prejudice. It seems to manifest itself in the notion of "I am damned because I am. . . . " Kurt Lewin, who seems to be the first to introduce the concept, explains, " . . . the individual has certain expectations and goals for the future. Belonging to his group is seen as an impediment to reaching those goals. This leads to a tendency to set himself apart from the group. . . . such frustration may lead to a feeling of hatred against one's own group as a source of frustration."[23] Among Jews and others who can pass, self-hate might lead to attempts to hide all traces of one's ethnicity or heritage. Preference given to light-skinned children (referred to as high yeller or bright) in black families seems to be indicative of self-hate. But, as has been noted by a number of authors previously, what can you expect when the mass society places a premium on being white? The principle that minority groups tend to identify with the more successful majority that surrounds them is a basic phenomena. This is especially true for those attempting to distinguish between the concept of a multiethnic society and one that is a melting pot. There is an inherent assimilation process that draws the minority groups to the periphery of their own group and, if possible, into the mass society.

Self-hate contributes to the development of the marginal individual who is drawn to the periphery of his or her own group and finds hiding her or his identity infeasible. This individual seeks acceptance among the outgroup and maintains some ties with his or her ingroup. The marginal person is frustrated by not being fully

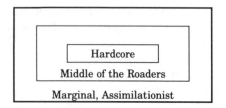

Figure 4. Degrees of Ingroup Association.

accepted by the majority, and this frustration leads to anger. But since the majority is too powerful and maintains the high status sought, the marginal person strikes out against his or her own group.[24] Lewin notes that when such individuals become successful in the outside world, they may become spokepersons for their minority group. Traditionally, these individuals tended to advocate assimilation.[25] However, in recent years, with the rise of multiculturalism, they have advocated a combination of assimilation and symbolic ethnicity. It is important to note that these leaders do not represent those members who are hardcore and anti-assimilationist. In the diagram above, the Middle of the Roaders represent those who fall between the two extremes. They are seldom aware of issues of assimilation and tend to quietly go with the flow. The hardcore members are acutely aware of assimilationists and often express disdain for the leaders. Yet they are hesitant to speak out; they want little or nothing to do with the outside or the marginal fringe.

For blacks, it may be a matter of crossing the color line if possible, or, if not, attempting to remove oneself from any involvement with other blacks, especially those poor blacks who are most stigmatized. Among those blacks who can pass as whites, it was estimated in the 1940s that the number crossing the color line was anywhere from 25,000 to 300,000 annually.[26] When society places a premium on being something other than what one is, the probability of self-hate and group distancing can be expected.

Another effect of discrimination is almost the converse of the above. In this instance, the individual develops a sense of pride and defiance against those he or she perceives to be the perpetrators of ethnic and racial discrimination. This attitude may be epitomized by the expression: "They can shove it." The rise of separatist groups might very well be a manifestation of this reaction to discrimination and hate prejudice. This pride and defiance may branch out in at least two directions. One includes the development of a stable and tolerant sub-society. This will probably occur if the emphasis is on self-reliance and pride. The other is the development of a hate-group whose members emphasize the bigotry and injustices of the majority to justify their group ties.

Being a member of a minority and constantly under the pressure of becoming a possible victim of discrimination tends to create certain patterns of behavior when the individual interacts with members of the majority. In some cases, it may result in a form of arrogant behavior, designed to test the tolerance of majority group members. In other cases, the individual may resort to acting out the stereotypic character that the majority group has established for his or her group. In both cases, there is probably some degree of hostility and distrust directed toward members of the majority. Members of the minority learn well to wear a mask. They also learn how to categorize the majority group member. This process of categorizing the outgroup member as fitting under one of a number of labels will often dictate which mask to wear. Quite often the defenses established upon the part of the minority group member will serve to distort reality and lead to spurious assumptions.

Relative deprivation is another social psychological effect of discrimination. This phenomena occurs when there is a "discrepancy between what one anticipates and what one attains."[27] The Civil Rights era of the sixties created a perspective in which minority group members no longer compared themselves to other members of their group, but rather to the mainstream of society. So while the plight of minorities improved, concomitant with these improvements were expectations that the quality of life would improve at a faster rate than actually occurred. When this did not happen, many members of minority groups felt more deprived than they had previously. The construct of relative deprivation partially may explain the popularity enjoined by minority, separatist and revolutionary groups. Feeling and believing that the "system" will never permit them to co-exist on an equal level as the majority, such group members accept the notion that they must either leave the system, a separatist move, or destroy the system, a revolutionary move. The former case might be illustrated by the Black Muslim movement. The Black Panther Party may have appealed to those seeking the latter.

These effects and reactions are by no means the totality of the repercussions of discrimination at the social psychological level. Further, it is essential to realize that, regardless of the amount of negative experiences one has encountered as a member

LOW←─────────AGGRESSION─────────→HIGH				
Avoidance	*Defamation*	*Acts Against Property*	*Assault*	*Murder*
Limted or	Verbal	Graffiti	Verbal	Limited
Select	Jokes	Light Damage	or	Genocide
Total	Labeling	Heavy Damage	Written	
	Name calling	Destruction	Physical	
	Accusations			
	Written			
	Jokes			
	Labeling			
	Name calling			
	Accusations			

Figure 5. Continuum of Aggression from Low to High.

of a minority group, he or she may be tolerant and accepting with regard to members of the dominant group. The most important principle regarding those who have been the victims of discrimination and those who have been the perpetrators is that each group is composed of individuals. As individuals, they will vary on how they perceive and relate to reality. However, as we shall see below, discrimination often begets discrimination, and hate often begets hate.

Scapegoating and Aggression

Ethnic and racial prejudices frequently are expressed by acts of aggression. For Allport, these acts of aggression were described under the rubric scapegoating. But as noted earlier, this seems to be a misapplication of the concept when applied to all forms of hostility. Nevertheless, I have followed his conception of a continuum of the degree of hostility with some modifications.

Aggression as a manifestation of hate prejudice can be seen along a continuum from avoidance to genocide. This continuum consists of the following: Avoidance, Defamation, Acts against Property, Assault, and Murder.

Avoidance as Hostility

We already have seen how avoidance may be acted in the form of discrimination. Here we shall augment this understanding by distinguishing between types of avoidance. Total avoidance consists of avoiding all members of an outgroup under virtually all conditions. The outgroup members are essentially treated as non-beings or untouchables. In the most extreme cases, members of the avoiding group will isolate themselves from the target group or groups so as to create a closed society. Total avoidance can even occur in a neighborhood with target group members living next door. It is almost as if the parties live in two totally different dimensions if not different worlds.

Limited or select avoidance takes place when one associates with outgroup members only when necessary. For example, an individual may have black or Asian clients or customers and therefore may maintain a limited economic relationship. But this same individual avoids any other social intercourse. In some cases, the avoiding individual or "avoider" may even employ a member of the target group but maintain a caste–like relationship with that person.

The effects of this type of avoidance maintains barriers between groups and results in the use of unchallenged stereotypes by members of both the ingroup and outgroup upon which to base their perceptions of one another. It also creates or reinforces feelings of distrust and disdain among both parties.

DEFAMATION

Defamation involves denigration of a group by communication. This may be verbal or written. Among the acts of defamation are jokes, labeling, name-calling, and accusations. Defamation may occur at either the intrasocial or intersocial levels. Intrasocial defamation refers to defaming a group without members of the target being present. Intersocial defamation involves calumnious and disparaging communication in the presence of the target group. In the case of written or printed defamation, intrasocial defamation would include literature that is limited in distribution to ingroup members, as in the case of a hate newsletter sent only to members of a hate group. Written intersocial defamation occurs when the message is made readily available for all members in society, as in leaflets handed out on a street corner or posted on telephone poles.

Jokes. In virtually every society there are jokes directed at various groups. These racial and ethnic jokes may be defamatory, positive, or unbiased. Still the fact remains that most racial and ethnic jokes are negative. They are inclined to draw upon negative stereotypes from which the "humor" emerges.

This can be illustrated by the following joke that in the first instance is the original version with the original target group. In the second instance the same joke is repeated, but the target group is changed.[28]

Original Version:

What's the new Webster's definition of the word Confusion?

Father's Day in Harlem.

Change of Target Group:

What's the new Webster's definition of the word Confusion?

Father's Day in Little Italy.

Using this illustration, in an informal survey with twenty white adults, the subjects found the first version either humorous or at least understandable. They perceived a connection between the joke and the stereotype of blacks as immoral and exceedingly promiscuous. When given the joke with Little Italy as part of the punch line, they failed to see any meaning in the joke.

A review of the jokes found in the publications *Truly Tasteless Jokes* and *Truly Tasteless Jokes X* indicates the following by group and stereotypic trait and number of jokes keying on the trait:[29]

Group	No.	Trait
Black	3	On par with animals
	3	Ignorant
	3	Play on word nigger, coon, or related
	4	Dishonest, criminal, violent
	2	Immoral, promiscuous
	1	Lazy
	11	Features, hair, skin, lips, sex organ
	2	Other negative
	7	Other not negative or ???
Jews	4	Lacking sexuality (women)
	15	Cheap, Rich, Materialistic
	1	Physical: big nose
	3	Other negative
	10	Other not negative or ???

Virtually all jokes related to Polish people illustrated that they were stupid, ignorant, or backwards.

Racial and ethnic jokes often are defended as being funny and harmless. The fact that they reinforce stereotypes tend to demean a group and its members, and help create a superordinate–subordinate relationship between groups, which is either ignored or castoff as being overly sensitive. Members of a particular minority, including a number of entertainers, resort to putting down their own group, and outgroup members use this in some cases to justify their own use of such humor. Nevertheless, the fact remains that negative racial and ethnic jokes are not necessary and probably do more harm than one might think.

Name Calling and Labeling. Name calling and labeling are very closely related, and one might ask whether there should be a distinction. I have selected to make this distinction with the caveat that in some cases the two concepts overlap, making a distinction somewhat useless. In other cases, the distinctions are of value. The act of labeling consists of associating a group and its members with some evil or undesirable element in society. Labeling has been used to express anger, fears, and frustrations. Name–calling, I suggest, is defaming by the use of disparaging descriptors, including racial or ethnic slurs and obscenities. The degree of hostility expressed by labeling and name–calling may be estimated by the content of what is stated and whether the target group is present. When done with the target group member being present, it should be regarded as more hostile than if done in the absence of a target group member. As a general rule, the more vicious the content, the greater the hostility.

Common labeling practices include associating Italians with criminal activity, especially organized crime. Rumors that New York governor, Mario Cuomo, had Mafia ties is one illustration of negative labeling. Anti-Semites tend to equate Jews with controlling the world's economy, and some adhere to the belief that they are tied to a fictitious group in Switzerland. Blacks have been labeled as dishonest, lazy, and oversexed (men). Unjustly labeling groups as communists or enemies of the state is still another form of labeling used to express hostility. Groups may be categorized and labeled differently depending upon social, economic, and political conditions at a given time and place. Japanese were labeled by masses of Americans as treacherous, sly, and inhuman during World War II. When they were no longer perceived as warring enemies but as economic rivals fifty years later, they were stigmatized as shrewd entrepreneurs and cutthroat competitors.

Name–calling or the use of disparaging descriptors, including obscenities, overlaps with labeling in some cases, but in other cases the use of these descriptors are often limited to a specific group. We

Group	Disparaging Name	Meaning or Association
Black American	Nigger	pejorative for Negro
	Jungle bunny	animal–like
	Porch monkey	animal–like
	Coon	ignorant, ineducable
	E.P.	earth people
	Sambo	happy and ignorant
	Pickaninny	animal–like (child)
	Uncle	elderly man
	Boy	any age
	Aunt	black woman
Italian	Wop	Without papers or from I "guoppo, meaning bold or handsome. Taken to mean a "dirty Italian"
	Dago	origin. of Spanish or Italian descent
	Grease ball	greasy hair and skin
	Spaghetti eater	self-explanatory
Jew	Kike	pushy, cheap, vulgar; used by assimilated German Jews toward Eastern European Jews
	Sheeny	"dirty Jew"
	Christ killer	self-explanatory
	JAP	Jewish American Princess, young women
Hispanic	Spic	possibly from spigotty meaning I do not speak English
	Beaner	from diet, beans
	Low Rider	from low slung auto
	Taco Bender	from diet, taco

Figure 6. Sample of negative labels used to describe racial and ethnic groups.

might speculate that the number of epithets for a particular group within a given society may reflect the degree of hostility toward that group. Some disparaging names used to identify groups or their members are listed above.

There are derogatory names for many other groups, Polish—Polacks; Japanese—Japs, Nips; Irish— Mick; French—frogs; Germans—Kraut; Vietnamese—Buddhaheads; white Americans—peckerwoods, honky; and so on. Although members of a given group might use these terms among themselves, it is regarded as totally unacceptable for an outgroup member to do so. For those who do not understand why this is so, consider the following analogy. It is one thing for a parent to call her or his child a spoiled brat. But it might be highly offensive for an outsider to do so. Furthermore, when names such as these are used among members of the ingroup, it often is accepted that the name–caller is doing so as a tongue-in-cheek comment.

Labeling and name–calling perpetuate negative stereotypes and breed mutual hostility. Most of these expressions are learned informally and are ingrained into the culture and society where they are used. The effect of being the victim of name–calling is long–lasting, if not permanent. The co-worker who even jokingly refers to a person by using a racial or ethnic epithet seldom realizes the damage created. First, it may leave an emotional scar on the victim, and, second, it creates a bitterness that may be irreversible. In 1983, a black radio talk show host and columnist Ken Hamblin worked the night shift for a Denver radio station. His white co-workers referred to him as the "night-nigger." Years later, Hamblin still remembered. Hamblin astutely observed, "They have no idea what it means [to be a victim of racial slurs]."[30] Racial and ethnic epithets and offensive jokes penetrate the victim's sinew, striking deep into the heart and mind, vibrating like a thousand drums, and yet, the victim often smiles or nods as if to say, "It's OK; it does not hurt." But hurt it does, and even this is an understatement.

ACCUSATIONS

Accusations consist of charging a group with some evil act or plot. The medieval blood libel against Jews is one such accusation. Accusations are usually transmitted by way of rumors. They are designed to create fear and call upon the authorities or masses to rise up in self–defense or retaliation. A common charge that has led to lynchings of blacks in the United States has been that of rape or attempted rape of white women by black men. During World War II, Japanese Americans along the west coast of the United States were accused of planting their crops in the shapes of arrows. These arrows, so the charge went, were designed to direct Japanese pilots to American bases on the mainland.

Accusations are a handy tool for demagogues to incite the masses and create sufficient fear in order to achieve greater power and control. For the workaday citizen, accusations and rumors may be used to undermine co-workers. As an economic and social weapon against racial and ethnic minorities, accusations are extremely effective when combined with stereotypes. Making accusations that fit the traditional stereotype of a group increases the credibility of the accusation—it fits what is already framed in one's perceived reality.

ACTS AGAINST PROPERTY

Hate acts against property most often include defacing property with graffiti. The use of graffiti serves two purposes. First, it provides the perpetrator with a tangible act against the victim while maintaining personal anonymity. Second, it lends itself to terrorizing the victim. Closely related to this form of vandalism are drive-by shootings, designed to intimidate rather than target an individual. Arson, fire bombings, and the use of explosives are probably the most violent acts against property.

In the two year period from 1989 to 1991, there were approximately two hundred acts of hate vandalism reported by the Southern Poverty Law Center.[31] These included attacks against schools, homes, synagogues, and churches. Most of these acts consisted of painting "KKK," swastikas, and racial or anti–Semitic slurs. Arsons during the same period totalled twenty–two. However, some acts were not proven to be racially or ethnically motivated. On the other hand, the Center collects only a sample of the total number of racial and ethnic violence perpetrated in any given period.

ASSAULTS AND MURDER

Assaults. An assault may be physical or verbal. Verbal assaults differ from name–calling and labeling to the extent that an assault must place the individual in fear for her or his safety. This usually is in the form of threat. Furthermore, the threat must be conceivable. In other words, if a person is told by another that the latter intends to crush the form by lifting up the Empire State Building and dropping it upon the intended victim, this probably would not be regarded as an assault. Verbal or written assaults include bomb threats, threat to kill, or threat to do other serious bodily harm.

Physical assaults encompass any offensive touching. This may range from slapping or pushing to utter mayhem. Battery is used in legal terminology to classify these attacks. Racially or ethnically motivated, physical attacks may be premeditated with or without a particular victim in mind. In recent years, there have been more spontaneous hate attacks—with the victim being in the wrong place at the wrong time.

MURDER

Murder, like physical assaults, may be spontaneous or planned. In the United States, many hate–related murders appear to be spontaneous when one isolated victim is involved. However, there have been murders in which selected victims have been targeted. Hate violence may result in murders along a continuum from one individual to genocide, the partial or complete destruction of all members of a racial, ethnic, or religious group.

Genocide most often requires the consent of the existing power structure in a society. It represents the highest degree of hostility of hate prejudice. The concept genocidal is sometimes used to describe the intent to kill substantially most if not all members of a group. In addition to the Nazi extermination of Jews and Gypsies, genocide and genocidal acts have been carried out against Carthaginians (146 B.C.), Native Americans (nineteenth century), Armenians (1915–21), Cambodians (1975-78), Igbo (Nigeria, late 1960s and early 1970s), Aché (Paraguay, 1970s), and Baha'is (Iran, 1980s).

Motives and Types of Haters

The acting out of hate prejudice may be viewed as a gamut extending from non-violent acts to the most dreadful forms of inhumanity. The reasons why people resort to these acts are varied and complex. Allport suggested seven motives that seem useful. These are: (1) frustration and deprivation, (2) guilt evasion, (3) fear, (4) anxiety, (5) self-enhancement, (6) conformity, and (7) tabloid thinking.[32] Although these terms will be used, I have taken the liberty to reframe some of his perceptions and disagree with others.

People who blame their deprivations on other groups and take coercive action against members of these groups are motivated by frustration and deprivation. The frustrated individual may develop a sense of hatred that eventually then turns to aggression. Another process may include fear. The feeling of being deprived may create fear and anxiety that, in turn, lead to hate and aggression. The thwarted scapegoater very well may fit this description. The thwarted scapegoater is usually frustrated in some important phase of life and cannot adjust. The individual often believes that he or she has earned or deserved a better life than the one being lived.

Fear and anxiety may be related to immediate life concerns such as when an individual has lost her or his job, or when one's home is about to fall to foreclosure. This immediate threat may then be generalized to include a diabolic plot, orchestrated by foreign or alien elements. One might even become convinced that the government is in the hands of some alien group.

One aspect regarding those whose hostility is based upon frustration and deprivation is the feeling of lack of efficacy, political, social, or economic. By blaming a tangible target or symbol of the target for personal deficiencies or deprivations, one can release his or her energies of frustration. In addition, the frustrated and deprived individual can rationalize that he or she is the true victim, and the aggression expressed is a matter of self-defense.

Closely related to the concepts of frustration-deprivation and anxiety–fear are guilt evasion and self–enhancement. Guilt evasion usually occurs when one cannot face up to those acts and decisions that have resulted in some negative condition or state. Hitler used guilt evasion as a tool by which he could blame others for the calamitous times that had fallen on Germany.

By projecting blame on others, not only do people evade guilt and responsibility, but, in the process, they can reaffirm their superiority and right to be regarded with dignity and respect. Self-enhancement also can be attained by attempting to create a superordinate–subordinate relationship. Even the telling of racial or ethnic jokes or using name–calling in a "friendly" way can produce a sense of superiority.

Conformity may motivate a person to take part in scapegoating or other acts of aggression. However, if one merely conforms to those norms of a group bent upon hate violence, it does not permit us to conclude that this is an acting out of prejudiced attitudes. In this instance there may be no anger, no hate. On the other hand, those who accept hate prejudices based upon their desire to be part of a group, may be hatemongers. To this extent, it may be said that they are motivated to express aggression.

Tabloid thinking is probably one of the most common motives for hate prejudices and aggression. It involves a simplistic view of the world. As noted in the chapter on stereotyping, the world is too complex for us to understand all of its intricacies. There is almost a natural tendency to reduce these to simple and understandable terms. Dividing the world into good and bad, and then advocating the good and seeking to destroy the bad, lends itself to seeking other groups as the imminent evil.

Allport also describes types of scapegoaters. The compulsive scapegoater is described as obsessed with delusions of persecution or paranoia. Here, we really are speaking about a mentally ill person or one close to mental illness, and it may seem that we can ignore these people as being rare. However, as we shall see in the next chapter, they can be rather successful and well-integrated into society.

In addition to the thwarted and compulsive scapegoater, Allport describes other types as being conventional, conforming, and calculating. The evidence is quite clear that committing violent behavior in order to be accepted in a group is quite common. One need only examine the mounting case studies on youth gangs to confirm this. But again, Allport's use of scapegoating fails to appropriately describe this individual. If one is acting out aggressively in order to achieve recognition by peers, then the concept of scapegoating does not fit—there is no projection or transference of blame.

His concept of the conventional scapegoater is one who has some problems coping with frustration but to a lesser extent than the thwarted scapegoater described earlier. This appears to reflect Allport's predisposition to categorize all hatemongers as abnormal or unable to cope with the trials and tribulations of daily living.

However, when we examine some of the motives for scapegoating, there may be cases where prejudices are acted out with very normal goals. For example, acting in a manner that improves one's self-image is not necessarily abnormal. In fact, most people seek to maintain or develop a positive image of him or herself. Putting down others to reach this goal is certainly not uncommon, and, although it may not be nice, it is not always an aberration. Using an entire class of people as the object of the put down is merely a step in this same direction. In other words, I am suggesting that what Allport describes as the conventional scapegoater may actually be a normal individual who has accepted a set of beliefs and feelings that reflect those stereotypes prevalent in a given society.

Calculating scapegoating is represented by those who seek power, leadership, and economic gain by playing upon the fears and prejudices of others. The calculating scapegoater may actually believe in what he or she espouses or may use hate rhetoric as a tool for personal gain. As we shall see in the forthcoming chapter, these individuals sometimes create "empires" and "churches."

CHAPTER 8

HATE GROUPS AND HATERS

Let freedom ring. . . . When we allow freedom to ring, when we let it ring from every village and every hamlet, from every state and every city, we will be able to speed up the day when all of God's children, black men, and white men, Jews and Gentiles, Protestants and Catholics, will join hands and sing in the words of the old Negro spiritual, "Free at last! Free at last! Thank God Almighty, we are free at last!

—Martin Luther King, Jr.

America's longest war is not to be found on the battlefields of distant lands, nor in the annals of military history. It has been and is being fought in the streets, homes, schools, and businesses throughout the United States. The source of this conflict resides in the hearts and minds of Americans, and it manifests itself in cruel and often violent forms of behavior.

It is Saturday night, December 20, 1986, and the temperature is hovering around 46 degrees under partly cloudy skies. Michael Griffith, his stepfather, and a friend are driving through the Howard Beach neighborhood of New York City. The car develops engine trouble. After pulling over to the side, the three men walk about three miles; they come to a pizza parlor, and ask to use the phone. After being told there was no phone, they order a pizza, complete their snack, and leave. Suddenly, they are surrounded by a group of white men. "Niggers don't belong here!" one yells. The whites attack the three blacks. Griffith, attempting to escape, is killed accidently while attempting to dash across a major thoroughfare.

On November 13, 1988, Mulugeta Seraw, an Ethiopian in his late twenties, is bludgeoned to death in Portland, Oregon. The murderers are Skinheads—youths bent on violence and fed on Nazi ideology. In Fallbrook, California, Tom Metzger, who publishes W.A.R. (White Aryan Resistance)—a hate tabloid that vilifies blacks, Jews,

and others, is linked to the Portland murder in a civil suit as insti-
gating the crime.

In the Crown Heights section of Brooklyn, August 1991, a car
driven by a Hasidic Jew accidently kills a black child, Gavin Cato,
and critically injures another. Outraged blacks attack the driver
and indiscriminately begin attacking any Jews they can find.
Twenty blacks attack Yankel Rosenbaum who is totally unaware of
what has happened. To chants of, "Kill the Jew," a black youth
draws a knife and murders Rosenbaum. Yosef Lifsh, the driver of
the car that hit young Gavin Cato, escapes the scene of the accident,
and blacks continue rioting, seeking to lynch Jews and especially
Lifsh. It matters little that Lifsh had saved two black children from
a burning building a year earlier.

Throughout the nation, individuals and groups still exhibit ethnic and racial hatreds and irrational passions. Why do they hate so?
What motivates these people? What beliefs and behaviors do they
exhibit? In this chapter we shall review some of these modern hate
groups and individual purveyors of racial and ethnic hatred in an
attempt to find some answers to these questions.

There are no less than 250 hate groups and hate mills in the
United States. A hate mill refers to an individual or small group—
business, if you will, that provides hate literature and in some cases
sponsors annual meetings and conclaves. These hate groups may be
classified along the political spectrum as left wing or right wing.
The most notorious and popularly known groups tend to be on the
right. They are predominately white supremacist groups with
blacks and Jews as their primary targets. Asians and Hispanics
form what might be regarded as secondary targets. The white supremacist groups also tend to be anti-Catholic, anti-homosexual,
anti-communist, and in some cases are opposed to the federal government in the United States. In the case of the latter, they often
claim that the United States is under the control of ZOG—Zionist
Occupation Government.

Notwithstanding that most hate groups in America are of the
white supremacist variety, ethnic and racial hatred is also found
among minority groups. The Nation of Islam or Black Muslim movement founded by Elijah Muhammad was without a doubt anti–
white—white people were described as white devils, and, in 1978,
Louis Farrakhan continued this racist approach. During the sixties
and seventies, anti-white prejudice also was expressed in the actions of the Black Panther Party. Whereas the Nation of Islam was
to the right of the political spectrum, the BPP was Marxist–Leninist in orientation.

Finally, organized hate is supplemented by individual purveyors of hate prejudice. These people may use literature from hate groups, or they may espouse their own theories designed to denigrate other racial or ethnic groups. In our treatment of hate groups and haters, we shall begin with white supremacist groups followed by an examination of the Black Panthers and the Nation of Islam. The chapter will conclude with two case studies of individuals who have embraced and professed bigoted beliefs.

White Hate

Among the white supremacists, we find five major categories: (a) the Identity Church Movement, (b) the Neo-Nazis, (c) the Ku Klux Klan, (d) the Posse Comitatus and (e) the Skinhead Movement. In addition, there are organizations that do not fit into any one of these categories. Furthermore, even the groups that can be categorized under different headings often share a number of common beliefs, and their members may have cross-group affiliations. For example, Thomas (Thom) Robb, who heads the Knights of the Ku Klux Klan, is also an Identity Church minister. The Aryan Nations, an Identity Church movement group under the leadership of Richard Girnt Butler, has followers who are Skinheads, neo–Nazis, and members of the Ku Klux Klan.

Identity Church Movement

Among the foremost hate groups in the United States are those that can be classified under the label of Identity Churches. Their source of righteousness and guide to action is their own brand of Christianity. There were approximately forty Identity Churches, located in about twenty-five states across the U.S. by the beginning of 1990.

Members are committed to the belief that God's chosen are the descendants of ancient Israel. These descendants are not Jews, but white Christians. Jews are regarded as Satan's seed, and are associated with communism and a conspiracy to control the world. They are the anti-Christ. Blacks are viewed as an inferior breed and often are cast in the role of pawns of Jews and the liberal left. As pawns, they commit crimes against white Christians and attempt to destroy the white race through "race-mixing."

Identity Churches also tend to share the belief that the United States is under the control of ZOG. While Christian precepts serve

Thom Robb, Grand Wizard of Knights of the Ku Klux Klan, addresses group in Denver, Colorado.

as a positive bonding force for church members, the beliefs that ZOG controls the government and that race mixing is a definite threat to their survival serve to provide negative forces that bind different groups together. The most active Identity organization by 1990 was the Aryan Nations.[1]

The Aryan Nations

The Aryan Nations is headed by Reverend Richard Girnt Butler, who is also the spiritual leader of the Church of Jesus Christ Christian. Butler claims that his movement is a continuation of the Church originally established by Wesley A. Swift in Lancaster, California. Butler began his professional career as an aeronautical engineer and served as a flight engineer instructor during World War II. By 1946, Butler had developed a major concern that the future of his nation and the white race was being threatened by "Jewish communism."[2]

In 1961, Butler met and began his tutelage under Wesley Swift. Swift, former Klan organizer and one of the founders of the Chris-

Aryan Nations Contingent in Pulaski, Tennessee, 1991.

tian Defense League, preached a gospel of Anglo–Israelism—a nineteenth century ideology that the true Israelites were Anglo-Saxons.[3] Following Swift's death in 1971, Butler assumed the Church's leadership and eventually moved its location to Hayden Lake, Idaho. It was here that Butler introduced the Aryan Nations or Call to the Nation.

For all practical purposes, the Aryan Nations and the Church of Jesus Christ Christian are almost synonymous. If a distinction must be made, one might suggest that Aryan Nations is the umbrella organization under which the Church resides. The basic theological beliefs of the Aryan Nations and Church of Jesus Christ Christian are summarized in the Kingdom Identity Message:[4]

> *We Believe* the Bible is the true Word of God . . . written for and about a specific people. The Bible is the family history of the White Race, . . . placed on earth through the seedline of Adam. Genesis 5:1

> *We Believe* that Adam–man of Genesis was the placing of the White Race upon this earth. Not all races descend from Adam.

Adam is the father of the White Race only. (Adam in the original Hebrew is translated: "to show blood in the face; turn rosy.") Genesis 5:1

We Believe that the true literal children of the Bible are the twelve tribes of Israel, now scattered throughout the world and now known as the Anglo–Saxon, Teutonic, Scandinavian, Celtic peoples of the earth. We know that the Bible is written to the family of Abraham, descending from Shem back to Adam. [An explanation follows extending the line to Isaac, Jacob] . . . whose name is changed to Israel (meaning: "he will rule as God.") Genesis 32:28; Exodus 12:3, 16:4, 19:20; Revelations 21:12

We Believe that there are literal children of Satan in the world today. These children are the descendants of Cain, who was the result of Eve's original sin, her physical seduction by Satan. We know that because of this sin there is a battle and a natural enmity between the children of Satan and the children of the Most High God . . . Genesis 3:15; John 3:12

We Believe that the Canaanite Jew is the natural enemy of our Aryan (White) Race. This is attested by scripture and all secular history. The Jew is like a destroying virus that attacks our racial body to destroy our Aryan culture and the purity of our Race. Those of our Race who resist these attacks are called "chosen and faithful." John 8:44; I Thessalonians 2:15; Revelations 17:14

We Believe that there is a battle being fought this day between the children of darkness (today known as Jews) and the children of light . . . the Aryan Race, the true Israel of the Bible. Revelations 12:10-11

We Believe that . . . [God] created pure seedlines (Races) and that each have a specific place in His order on this earth. . . . We know that man (Adam) was given the command to have dominion over the earth and subdue it, but that, in great part, our Race has been deceived into rejecting this Divine order. . . . There is no race hatred in this statement. It was and is the plan of . . . [God] to bless all through the seed of Abraham.

We Believe in the preservation of our Race, individually and collectively. . . . We believe our Racial Nation has a right and is under obligation to preserve itself and its members. Isaiah 54:17

We Believe that the redemptive work of Jesus was finished on the Cross. As His divine Race, we have been commissioned to fulfill His Divine purpose and plan: the restitution of all things. John 6:51.

•••

According to this belief system, the twelve tribes of Israel are now the following Aryan Nations: Denmark, Norway, Finland, Germany, France, Italy, Holland, Spain, Iceland, Great Britain, Canada– U.S.A., and Sweden.

In the creed set forth above, there is no mention of blacks, Asians, or other groups. Indeed, most the articles in the Aryan Nations' publication, *Calling Our Nation,* seem to focus upon Jews as the prime enemies of the white race. Briefly, the content of articles suggests that it is the Jews who control the media and Hollywood. They spew immorality across the nation. The economy and the political structure is in the grip of Jews. Even the Presidents have sold out to the Jewish communist cartel.

Blacks are viewed as a major threat to the survival of the "White Race," and the "Ultimate Abomination" is described as race mixing. "Today YOU can escape the terror of the black ghettos and Brown Barrios. Your children and your children's children will have no refuge. The DEATH OF THE WHITE RACE is neither imaginary nor far off in the distant future."[5] Asians and other non-whites are viewed as invading the United States through immigration.

The government's affirmative action program is targeted as another weapon designed to destroy white Americans. The following content appeared in a flier during the 1980s:

ATTENTION: WHITE MEN
LOST YOUR JOB DUE TO "AFFIRMATIVE ACTION"?
DENIED EARNED PROMOTIONS DUE TO "AFFIRMATIVE
ACTION?
DENIED JOBS BECAUSE YOU ARE WHITE?
  ARE:
  YOUR WIVES, MOTHERS, OR SISTERS DREADING
TO WALK THE STREETS FOR FEAR OF BEING
DISFIGURED OR RAPED?
    YOUR FACTORIES CLOSING AND "THE THIRD WORLD"
  SELLING YOU YOUR OWN PRODUCTS?
WOULD YOU RATHER
BE SOVEREIGN WHITE MEN AS WERE YOUR FOREFATHERS. . .
                    TO
REALLY OWN YOUR OWN HOMES, MARRY AND RAISE
FAMILIES OF YOUR OWN KIND———
ENJOY THE FRUITS OF YOUR LABORS RATHER THAN
HAVING THEM ROBBED FROM YOU?

> ... live in a moral society where the crimes
> of sodomy, pornography, rape, murder, usury,
> treason, child molesting, etc. are capital
> crimes?————— ...[6]

The Aryan Nations is not an isolated group. It has connections with members of the Ku Klux Klan, neo–Nazis, and other Identity movement groups. During the first half of the 1980s, members of the Aryan Nations formed what became the Bruders Schweigen, more popularly known as The Order. Its short history was marked by violence, robbery, and murder.

THE ORDER

The rhetoric of hate and racial purity, and the need to combat the Satan–Jew, and the danger of race–mixing eventually led to the belief that action must replace mere words. If the white race were to survive, then something has to be done. These thoughts were deeply embedded in the psyche of Robert Mathews, white supremacist and follower of the Reverend Butler.

In 1983, Mathews and eight fellow racists met in Metaline Falls, Washington, at Mathews's compound. The nine men, including Mathews, David Lane, Bruce Carroll Pierce, Richard Kemp, Daniel Bauer, Randy Duey, Denver Permenter, Kenneth Loff, and William Soderquist each took the oath of the Silent Brotherhood that included the words: " ... to join together in holy union with those brothers in this circle and to declare forthright that from this moment on I have no fear of death, no fear of foe; that I have a sacred duty to do whatever is necessary to deliver our people from the Jew and bring total victory to the Aryan race."[7]

One of the main guides for the Brotherhood's action was the *Turner Diaries,* believed to be written by William Pierce under the pseudonym of Andrew McDonald. The *Turner Diaries* is a novel in which white supremacists faced with the demise of white racial purity carry out a struggle against the forces of evil—race traitors, Jews, and the Jewish–controlled government of the United States.[8] According to the novel, the white revolution begins in 1991 and comes to full bloom by 1993. In carrying out the white revolution, supremacists attack federal agencies and public utilities; race traitors are hung; and all Jews throughout the world are murdered— Tel Aviv is wiped out with a nuclear bomb. It is this book that helps guide the Brotherhood in its quest for a White Bastion—a white state within the United States.

At their initial meeting, the true-to-life Silent Brotherhood maps out its strategy. It is decided to carry out assassinations of Jewish leaders or those identified as puppets for the Jewish cartel. But they fail at this time to target any one person for immediate liquidation. Another major concern was developing the material requisites to bring about a successful revolution. Certainly, they must have a war chest, but how can one be procured in short order? Their conversation drifts to the notion of robbery, but the Bible says "Thou Shalt Not Steal." It is finally decided that robbing pornography shops, drug dealers, and pimps—especially black pimps, would be morally correct.

The Silent Brotherhood then proceeds to hit drug dealers and pimps, but the effort fails, and they finally resort to robbing a pornography establishment. The crime fetches a few hundred dollars—not enough for a revolution. Undaunted, The Order, as it is popularly called, extends its criminal activities to include bank robbery and to engage in counterfeiting activities. With relatively greater success, they are able to send donations to other white supremacist groups and are now counting their cache in the thousands of dollars. New members are added until there are upwards to forty or so members, including Gary Yarbrough.

While pursuing their goal of creating a war chest, Mathews decides the time has come to let the world know of the revolution. An assassination is planned, but the victim is not to be some major player in the government or so-called Jewish magnate in control of the media. Target number one is to be an off-the-wall radio talk show host in Denver. David Lane, whose hatred for talk show host Alan Berg was beyond seething, recommended the hit. On Monday, June 18, 1984, as Berg was leaving his Volkswagen bug in his driveway, Bruce Carroll Pierce sprayed him with .45 caliber rounds fired from a MAC–10 submachine gun. Looking on, the driver of the getaway car, David Lane, reacted nervously by defecating in his pants. The deed was done. The glory of the White Aryan revolution was announced, notwithstanding the fact that the group could not publicly announce its responsibility.

In July, the Brotherhood robbed a Brink's armored car near Ukiah, California, approximately 105 miles north of San Francisco. Their take was approximately three and a half million dollars. But Robert Mathews made one major mistake; he left his weapon

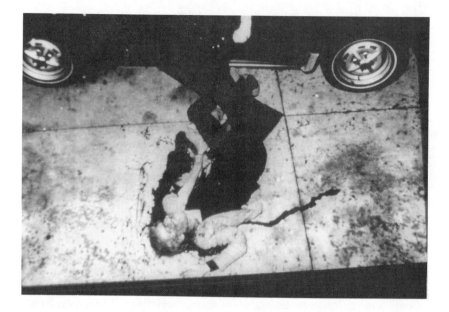

Alan Berg murdered by the Order. Credit: MAGIC Team.

behind. This error and information obtained by Denver police detective Dan Malloy eventually led to the somewhat inglorious end of The Order.

According to Malloy, David Lane was known to police intelligence as a white supremacist.[9] Periodically, intelligence would update their files on such individuals as to their whereabouts and activities. During a meeting with an informant in late January or early February 1984, Malloy learned that David Lane was in Denver and in the company of one Gary Lee Yarbrough. Yarbrough was described as an ex-convict and a member of the Aryan Nations who worked on the Butler compound at Hayden Lake, Idaho. The informant stated that Lane planned to leave Denver and "he was going into deep cover." In other words, Lane wanted to "lose his identity."

At this time, The Order was unknown to the police and the Federal law enforcement agencies. Crimes were being committed, but there was no evidence as to their perpetrators or even their connection with one another. Therefore, Lane's departure from Denver seemed to be unrelated to any of the foregoing events. Lane's marriage had broken up, and he had either left his job or was fired. It was concluded that Lane was probably seeking a new start in a new environment. There was no suspicion that he was associated with a hate group engaged in criminal activity.

Immediately after the murder of Berg, a major case squad was formed consisting of 65 detectives under Denver police command personnel. Their first task was to investigate various aspects of Berg's life and to determine if a lead could be developed pointing to probable suspects. At that time, David Lane's name was supplied as a local, militant, white supremacist. Lane had called Berg on his radio program a number of times, and the two had engaged in altercations. Lane was especially angered by Berg's treatment of white supremacists, Reverend Pete Peters and Colonel Gordon "Jack" Mohr, during a previous interview on the talk show. Lane was only one of several suspects. Since there was no information about Lane's whereabouts, the follow-up on Lane was somewhat suspended.

By now, the August Ukiah robbery had taken place, and the F.B.I. was pursuing the case of the armored car robbery. The federal investigators traced the weapon that Mathews left behind to Andrew Barnhill, a fellow Order member and currently in the C.S.A. (a militant Identity Church group) compound in Arkansas.

Law enforcement investigators had known about connections between and among various supremacist groups, but now they began to discover the linkages between extremist groups and their members and criminal activities. The F.B.I. set up surveillance teams to monitor white supremacists, and one surveillance location was the house of Gary Yarbrough. As the result of a confrontation between Yarbrough and the F.B.I., his house was raided, and the MAC-10 submachine used to kill Berg was found. The weapon to kill Berg and the Ukiah robbery now connected up with a white supremacist group—the Silent Brotherhood had been discovered.

Mathews was tracked down and killed in a shootout on Whidbey Island north of Seattle. More specifically, according to a police intelligence officer, Mathews became a "crispy critter" when his cabin was ignited by a flare and engulfed in flames. David Lane, the driver of the getaway car in the Berg murder, was sentenced to no less than 190 years. Bruce Carroll Pierce was sentenced to over 250 years for his criminal activities, including the murder of Berg. Other members of The Order rolled over as informants or plea bargained to receive shorter prison terms. Some informants were released on probation. But Butler's Aryan Nations and other groups that may have benefitted from the money obtained in the robberies are still operating. The seeds of racial and ethnic hatreds continue to be planted in the minds of both young and old through the dissemination of hate literature and related activities.

REFLECTIONS ON THE SILENT BROTHERHOOD

The Silent Brotherhood may be viewed as a fringe, one-time occurrence, or it may be regarded as an ominous sign of what can be expected in the future. Anti-terrorist task forces of the F.B.I. and other law enforcement agencies may keep track of extremist hate groups, raid them, and even put some out of business, but they obviously cannot prevent people from hating or resorting to violence. In fact there are times when local and state law enforcement agencies are required to protect racist groups during public demonstrations.

The feelings, fears, and beliefs of people eventually find their way into action. The Silent Brotherhood was just that, the logical end of the rhetoric of hate. When Detective Malloy, who had spent over twenty years investigating hate groups, was asked to reflect upon the potential of another group emerging, he stated "Yes. Certainly, there is going to be another coalition of these groups. The hardcore of these groups are going to get together again." Malloy also pointed out that The Order spread over twelve to thirteen states, and, if they had been more careful and structured themselves better, they could have become a most formidable organization.

The Order did not emerge as some unrelated or isolated phenomena. It reflected a set of past and current beliefs. The true believers in The Order did not view themselves merely as white supremacists intent on destroying subhumans. They believed that their very existence was threatened by Jews and race–mixers, by ZOG and liberals who were plotting to destroy their person and heritage. As bizarre and insane as The Order's philosophy and purpose may seem, it would be a considerable error to ignore its logic and its appeal to those who can accept its tenets. And the acceptance of bizarre tenets is as old as religion itself. The Order's strategic goals were no less mad or illogical than the goals of millions of people throughout the world. Once a myth is accepted as truth, that which flows from it is often a logical result. Few will argue with the statement that there is no justification in denouncing anyone's religious beliefs if one accepts the concept of "freedom of religion." On the other hand, how do we deal with belief systems based upon hate and concepts of racial and ethnic supremacy?

One primary step in combatting racial and ethnic hatred and violence is through education. Thus far, social education in most schools, in most social studies curricula, has assisted racism and hate violence by remaining passive, ignoring the study of hate groups and the nature of prejudice. Without a knowledge base of just what these groups advocate and without an understanding of the development of hate prejudice, youths will continually be drawn to these groups and their beliefs at the right time and in the right place. One can learn about it in school or on the street. If schooling is to prepare the child for the real world, then it must address the issues in that world.

If Bobby Mathews had learned about the nature of prejudice and the myths of racism in the classroom, would Alan Berg have been murdered? Would the Order have even been formed? Or would Mathews have been a middle–class family man shaking his head and wondering what is wrong with hatemongers like Richard Butler? What would have been his reaction when hearing about a paramilitary, white Christian supremacist group in the Ozarks? Would he have been interested enough to even learn its complete name, the Covenant, the Sword, the Arm of the Lord?

The Covenant, Sword, and Arm of the Lord

The Covenant, the Sword, the Arm of the Lord (C.S.A.) was eliminated shortly after the fall of The Order. As an Identity Movement organization, the C.S.A. differed from Richard Butler's Aryan Nations and Church of Jesus Christ Christian in that C.S.A. was a survivalist, paramilitary, communal organization. Under the leadership of James Ellison, the C.S.A. established a compound in Arkansas on the Northeast tip of Bull Shoals Lake, near Pontiac, Missouri, at the Missouri–Arkansas border. It was called Zarephath–Horeb and was set on 224 acres. Entry by land to the compound could only be made through Missouri.

The physical layout of Zarephath–Horeb took fields of fire into account. Land mines were set and access was likened to a battlefield with defense perimeters. In the event of invasion, one could fire in all directions from the church steeple. The population varied from time to time, but it usually consisted of between twenty and thirty families. This was the training ground for the white supremacist army. It was also the source of weapons—manufactured from scratch or modified from existing legally purchased weapons or those stolen by C.S.A. members who had served in the United

States armed forces. The weaponry also included rocket launchers and similar high explosive items.

The C.S.A.'s philosophy was relatively simple. The day would come when anarchy would over take America. Jews, the seed of the Devil, race mixers, blacks, and other minorities would attempt to bring doom and decadence to American cities; in fact, this had already been going on for some time. Average white Americans would be limited in their ability to ward off this evil, and it would be left to the C.S.A. and others of similar ilk to provide for the final defense of White Christian Americanism.

The following excerpts from a C.S.A. brochure provide a brief overview of the concerns of the C.S.A.:

> The Beast of Daniel 2 and Revelation 17 is beginning to fall. People are resisting the Government as they never have before. Aryan Adamkind will only get pushed so far and then He will push back! That old serpent, the Devil, and Satan, our enemy, knows the time is short. His Jewish seed is scared and running, vomiting a flood of propaganda as a final thrust against us. Soon the government and kingdoms of this world shall become the Kingdom of our Lord and of His Christ! Hallelujah!
>
> For years, people have preached anti-taxes, anti-jew [sic] anti-fed, etc. This is not bad! It was needed. However, too much effort and finances were expended preaching on these subjects, while the enemy continued to build their forces and thereby tearing ours down. The time has arrived for all of us to apply POSITIVE FAITH . . . Instead of coming out against the school system with its Humanistic teachings, we need to take our children out of public school and teach them at home. Instead of preaching and teaching against the jews and other races, we need to teach our people the historical, racial, physical, and spiritual significance of our race and the godly place and purpose of the other races. . . . By releasing the genetic code in ourselves and our children, we can develop a platform of Christian Nationalism, a platform whereby *every* thing that we do is geared towards enhancing our race, our faith, and our heritage.[10]

The C.S.A. offered a Defense Training Survival School that included a number of paramilitary instructional topics divided into courses. Each course was designed for 2.5 to 5 days, and it was stressed that all courses were "taught by Christians from a Christian point of view."[11] The courses included: 1. Basic Rifle and Pistol, 2. Weapons Proficiency, 3. Natural Wilderness Survival, 4. Urban

Warfare, 5. General Military Fieldcraft, 6. Personal Home Defense, 7. Christian Self–Defense, and 8. Christian Military Truths.

These courses were being offered and the above words published during the same time that The Order was carrying out its wave of crime. Even before the Mathews's gang had formed, C.S.A. leader James Ellison had declared that robbing and violence against the enemy was justified according to the Bible.[12] The connection between the C.S.A. and The Order included many common members. One was Andrew Barnhill, whose weapon Mathews used and subsequently lost during the Brink's robbery in Ukiah, Washington.[13] In 1985, the C.S.A. was terminated by the arrests of its leader and members. Ellison and his lieutenants were convicted on charges of racketeering and illegal weapons. Ellison and follower Kerry Noble agreed to testify for the government against other extremists in 1988 for which they received a reduced sentence and were admitted into the witness protection program. As can best be determined, James Ellison is currently somewhere in the United States under an assumed identity.

The LaPorte Church of Christ

Although no case was made against Pastor Peter J. Peters, a number of law enforcement intelligence investigators believe that he may have been the recipient of money from The Order. Peters's Church draws between 200 and 300 worshipers in LaPorte, Colorado. His message is a hate mosaic covering a number of social issues.

Peters's first principle, around which everything else revolves, appears to be the conflict between Christ and the anti-Christ. In an assault against the Anti-Defamation League of B'nai B'rith, Pastor Peters identifies some of his concerns. He refers to the ADL as an "organization that hates Jesus Christ, removes Bibles from schools, fights against America being a Christian nation, supports hateful Zionist Arab murderers in Israel, etc."[14] In his literature, Peters indicates a strong sense of being persecuted. This belief or feeling of persecution is a common thread among a number of the Identity Churches. In the case of Peters, when any publicity or events adverse to him take place, he seems to view it as a communist Jewish conspiracy and then finds consolation in some Biblical reference.

After two reporters attended his family Bible camp and published their story on Pastor Peters and his activities, Peters responded that "attacks from such small timers are comparable to the curses, abuses, and stones Shimei threw at David (II Samuel

16:5–8)."[15] In his opposition to gun control, Peters advertised a flier entitled "Everything You Wanted to Know About Gun Control." The advertisement contains a drawing of "Uncle Sam" saying: "I Want Your Gun for your own good and Welfare for my child. Give it to Uncle and I'll give you something in return." The reader is directed to turn the page. On page two it is revealed that "Uncle Sam" is actually a Soviet Bear holding a hammer and sickle dripping with blood. Next to the drawing are the words: "Beware of False Prophets, who come to you in sheep's clothing but inwardly are ravenous wolves."[16] In this flier, also, Peters advertises a "tract" entitled *The Bible: Handbook for Survivalists, Racists, Tax Protestors, Militants, and Right–Wing Extremists* by none other than Pastor Pete Peters himself.

This review of three somewhat different types of Identity Church Movement groups provides a fairly broad overview of the movement and its variations. While we could review other groups, it would lead to ennui since most of them espouse very similar ideologies and goals.

Although other hate groups such as neo–Nazis and the Ku Klux Klan share some basic tenets with the Identity Churches, there are differences. As we shall note in the following, some neo-Nazi groups are Odinist and anti-Christian. Many Skinheads regard the religious moral espoused by Church leaders as restrictive.

Neo–Nazis and Skinheads

The neo-Nazi movement began to appear shortly after World War II. Germany, divided, occupied, and in ruins, still had those who adhered to the Third Reich and its mission. Reports of a remnant of Hitler's "Greater Germany" were few and sparse in content. In the United States, neo–Nazis began to gain notice in the 1950s. The rise of neo–Nazism may be attributed to the usual white supremacist beliefs along with a strong anti-Communist orientation left over from the McCarthy period of the early fifties. In addition, there seemed to be an almost natural affinity for the symbols of the Third Reich, from the swastika to goose stepping, from the banners and clicking of heels to the alliance of a great new race. The stereotype of the Nazi Hun was being replaced by the blood-curdling, goose stepping Communist. George Lincoln Rockwell might be regarded as the father of American Nazism during the post World War II era.

Rockwell's American Nazi Party, located in Arlington, Virginia, was limited to relatively few members, ranging in number from ten to twenty during the sixties. His message was Americanism, Nazi-style—send the blacks to Africa and the Jews to ovens. In 1967, Rockwell's murder by fellow Nazis resulted in a power struggle for leadership. His successor turned out to be Matthias Koehl. One of Koehl's first moves was to change the organization's name to the National Socialist White People's Party (NSWPP) in 1967. The NSWPP failed to coalesce and, while numerous Nazi groups emerged, they did not unite. By 1985, Koehl had moved the organization's headquarters to New Berlin, Wisconsin, and again changed the group's name to the New Order. During the 1980s, the Nazi movement consisted of a number of independent groups or individuals producing and disseminating Nazi literature.

White Power

While Koehl's New Order was relocating and seeking a new Nazi nation within the United States, Gary Rex Lauck, alias Gerhard Lauck, was pursuing the work of his NSDAP–AO (National Socialist German Workers' Party–Foreign Organization). According to Lauck, the concept of "White Power" originated in 1966 when Dr. Martin Luther King, Jr. "and his filthy, black hordes tramped into" the white neighborhoods of Chicago.[17] Upon seeing whites yelling "White Power!" and throwing rocks and bottles at the blacks, George Lincoln Rockwell, the American Nazi leader at the time, decided to print and distribute "White Power!" posters. Having established that the concept emerged from the masses of white people, Lauck explains the meaning of "White Power."

He states, "We believe that America and all civilized society are the exclusive products of White man's mind and muscle. We believe the White race is the Master Race of the earth." For Lauck and, no doubt, many others of like ilk, white people are the "Master Builders, Master Minds, and Master Warriors of civilization."

Unlike the shakers and movers of the Identity Movement Churches, Lauck's Nazis accept all people regardless of their national heritage or religious or non-religious beliefs—so long as they are "White." Obviously, this does not include Jews.

The goals of the NSDAP–AO are to obtain a strong unified national government in the United States by and for white people. The development of a strong and unified state requires a nation that is socially unified. Therefore, Lauck refers to his people as "social racists." Adolf Hitler is idolized because "he laid down the ideas of

National Socialism," and unified Germany and then Europe against "Asiatic Communism."

Within this ideology, there is the belief that, once this government is realized, unemployment will cease to exist because "unproductive niggers, spics, and other racial low–lifes" will be gone. Furthermore, the economy will stabilize, as its control is taken away from international Jewish bankers. With the removal of blacks from society, tax money will no longer be needed to integrate schools and educational standards will be raised to their former high levels. There will be no slums or "bad neighborhoods because the sub-humans . . . will be gone forever." It also means the end of white women being raped as well as the high crime rate.

In order to achieve these goals, Lauck calls for a national white movement made up of people of all ages. Children are expected to distribute and post "White Power" stickers beginning at age seven. High school students should battle "niggers on the streets," and college students are assigned the role of writing articles to spread the truth about "White Power." Workers between the ages of twenty and fifty are regarded as "Stormtroopers." The elderly are encouraged to provide financial support. This, then, is what is meant by "White Power"—American Nazi style.

The National Alliance

William L. Pierce received his doctorate in physics from the University of Colorado at Boulder. During the sixties, he worked with the National Socialist White People's Party. In 1974, Pierce founded the National Alliance. Notwithstanding the fact that it holds an annual conference, the National Alliance is primarily a Nazi publication mill. Its primary publication, the *National Vanguard,* warns of racial pollution, Jewish conspiracies, and the like. The Holocaust is treated as fiction, and Nazi war criminals are defended. The fact that Michael Jackson and Eddie Murphy are popular with American youths is viewed as proof of American decadence. A major and constant concern is the power of ZOG. One of Pierce's major claims to fame in the hate circuit is his book, *The Turner Diaries,* which was written under an assumed name. As we might recall, this book seems to have had an influence on the formation of Robert Mathews and his Silent Brotherhood.

CHURCH OF THE CREATOR AND RACIAL LOYALTY

One of the popular emblems among young racists and especially among a number of Skinheads is the "W" (White race) topped by a crown (racial superiority), and halo (purity of blood) above. This emblem represents the Church of the Creator headed by Ben Klassen who refers to himself as the Pontifex Maximus. Klassen claims to have immigrated to the United States from the Ukraine. He was trained as an electrical engineer, invented the electric Can-O-Matic opener, served as a state representative in the Florida legislature, and worked in real estate before his retirement. When it comes to identifying the "Five Greatest Leaders of White Thought," Klassen is no shrinking violet. His list contains Gobineau, Darwin, Nietzsche, Hitler, and Ben Klassen.

Klassen, who is in his mid-seventies, was expected to be succeeded by Rudy "Butch" Stanko upon Klassen's death or retirement. Stanko, who uses the title reverend, had been in the meatpacking business until he was charged by the Federal government with supplying tainted meat for the School Lunch Program. Sentenced to serve time in the Federal prison system, Stanko refused probationary early release and opted to serve his maximum time. He was released in November of 1991. In his book, *The Score,* Stanko claims that Jews control the meatpacking industry, the banking system, the media, and the Federal government.[18] During 1992, Klassen seemed to distance himself from Stanko, and the latter's chance for the title Pontifex Maximus began to fade.

The Church of the Creator seems to be somewhat of a fiction as churches go. Notwithstanding that Klassen did build a church, Bob Scott, a reporter with the *Asheville Citizen,* has stated that no more than three people have been seen around the Klassen property.[19] There are supporters in other areas, such as Eric Hawthorne in Toronto and Charles Eidson of Tampa, Florida, but it is unknown if there are any organized groups. Although the extent and activity of Church members beyond Otto, North Carolina, is questionable, Klassen's hate literature mill is quite real. The main publication of Klassen's Church of the Creator is the racist paper, *Racial Loyalty.*

In the August 1989 issue of *Racial Loyalty,* Klassen finds it necessary to remind his readers that the "Creativity Movement" is not an illegal or underground organization. In describing this legal status, it is noted that "the deadly merciless, RACIAL WAR between the intellectually inferior (but well organized and prolific) Jew, mud, nigger subspecies, and the intellectually superior (but disorganized and nonprolific) White subspecies is already on . . . "[20]

This statement provides a basic summary of Klassen's worldview. The rest is rhetoric, as shown in his statement: " . . . please remember that you [white man] are already suffering [from] tyrannical Jewish oppression and reprisals in the form of confiscatory

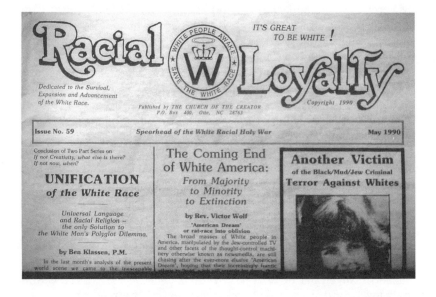

Masthead of Ben Klassen's paper. Klassen heads the Church of the Creator.

taxation, affirmative action, forced busing, jewsmedia–generated brainpollution, and the black/mud/jew criminal terror against Whites in the city streets.... The mad Jewish plan is to exterminate all White people by the year 2000." The messages usually end with some advice on what action to take. This includes "renting a post office box (without the knowledge of your spouse or in-laws, if need be) and send us financial support in the form of bank or postal money orders (instead of the more traceable personal checks)...."

Although some may think that with a name like the Church of the Creator, the Pontifex Maximus would be sponsoring an Identity Movement Church, nothing could be further from the truth. If anything, the theology of the Church of the Creator is more akin to Odinism. Religion is a weapon for Klassen and the Creativity movement, "the same weapon the Jews have used ... "[21] But what is proposed is not Christianity or any perverted form of it. Rather, Klassen suggests that Judeo–Christian holidays, Christmas, Easter, etc., are hoaxes and should be rejected. Creativity holidays such as the vernal equinox, summer solstice, winter equinox, and autumnal equinox should replace them. Klassen also calls upon all white people to reject "the day of birth of a mythical Jewish bastard and the even more absurd day of resurrection of a mythical Jew on the Stick." The Creativity calendar also would "foster healthy and noble White family traditions and ceremonies . . . " These would include birth, puberty, marriage, and death. Finally, White parents are encouraged to provide their children with classical Roman, Greek, and other pagan names.

The Church of the Creator follows a line similar to the other Nazi groups—international brotherhood among all White nations, protection of the pure, white bloodline, and a war of extermination against the mud races, including Jews, blacks, Asians, and other non-whites.[22] Like most white supremacist groups or orators, the call is always urgent to save the white race from race–mixing and eventual extermination through pollution.

WAR: White Aryan Resistance

> "This is WAR hotline. How long, White men, are you going to sit around while these non–White mud races breed you out of existence? They have your jobs, your homes, and your country. Have you stepped outside lately and looked around while these niggers and Mexicans hep and jive to these Africanized rap music? While these Gooks and Flips are buying up the businesses around you? San Diego is going down the toilet just like L.A. This racial melting pot is more like a garbage pail. Just look at your liquor stores. Most of them are owned by Sand niggers from Iraq, Egypt, or Iran. Most of the apartments are owned by the scum from India, or some other kind of raghead. Pretending is not going to make it go away. It was good to see the East Germans run the non-Whites out of their country this week. This here racial melting pot was spread by the poisonous seeds of Judaism. They are like maggots eating off a dead carcass. When you see what these Jews and their white lackeys have done, the gas chambers don't sound like such a bad idea after all. For more information write us at P.O. Box 80272, San Diego, California, 92138 and . . . any of you out there who would like to start a White Student Union on your high school or college campus can write the White Student Union at P.O. Box 151635, San Diego, California, zip 92175. And remember, this time the world, this is WAR."[23]

This is the type of message one may receive by dialing into a White Aryan Resistance phone message in a number of states. The White Aryan Resistance or WAR is the creation of Tom Metzger. WAR is dedicated to the establishment of a White "Aryan" world void of any group that does not fit into this category.

For Metzger, race is the only issue. He rejects any personal so-cial beliefs that may interfere with white racial separatism. Metzger differentiates between two classes of supremacists, Warriors and Priests.[24] Warriors, be they National Socialists, Klansmen, Odin-ists, Identity Christians, Atheists, or Agnostics, have race as their first priority and are willing to leave other views aside. Priests, on the other hand, may have race as a major issue, but it is secondary to a particular religious dogma. Although Metzger is critical of those movements or groups that place other issues above race, he maintains an open line of communication with other such groups.

The WAR message can be received through a telecommunica-tions network, on public access television (the program "Race and Reason"), or by subscribing to Metzger's paper, *WAR*. The paper is one of the most scurrilous and repugnant of the racist publications as can be surmised from a sample of its cartoons and illustrations.

A major target of adult racist groups is the youth market. Metzger has tried to appeal to young whites—especially Skinheads. The following letters appearing in two issues of *WAR* were attrib-uted to Kristina H. at age 12 and later at age 14.[25] There is no in-dication that she is a member of the Skinheads, but the letters may indicate how a young true believer views her racial world at two in-tersections of time and place:

> Being White is NOT a Crime
> Age 12
>> White and proud
>> That's what I am
>> Storming the streets
>> Getting rid of the trash
>> What's wrong with knowing
>> your race is strong?
>> Aryan people unite against-
>> Drugs, Race–Mixing, and Crime.
>> Brothers and Sisters stand by my side,
>> Join the fight for what's right.
> Letter to Editor
> Age 14:

> Let us forever banish the myth that all White women should have "37" by "26" by "37" measurements, practically hairless, and always stay at home with housework. That is the image the Jews are portraying women to be. . . . mindless, prideless, bim-bos. These lip–suctioned, silicone injected, "females" would never fight for their Race or even bare [sic] a child. It sickens me

to see Aryan men trying to make their partners live up to (stoop
low enough to) imitating these air–brushed magazine photos.
A true Aryan female has hips to bare [sic] a child, breasts to feed
it with, and energy to fight for her race.

—WHITE POWER.

In 1991, the Southern Poverty Law Center pursued a civil suit
against Metzger for contributing to the murder of the young Ethiopian, Mulugeta Seraw, in Portland by Skinheads. It was charged
that Metzger had encouraged such racial violence in his paper and
on his talk shows and that this influenced the perpetrators. A judgment of over $10 million was levied against Metzger. Notwithstand-
ing this suit, Metzger remains in business, directing much of his
energy toward the support and recruitment of Skinheads.

Skinheads

The Skinhead movement began in Great Britain during the
late sixties and has spread to the United States as well as Germany
and other western and central European states. The rise of Skinheads in Britain was a white youth reaction to the influx of Indians,
East Indians, and other individuals racially different from the majority of the Commonwealth. Since the sixties, racial violence in
Great Britain has been prevalent, usually involving conflicts between immigrants and the lower middle class whites.

The term *Skinhead* refers to the shaven heads of its members.
In the United States, Skinhead members generally range from approximately 11 years of age to 23. However, there are Skins, who,
having immigrated from England, are in their thirties. The estimated number of American Skinheads varies from 3,000 to 5,000,
but there may be as many as 10,000. In addition to the shaven head
among male members, their "uniform" consists of Doc Marten boots
("docs"), suspenders ("braces"), tattoos ("tats" or "ink"), and flight
jackets ("flights" or "bombers"). Trousers may vary from drab green
military fatigues to black jeans. Emblems sewn on their jackets
usually consist of the swastika, Celtic cross, an American flag on
either the left or right shoulder, a Confederate flag on the opposite
shoulder, and other insignia, such as the South African three 7's.
Occasionally, the halo crown W of the Church of the Creator may be
seen. More recently, the shaven head has been more or less limited
to new members and may no longer be regarded as a factor in recognizing a member of the movement. Male members refer to their
shaven haircuts as buzz cuts. Females, called Skinettes or Birds,

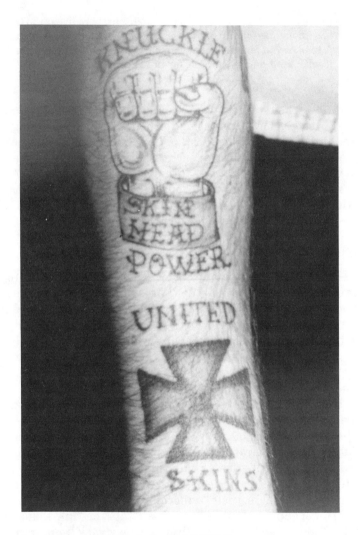

Arm tattoo of a Skinhead. Credit: MAGIC Team.

also shave their heads but leave the bangs and fringes on the back and sides. These haircuts are called buzz fringes or just fringes.

From initiation to exiting the movement, the period in which most teens are active as Skins lasts about six months. Those who remain in the movement for any appreciable length of time may become entrenched and eventually move onto adult groups such as the Ku Klux Klan, another neo–Nazi group, or an Identity Church. The

Shawn Slater, Exalted Cyclops. Slater was scheduled for promotion in the 4-K to Grand Titan in October 1992.

latter is less appealing, due to the more restrictive religious orientation. The Ku Klux Klan, Metzger's WAR movement, and Butler's Aryan Nations have made concerted efforts to recruit Skinheads. One major success among adult racist groups has been the recruitment of Shawn Slater into the Klan. Slater moved in rank from novice to Exalted Cyclops within approximately one year. An Exalted Cyclops heads a local chapter or Klanton.

The Skinhead lifestyle contrasts sharply with that of gangs. Skins are opposed to hard drugs, but are heavily into beer drinking. Drugs are viewed as something limited to the "mud races." Skins also emphasize monogamous relationships between male and female members, whereas some gangs share their females. Should a young woman enter the movement and pass herself around to male members in order to become more acceptable, her membership generally will be terminated.

In terms of organizational structure, the Skinheads are a loose affiliation, and rivalries among subgroups are almost non-existent. However, one must distinguish between Skinheads and Sharps. Sharps dress like Skinheads and claim to be Skinheads against

Skinheads often appear to protest Martin Luther King Day in January and to celebrate Hitler's birthday in April.

racism. Sharps are described as "Shit talkers," and tend to avoid actual combat with Skinheads. Nevertheless, a fight between these two groups should not be construed as an internecine conflict. Likewise, Trojan Skinheads, who are homosexuals, should not be confused with authentic Skinheads. In fact, Skinheads not only view homosexuals as perverts, but they have been known to act out violently against the homosexual community.

Race or, more specifically, white racial purity is the main item on the Skinhead agenda. "Being down for one's race" refers to defending one's white racial pride and white family or nation. The most common activities among Skinheads are the distribution of racist materials, demonstrations, writing graffiti, fighting, and partying. Public demonstrations usually take place as counter-demonstrations against such occasions as a Martin Luther King Day parade. There also have been joint Klan–Nazi–Skinhead rallies in some cities.

Early speculations on the background of youths who join the Skinhead movement suggested that most of the members are from broken homes and the lower middle class. They also were described

Samples of hate literature shared by various white supremacist groups.

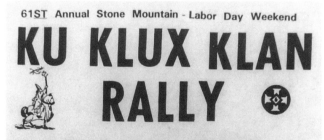

61ST Annual Stone Mountain - Labor Day Weekend

KU KLUX KLAN
RALLY

August 31, Saturday, City of Stone Mountain, End of Lucille Ave 7 PM
Sponsored by Southern White Knights, Knights of the KKK

On Saturday, August 31, at 1:00 PM, hundreds of White Christian Patriots will march through downtown Gainesville, Ga. to protest against the failure of our government to arrest and deport the 25,000 illegal alien Mexican wetbacks who are ruining this once beautiful North Georgia town. Many are alcoholics, use drugs, rob, rape, molest White women and have caused a crime wave ! We want to focus the national spotlight on this grave problem in order that Gainesville can overcome this crisis. We urge all White Christian Citizens of Gainesville to come and join in with this march. Meet at the Georgia Mountain Center parking lot at 12:00 noon, Saturday, Aug.31. Most White people just take the attitude "let somebody else do it - I don't want to get involved." Well, here is your opportunity to have your voice heard - We demand that all illegal aliens be deported according to the LAW !

Later in the day at the rally field in Stone Mountain we will have the nation's finest White Patriots speak and meet you personally. The following are only a few national leaders who will speak. J.B. Stoner, leader of the Crusade Against Corruption; Imperial Wizard J.W. Farrands; Dr. Ed Fields, editor of THE TRUTH AT LAST; Dave Holland, of The Southern White Knights, Imperial Wizard, James R. Venable; K.A. Badynski from Seattle, Wash., Rev. Thom Robb from Arkansas, Greg Walker, Dale Reusch from Ohio, Michael Lowe from Texas and Ed Novak from Chicago.

March:	August 31, 1991
Time:	1:00 PM
Where:	Georgia Mountain Center, Gainesville, GA
Rally:	August 31, 1991
Time:	7:00 PM
Where:	Lucille Ave, Stone Mountain, GA

Bring your friends for an enjoyable evening of good fellowship at a "Whites Only" event ! Enjoy old fashioned hot-dogs, hamburgers and soft drinks will be available. Klan jewelry, literature and T-shirts will on display. Come out and have a good time !

Bring yourself a lawn chair and see the giant TRIPLE CROSS LIGHTING.

National Office
P.O. Box 164
Conyers, GA

Directors Office
P.O. Box 476
Redan, GA 30074

White People Unite - Stand Up For Your Rights !

Klan Announcement.

as school dropouts and loners who had a propensity for violence. While this is still true for a number of Skinheads, there have been some notable changes. More and more middle–middle and upper–middle class, full–time students have entered the movement. Furthermore, many of these youths come from intact households. Currently, it may be said that the profile of a Skinhead does not differ significantly from any typical teenager.

The Skinhead movement provides a group identity for white youths along somewhat the same lines of minority gangs—Bloods, Crips, Vice Lords, and Disciples. But this is the only similarity. The concept of race is a mark of pride and superiority around which members can rally. It also serves as an outlet for some youths who are seeking their own identity in counterposition to the values and mores of their parents. In other words, it offers an opportunity to engage in youthful rebellion common among adolescents.

Another reason for joining the Skinhead movement is the resentment created by the perception that minorities are given preferential treatment in schools and in the workplace. In some cases, white students find the Skinhead movement a psychological and tangible defense against the threat of minorities, especially those who have perpetrated acts of violence against whites, either in gangs or individually. Regarding the latter, one should keep in mind that when an ethnic or racial minority group member commits a wrong, that wrong often is generalized to all members of that group—especially, if it reinforces some traditional stereotype.

The Ku Klux Klans

Today, the term Ku Klux Klan is somewhat misleading as there are a number of independent Klan organizations. The two most active and largest groups are Tom Robb's Knights of the Ku Klux Klan and James Farrends's Invisible Empire, Knights of the Ku Klux Klan. The Klan represents the oldest active supremacist group in the United States. Following its rebirth in 1915, the Klans' membership reached approximately 5,000,000 by 1925.[26] According to Danny Welch of the Klanwatch Project, the five million estimate was the result of a thorough research carried out by the Center's staff.[27] Other estimates range between three and four million, and one source puts the total in 1925 at 8,904,871.[28]

At that time, the Klan operated on two levels. At the public level, the Klan preached Americanism and expanded its targets of opposition against blacks, Catholics, and Jews to include Communists, Asians, bootleggers, dope peddlers and users, nightclubs, houses of prostitution, premarital and extramarital sex, and other behaviors regarded as immoral.[29] It worked toward dominating the American political landscape from the local town sheriff and mayor to the Congress. Working clandestinely, Klan members carried out a reign of terror against its enemies while denying charges of murder, burnings, and beatings.

Eventually, internal strife, exposure of the Klan's violent activities, and a general repugnance to such violence in both the North and South led to a decline of Klan membership. By 1930, the Klan was reduced to under 35,000. Eventually, this number would fall to between an estimated five and ten thousand during the seventies and eighties.[30] Furthermore, this relatively meager membership was spread among various Klan organizations: United Klans of America, Invisible Empire, Knights of the Klux Klan, Christian Knights of the Ku Klux Klan, Florida White Knights, Ohio Knights, Independent Order of Knights, Confederate Independent Order Knights, and others.

The 1980s were a mixture of highs and lows for the Klans. In March 1981, a black teenager, Michael Donald, was beaten and hung. Two leaders of the United Klans of America (Tuscaloosa, Alabama) were found liable for the murder of Michael, and his mother, with the aid of the Southern Poverty Law Center, sued for damages in a federal court. The court awarded Ms. Donald $7 million in February 1987. The ruling virtually bankrupted the United Klans.

The following year, civil rights activist and Atlanta Councilman Hosea Williams, Georgia State Representative James W. McKinney, and Morris Dees, the head of the Southern Poverty Law Center, spearheaded a suit against the White Knights of the Ku Klux Klan and the Invisible Empire Knights of the Ku Klux Klan. The suit resulted from a violent disruption by whites and Klan members of a 1987 civil rights march in Forsythe, Georgia. The march was held in commemoration of Martin Luther King's birthday. Dees had asked that $1.5 million be awarded the plaintiffs (all black people of Georgia). Approximately one million dollars was awarded.

During this same period, David Duke, founder of a neo–Nazi group and one time Imperial Wizard of the Knights of the Ku Klux Klan, was elected to the Louisiana State Legislature. Duke maintains strong Klan support and in November 1991, ran for the Louisiana Governorship. Although Duke lost by 22%, he received 55% of the white vote. In 1982, neo–Nazi Tom Metzger won 2.8% or 75,593 votes in the California Democratic primary for the U.S. Senate. Duke, by contrast, acquired over 681,000 votes. David Duke's strategy was to provide a relatively moderate platform in terms of his past experience as a neo–Nazi and Klansman. His program played down white supremacy and focused on the evils of affirmative action, street crime, and the welfare system.

As for the Klans, the Knights of the Ku Klux Klan, with its national headquarters in Harrison, Arkansas, was the fastest growing and possibly the most powerful of America's supremacist groups.[31] The Knights (KKKK) seemed to follow the strategy of Duke—to create a new, more moderate image. Reflecting upon Duke's bid for the governorship, Grand Wizard Thomas (Thom) Robb stated that fu-

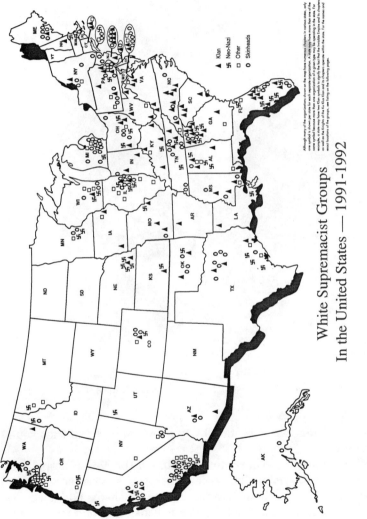

White Supremacist Groups
In the United States — 1991-1992

Location of Hate Groups in U.S.A. Courtesy of Klanwatch/Southern Poverty Law Center.

Grand Dragon Edward Novak (left) in security uniform of the
4-K; Mathew Hale (right), Neo-Nazi, Peoria, Illinois.

ture Klan leaders "will be taught to avoid statements that sound
hateful and turn people off."[32]

While it is still too early to determine if the KKKK actually intends to shed its violent activities, there have been some radical
changes from the past two decades. The white sheets and hoods are
being replaced by the security uniform, consisting of a white shirt,
black tie, Klan emblem (a cross with a drop of blood in the center),
black trousers, and black boots. As for the Klan line, there are indications that the Klan will move to a "more moderate" racist
stance regarding the disposition of minorities. Furthermore, the
Klan is beginning to emphasize Christian moral principles and the

Anti-Klan demonstrators at Klan 1991 celebration in Aurora, Colorado.

importance of the family. This emphasis is nothing new; it was used by the Klan in the 1920s. Finally, the Klan is outlawing the use of swastikas and other Nazi symbols and flags. However, there are other indications that Klan activities and beliefs may not be radically different from the previous attacks on blacks and others. During 1989, there were no less than twenty cross–burnings and instances of violence by those associated with the Klan, including beatings and murders.[33] In a letter distributed to high school students in the metropolitan area of Denver in October 1991, the following message is presented:

WHITE KIDS—BEWARE OF THE LIES OF RACE TRAITORS
RACE TRAITORS ARE TEACHING IN THE SCHOOLS OF AMERICA IF THEY ARE TEACHING THE LIE THERE IS NO DIFFERENCE IN THE RACES EXCEPT THE COLOR OF SKIN.

ASK YOUR TEACHER, "WHY IS IT THAT A BONE DOCTOR CAN TAKE A PILE OF CENTURY OLD BONES AND SAY THEY CAME FROM A WHITE MAN OR A MAN OF COLOR?" CERTAINLY THERE IS NO SKIN LEFT.

ASK YOUR TEACHER, "WHY IS IT THEN THAT NEGROS [SIC] HAVE SICKLE CELL DISEASE IN COMMON WITH DEER, MONKEYS, APES, AND GORILLAS

Symbol of the 4K. Note that the cross corners and border around the blood make up 4 "Ks".

WHILE PURE WHITES ARE NEVER KNOWN TO HAVE THIS DISEASE OF ANIMALS?"

TELL YOUR TEACHER TO READ GENESIS WHERE IT SAYS "GOD CREATED MAN AFTER HIS OWN IMAGE" (WHITE RACE). GOD MADE THE ANIMALS AFTER THEIR OWN KIND NEGROS, APES, MONKEYS."—THE BEASTS IN THE BIBLE.

THE MAIN LAW OF GOD IS SEGRAGATION [SIC] OF THE RACES. THE MIX
OF WHITE AND BLACK WILL *NOT* HAVE A SOUL. READ EZEKIEL 14:11–21
AND DEUT. 23:2.

. . .

ASK YOUR TEACHER "WHY IS IT THAT A NEGROS [SIC] HAIR CAN BE
MADE INTO CLOTH AS IS TRUE WITH SHEEP OR ANY OTHER ANIMAL
WHILE WHITES' HAIR CANNOT?"[34]

Since its decline more than sixty years ago, it seems almost inconceivable that the Klan could re-emerge as a viable force. However, there are indications that the Klan is beginning to evolve
toward a more sophisticated incarnation. The leadership is focusing
upon youths and providing a less regular if not less hateful message. For example, the KKKK paper, *White Patriot,* does not carry
any of the obscene cartoons or messages found in *Racial Loyalty,
WAR,* or *Calling Our Nation.* This attempt to gain respectability
worked in 1921, and there is no evidence that it cannot work today.
One of the most important factors regarding the Klan is the fact
that they have returned to the open political arena.

Sheriff's Posse Comitatus

The Sheriff's Posse Comitatus was founded by Henry L. Beach
and William Potter Gale in 1969.[35] Gale, an avid racist and anti-
Semite who died in 1988, had been active in the Identity Church
Movement and had been associated with Wesley Swift and Richard
G. Butler. The Posse is described as a loose affiliation of "semi-
autonomous units" with membership being estimated at between
2,000 and 10,000 members.[36] The organization predicates its position on the principle that the true seat of government is at the
county level. From this proposition, it follows that the "County
Sheriff is the only legal law enforcement officer in these United
States of America."[37]

Using the Constitution of the United States as the basis for its
opposition to acts by the federal government, the Sheriff's Posse Comitatus raises a number of objections, most of them related to taxation. The Federal Reserve System is targeted as an unlawful
institution. The Constitution, it is argued, does not permit the government to establish a "privately owned Federal Reserve System
which pays no taxes and is not audited nor subject to regulation by
any agency of the Federal Government."[38]

The Internal Revenue Code is viewed as a violation of both
"God–given and Constitutional Rights." A major violation identified

includes the requirement of citizens to file income tax returns. According to the Posse, this requirement violates their rights under the 4th, 5th, and 7th Amendments to the Constitution. If a citizen refuses to file a tax return, the Posse position is that since there is no right to tax, any government official who attempts to legislate, enforce, or judge a person for refusing to file tax returns or pay taxes should be arrested by the County Sheriff and tried by a Citizen's Jury.

The Posse advocates a strong anti-Semitic message. According to Posse leader James Wickstrom,

> The Jew-run banks and federal loan agencies are working hand in hand, foreclosing on thousands of farms for the Jews. The federal government follows a well-regulated plan that goes hand in hand with the Jewish money barons who pay off the politicians who control the farm crops ... the farmer sells his hard-earned self-invested crops to the local Jewish governed cooperative, in turn practically giving our crops to the enemy for nothing.[39]

The Posse objects to gun control, government legislation and court actions related to education, schools, and environmental protection. Members of the Posse have engaged in kidnapping and murder. Finally, a number of Posse members have been associated with the Klan, Identity Church Movement, and other white supremacist and anti-Semitic groups.

Among those extremist groups or individuals who seem to share similar beliefs and feelings with members of the Posse Comitatus are: Willis Carto (Populist Party and Liberty Lobby; publication: *The Spotlight*), Lyndon H. LaRouche (National Caucus of Labor Committees and American Agricultural Movement; publication: *New Solidarity*), and Roderick Elliot (National Agricultural Press Association—NAPA; publication: *Primrose and Cattleman's Gazette*—now defunct.)

Like other hate groups, the Sheriff's Posse Comitatus provides both an anchor and an outlet for those who view their world as threatened and in the grips of some sort of conspiracy. These organizations give their adherents a sense of self-righteousness created by the notion that others also believe and feel as they do. It also provides a basis for determining the causes of perceived evils. By casting blame on blacks, Jews, and others who are perceived as innately different, the "evils" and "ills" of the world are given a tangible target or set of targets. Once individuals can identify a tangible target, they are able to vent their frustrations and hatreds toward such targets and their symbols.

Minority Against Majority

Hate prejudice is not limited to any one group, ethnic or racial. Nor is it limited to those groups who are identified with the sociological majority. Victims of racial and ethnic hatreds also may exhibit prejudiced and racist beliefs and behaviors. The causes for the rise of organized hate among minority groups may be explained as a reaction to victimization in which the victim fights hate with hate. Or it may be an attempt to establish a sense of reverse superiority—a form of "if you think you're superior, then we will think we are superior." Another explanation may be that, in a society where the concept of racial or ethnic supremacy is part and parcel of the values of the society, it is quite natural for groups to adopt these values and adjust them to fit their particular ingroup.

Finally, the establishment of a doctrine of reverse racial superiority may be viewed as an outgrowth of a separatist movement. In order to wield group cohesion and establish a sense of independence from what is perceived as a hostile mass society, some minority groups may employ the same methods and ideologies espoused by hate groups of the sociological majority. Whether or not any of these explanations seem plausible is a matter of debate and perception, but one thing is clear; hate does seem to beget hate. The cases of the Black Panther Party and the Black Muslim Nation illustrate this very notion.

The Black Panther Party

Goal gradient behavior refers to the phenomena that occurs when an individual or group begins to achieve its goals. The closer one comes to realizing such achievement the more active he, she, or they become. The Black Panther Party emerged in 1966 at the height of the Civil Rights Movement in the United States, and it is very possible that this organization does reflect an example of goal gradient behavior. But regardless of the socio–psychological theories that can be suggested to explain the rise of the Black Panthers (BPP), the fact is that they rose up against what they perceived to be a white racist government. Their political philosophy was Marxist–Leninist, and their goal was black liberation. Our concern in examining the BPP is to garner those aspects of the party's beliefs and activities that relate to the question of racial and ethnic hate. However, as we shall see, the BPP was not a racist group.

In October 1966, the BPP published its political platform entitled "What We Want—What We Believe." This consisted of ten points:

1. We want freedom. We want power to determine the destiny of our Black community. . . .

2. We want full employment for our people.
   We believe that the federal government is responsible and obligated to give every man employment or a guaranteed income. We believe that if the white American businessman will not give full employment then the means of production should be taken from the businessmen and be placed in the community . . .

3. We want an end to the robbery by the CAPITALIST of our black community.
   We believe that this racist government has robbed us and now we are demanding the overdue debt of forty acres and two mules. Forty acres and two mules was promised 100 years ago as restitution for slave labor and mass murder of black people. We will accept the payment in currency. . . . The American racist has taken part in the slaughter of over fifty million black people; therefore, we feel that this is a modest demand that we make.

4. We want decent housing, fit for shelter of human beings. . . .

5. We want education for our people that exposes the true nature of this decadent American society. We want education that teaches us our true history and our role in the present–day society. We believe in an educational system that will give our people a knowledge of self. . . .

6. We want all black men to be exempt from military service.
   We believe that black people should not be forced to fight in the military service to defend a racist government that does not protect us. We will not fight and kill other people of color in the world who, like black people, are being victimized by the white racist government of America. We will protect ourselves from the force and violence of the racist police and the racist military by whatever means.

7. We want an immediate end to POLICE BRUTALITY and MURDER of black people.

8. We want freedom for all black men held in federal, state, county and city prisons and jails.
9. We want all black people when brought to trial to be tried in court by a jury of their peer group. . . .
10. We want land, bread, housing, education, clothing, justice and peace. And as our major political objective, United Nations supervised plebiscite to be held throughout the black colony in which only black colonial subjects will be allowed to participate, for the purpose of determining the will of black people as to their national destiny. . . . [40]

Although these principles of beliefs and demands indicate a strong disdain for white America, it does not indicate a racist philosophy of superior and inferior racist groups. But hate prejudice against whites was part and parcel of their activities.

Among other activities, the Black Panther Party instituted free health clinics and a free breakfast program for youths. During the summer, liberation schools for children ranging in age from 2 to 13 were established. The curriculum for some of these schools included such topics as Revolutionary History Day, Revolutionary Culture Day, Current Events Day, Movie Day, and Field Trip Day.[41] In these schools, children learned songs that told of "the pigs running amuck and Panthers fighting for the people."[42]

The near racist features of the BPP were exhibited in *The Black Panther* newspaper. The cartoons featured encouraged violence against white police depicted as pigs.

Some may argue that the Black Panther Party and its assault against the "white racist American government" with its "pig police" was not racist. Rather, the BPP emerged as a reaction stemming from frustration and anger of having been denied equal rights. Regardless of what rationalizations are used, the BPP did advocate violence and express strong hate prejudice against their perceived enemies. But what may be more important about the Black Panthers is the legacy and perceptions they left behind.

The following two excerpts from Panther apologist and *Ramparts'* editor Gene Marine's *The Black Panthers* provide a clear connection between the rise of Afrocentrism and black ethnocentrism in the early nineties. The first excerpt describes the pride in African culture and the contributions of Black Americans. The second provides a black power perspective of the essence of the "Black liberation movement."

"THE HEIRS OF MALCOLM NOW STAND MILLIONS STRONG ON THEIR CORNER OF THE TRIANGLE, FACING THE RACIST DOG OPPRESSOR AND THE SOULLESS ENDORSED SPOKESMAN. THE HEIRS OF MALCOLM HAVE PICKED UP THE GUN."

Huey P. Newton
Minister of Defense

Black Panther cartoon from late sixties shows disdain for police.

Out of Africa's long and proud heritage of civilization and art—a heritage as long and as proud as Europe's, and one whose "discovery" still makes a racist America too uncomfortable for it to be given its due in any but a very few school systems—many excited blacks have begun to regain a sense of the value of their own past, an understanding of the fact that their roots run as deep and in soil as rich as those of the Greeks or Jews, and far deeper than those of such upstarts of civilization as Irishmen or Germans.[43]

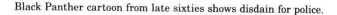

Stokely Carmichael and the Black Panthers believe, and believe profoundly, that black dignity and black liberation are not possible in the United States without profound changes in the system . . . They believe . . . that America will not suffer a revolution peacefully because racism is built so deeply into the American structure—into its foreign policy, into its profit system, and into its daily social life—that the country cannot stay as it is and purge racism.

This, and not "black racism," is behind student demands for black studies departments administered independently by blacks. They have been conned into white values by a racist educational system for so long that they simply don't trust us whites anymore. They have rejected the goal that the best–willed whites still put forward—"integration" means joining *our* white society, with our white values (which we don't even realize are white) and our blondes-have-more-fun culture and our insistent clinging to the same system which to them, for three hundred years, has meant oppression and horror.[44]

There are challenges in Marine's descriptions, and these same challenges can be expected to continue to reappear until the white–black conflict is resolved. In the sixties, blacks revolted in various ways, and, from a social psychological perspective, this revolt might be viewed an example of the frustration–aggression hypothesis on a massive scale. But regardless of which perspective is taken, two things emerged. First, the day of "Up against the wall, mother-fucker" had ended. Second, blacks would never again be passive recipients of what they perceived as a white racist society. The seeds for continued white–black confrontations of even the most violent kind remains a real potential in the United States.

Black Muslims

The Black Muslim movement in the United States has a tradition of being anti-white and racist in its pronouncements. Unlike the Black Panthers, the Black Muslims are right wing racists as opposed to the leftist, Marxist–Leninist Panthers. The Black Muslims were founded by Wallace Fard, who took the name Wali Farad Muhammad, in Detroit in 1930.[45] In 1931, Fard opened a temple in Chicago, and three years later, he literally disappeared, never to be heard from again.

In Fard's place came Elijah Poole, whose Muslim name is Elijah Muhammad. Under the leadership of Elijah Muhammad, the Nation of Islam, the actual name of the movement, prospered into a "multi-million dollar empire"—owning "chains of stores, restaurants, distributorships, and one Chicago bank."[46] Unlike the declining membership of the Klan and other white supremacist groups, the Black Muslim membership reached over one-half million by the end of the sixties. Elijah Muhammad preached against the "white devils," and forecast that they would soon be destroyed by a holy fire. Whereupon the original peoples of the world, the black race, would assume their rightful role as earthly masters. In addition to these declarations, the ideology of Black Muslims included the belief that the pig was a hybrid of a dog, rat, and cat; white people were created by a sorcerer who "botched an experiment on subhuman creatures."[47] In the Black Muslim newspaper, *Muhammad*

Speaks, each issue included a summary of "What the Muslims Believe" and "What the Muslims Want." In reading the following list of Beliefs, one might find it rather interesting to compare these with the tenets set forth earlier by Butler and his Aryan nation Church of Jesus Christ Christian.

1. We Believe in the One God Whose proper Name is Allah.
2. We Believe in the Holy Qur-an and in the Scriptures of all the Prophets of God.
3. We Believe in the truth of the Bible, but we believe that it has been tampered with and must be reinterpreted so that mankind will be snared by the falsehoods that have been added to it.
4. We Believe in Allah's Prophets and the Scriptures they brought to the people.
5. * . . . we believe we ["so-called Negroes"] are people of God's choice, as it has been written, that God would choose the rejected and the despised. We can find no other persons fitting this description in the last days more than the so-called Negroes in American. . . .

   • • •

7. We Believe this is the time in history for the separation of the so-called Negroes and the so-called white Americans. We believe the black man should be freed in name as well as in fact. By this we mean that he should be freed from names imposed upon him by his former slave master. . . .
8. We Believe in justice for all, whether in God or not; we believe as others, that we are due equal justice as human beings. We believe in equality—as a nation—of equals. We do not believe that we are equal with our slave masters in status of "freed slaves."
9. We Believe that the offer of integration is hypocritical and is made by those who are trying to deceive the black peoples into believing that their 400-year-old open enemies of freedom, justice, and equality are, all of a sudden, their "friends." Furthermore, we believe that such deception is intended to prevent black people from realizing that the time in history has arrived for the separation from the whites of this nation. If the white people are truthful about their professed friendship toward the so-called Negro, they can prove it by dividing up America with their slaves.

   • • •

12. We Believe that Allah (God) appeared in the Person of Master W. Fard Muhammad, July, 1930; the long–awaited "Messiah" of the Christians and the "Mahdi" of the Muslims. . . . [48]

As for what the Black Muslim want, Elijah mentions, equal justice, freedom of black inmates in jails and prisons, equal opportunity in society, the end of police brutality, exemption from taxation until equal justice is attained, and equal education of the young, but in separate schools. As for education of black children, they are to be taught by black teachers. Furthermore, girls are to be sent to "women colleges and universities."

In addition to these wants, Elijah calls for a separate state or territory for blacks. This territory need not be in the United States, but it must be rich in fertility and minerals. For the first 20 to 25 years, the "former slave master" (the United States government) should be obligated to supply all the material needs of the black people until they are able to be self-sustaining.[49]

Given this racial separationist orientation, it should not be surprising that Thomas Metzger of the White Aryan Resistance donated $100 to the Nation of Islam some years later following a speech by Louis Farrakhan.[50] After Elijah's death, his son Wallace (Warith) Deen Muhammad took over the reins of the movement and eventually permitted whites to join. Farrakhan split from the group and set up his own branch. After Warith Deen's faction eventually dissolved, Farrakhan became the undisputed leader of the Nation of Islam.

To the anti-white racism of his predecessor, Farrakhan added a heaping dose of anti-Semitism, blaming Jews for introducing alcohol into the black communities, controlling the media, promoting negative stereotypes of blacks in movies, and a host of other evils and ills found in the black community. He has praised Hitler as "being a great man" and accused Jews for "using God's holy name as a shield for your dirty religion."[51] But unlike white racists, who acknowledge their racism with pride, Farrakhan strongly condemns charges of racism and anti-Semitism:

Can you imagine any white writer, any of you to have the unmitigated gall, the un-mit-i-gat-ed gall, to call me, a victim of white racism, a racist. I'm a victim of your bigotry, and now you call me a bigot . . . "[52]

And so we have it. People, organized, belonging to their respective groups, seeking empowerment and spewing hatreds. This, then, is America at the eve of the twenty-first century; Americans thinking and acting along their separate racial and ethnic lines.

But one need not be a hate group activist in some survivalist or supremacist group in order to take advantage of the hate literature of hate groups or to espouse the hate–line. Indeed, individual cases of hate prejudice are as common as organized hatemongering. Consider, for example, the case of English teacher, Dorothy Groteluschen, at Hinkley High School in Aurora, Colorado.[53]

Individual Purveyors of Hate Prejudice

Miss Groteluschen and the Holohoax

Responding to charges of providing students with misinformation, Ms. Groteluschen in 1990 claimed she was merely giving her students another perspective. Groteluschen had provided her students with materials that claimed Jews were not murdered under Nazi rule. According to one article distributed, "Swindlers of the Crematoria," Jews starved and were not murdered. Further the article, published by the Christian Defense League, continues, "The truth is more likely that the Jews said to have been exterminated, and are truthfully no longer in central Europe . . . found new homes for themselves in Israel and the United States."[54]

Claiming she used the term "holohoax" merely to liven up her English honors class, Groteluschen also allegedly stated, "The Jews had an illness, and that is the reason they died in large numbers." At the bottom of an article she distributed in class, a note from the editor warned, "Make sure your patriotic books do not fall into the hands of Jews."

What makes the story of Groteluschen even more interesting is the fact that the Aurora Teachers Association defended Groteluschen when the oft–viewed as liberal American Civil Liberties Union (ACLU) seemed to support District's decision to demote her from chairperson. Furthermore, according to a former student who had Ms. Groteluschen some years earlier, it was common knowledge that she was engaged in teaching bigotry. In 1991, David VonFeldt stated the following:

> In the fall of 1985, I attended Hinkley High School in Aurora, Colorado. During the year, I was enrolled in the typical courses for a

junior in high school. One of these courses, Honors English II, was not so typical. Miss Dorothy Groteluschen taught our class many things, one of which was that the Holocaust was a holohoax.

She would, I am sure, beg to differ. She would say that she did not teach us that the holocaust was in fact a holohoax. To us, the students in her class, what she said was her truth, and though I, and I am sure many others, thought that she was full of hot air, I am sure with others she planted an ill–begotten seed of doubt. This doubt was a doubt that the real truth that multitudes of Jewish people were slaughtered by a group of people known as the Nazis. To those who had the temerity to question her on her statement about the holohoax, she offered to bring in "substantiated" evidence as written in non-mainstream literature.

She said that there are always two sides to a story, that the most popular side makes history. Her side was less popular, so therefore, received less attention, and less belief.

It was rumored around school that Ms. Groteluschen was a Nazi. Students and teachers alike recognized the "humor" in the way in which Miss Groteluschen portrayed an obvious truth in such a distorted way.

I do remember that at the beginning of the year one of my friends who had Miss G. said that I would do all right because my last name was German. On the first day of class when Miss Groteluschen called my name for roll, she said, "VonFeldt, what a nice German name." Then she spoke a few words to me in German, which I answered back in German, and proceeded with the class. It was rumored that if you had a German name, that you would do well in her class, but if you had a Jewish name, that you should drop her class at the earliest possible time. . . .

Six years later I look back at this event and I am surprised that so many of us, for countless years before and since, sat through her class and listened to her distorted view of what was a very significant historical event. . . . [55]

When Ms. Groteluschen began legal proceedings to be reinstated as department head and to regain back payment lost as a result of her demotion, the School District of Aurora reinstated her along with the chair's back pay, stating that a court case would be too costly.

When we examine the Groteluschen affair in relation to organized hate groups, it should become clear that bigotry is not limited to the latter. How could teachers and school administrators remain silent to what was being purveyed by Groteluschen? How could a teacher's union or association defend this type of teaching? But then again, we might ask, why does the study of hate groups and prejudice seem to be ignored by so many teachers and curriculum developers?

Professor Jeffries: Ice People

The next case involves Professor Leonard Jeffries of the City College of New York. Jeffries, an African American, is the former chairperson of CCNY's the African–American Studies Department. During his tenure as chairperson, he served as a consultant to the New York State educational commissioner. As a consultant, Jeffries was to assist in the creation of a more multicultural social studies curriculum. In the early nineties, Jeffries came under attack for a number of beliefs that he had espoused in speeches and in his teaching.

According to Jeffries, those people who are of European descent may be properly referred to as "ice people." The socio-racial character of these people is described as materialistic and greedy. Furthermore, they have a basic need to dominate other cultures and races.[56] On the other hand, people of African descent, referred to as "sun people," are humanistic and ruled by the three "C's, communal, cooperative, and collective spiritual development."[57] In addition, Jeffries reportedly presented his students with material contending that, since black people have more melanin, the determining factor for skin pigmentation, they are intellectually and physically superior to whites.[58]

The concepts of "sun people" and "ice people" were explained by Jeffries as follows:

> We have not created any concept of ice and sun. Ice and sun are very real and very scientific. We are sun people, people of color because of the sun. The melanin factor. Europeans have a lack of melanin and have lost a great of it because much of the European development has been in the caves of Europe where you do not need melanin. So the factor of the ice is a key factor in the development of the Europeans, biologically, culturally, economically, socially. And what we are talking about is the values that are transmitted from ecologies. . . . your economy which is related to your ecology begets your sociology which is related to your politics.[59]

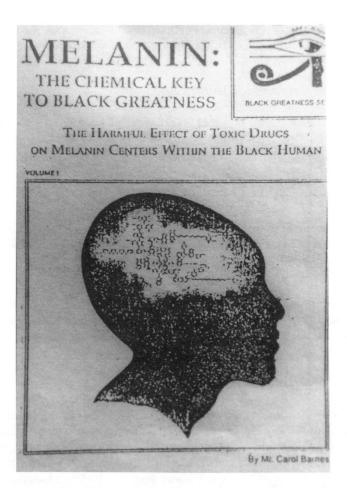

Afrocentric books such as this one often condemn white people and exalt blackness.

The beliefs Jeffries espouses, either his own or those of others that he accepts as fact, seem curiously similar to those of early racial theorists or current white racists. The exception, of course, is that the superior group is not white but black. Consider the following:

On Religion:

"Africans had put the concept of the oneness of God before the ancient Hebrews."[60] As for Christianity, the oldest Christian nation is cited as Ethiopia. Furthermore, he claims that the true people of the Bible were not European but African or "people of mixed African blood."[61]

On the Origin of the Human Species:

"Dr. [Cheikh Diop] says there is only one human race and it's the African race. Everything else is a mutation of African genes. That's the scientific and historical data. That's what we stand on."[62]

On the Development of Civilization:

"First World were African people, people of color, sun people. Everybody else comes after that. . . . We are the mothers and fathers of civilization. We developed science, mathematics, philosophy. And we stand on that."[63]

Jeffries's racist and anti-Semitic pronouncements eventually led to his dismissal as chairperson. Unlike the Colorado teacher, Dorothy Groteluschen, he was not reinstated.

Where Does It Lead?

"We live in an unruly and uncivilized world," said the former Associate Justice of the Supreme Court, Arthur Goldberg.[64] This is how he tried to explain the fact that we seem to have done little in the creation of a better, more tolerant, less violent world. In the struggle to seek a better world, there seems to be the implicit belief that a better world for me and my kind can only come through empowerment at the expense of others.

At the 4th National Conference on Racial and Ethnic Relations in American Higher Education in June 1991, a group discussion centered on the need for people of color, feminists, and homosexuals to strip power from the white males who were perceived as the power structure in American society. This need was regarded as the essence of political correctness. I asked why the goal could not be to seek equality and sharing of power. The response was narrow and sharp—"They will never share their power." This reply well illustrates Lippmann's concept of stereotype—this quality of adding to reality one's own expectation of what is, and it helps explain where we are and why Justice Goldberg's words were so perceptive.

CHAPTER 9

HATE PREJUDICE AND EDUCATION

> We want to have a better world,
> We want to work, we must not die.
>
> —Eva Pickova, age 12

Hate prejudice, racism, and ethnoviolence continue to be major critical problems for society, problems that demand the attention of social educators. This is not to say that education alone can stem the constantly recurrent tide of hate, but rather that schooling does have a role in seeking a more integrated and tolerant society. In order to determine just how educators might address this problem, it is necessary to have some awareness of the social landscape within which the problems of hate prejudice and racism reside.

Multiculturalism and the Melting Pot

Since the civil rights movement of the sixties, a definite trend toward emphasizing the multicultural character of the United States has emerged. This concept of a multicultural state seems to be in contraposition to the goal of a homogeneous society and the concept of the "melting pot." There are three essential differences between the two concepts. First, the concept of a "melting pot" describes both a process and a condition. Multiculturalism describes a condition only. Second, the "melting pot" emphasizes various degrees of assimilation, which is not necessarily true about multiculturalism. Third, the "melting pot," being an older concept and introduced during the period of Social Darwinism, is tinged with racism by the exclusion of certain groups. Multiculturalism, on the other hand, refers to all cultures and racial groups. These differences will be addressed in the following discussion.

While some observers may regard the multicultural and "melting pot" concepts as distinctly and diametrically opposed, it

233

MULTICULTURALISM	MELTING POT
Separatist.....Coexistence.....Integrationist.....Assimilationist.....Amalgamation	

Figure 1.   Continuum of Multicultural versus Melting Pot.

probably is more accurate to describe them as existing along a continuum as illustrated above.

America as the Melting Pot

The "melting pot" theory recognized three attributes of American society. First, it recognized a dominant mass culture whose members would be identified as Americans. Secondly, it acknowledged that the United States consisted of people from a variety of ethnic and racial groups. Third, it accepted as the logical goal of American society that people would shed most of their cultural heritages and enter the mainstream of American social, political, and economic life. Over time, the melting pot theory was interpreted differently based upon varying degrees of assimilation. We might label these interpretations or perspectives as amalgamationist, assimilationist, and integrationist.

AMALGAMATIONISTS

The amalgamationist perspective was the most tainted with racist notions. Not only did it exclude non–white racial groups and their cultures, in some cases it precluded Eastern and Southern European immigrants from assimilating. In addition, those holding this perspective anticipated that Americans would emerge as a new race—quite superior to those in other nations. This race would be physically white and culturally American, reflecting a heavy dose of Anglo roots combined with various other European strains. From a cultural perspective, it was regarded that America would become a homogeneous society. New immigrants would shed their ethnic origins.

This conception of American society is more or less the original view of the "melting pot" theory and was contested by anti-assimilationists who claimed British ancestry.[1] These individuals viewed the "melting pot" as a degenerative force, weakening the pure Anglo race that, from their perspective, founded the nation.

Opposition also came from "pluralists" who foresaw America as a blending of cultures or a composite ethnos with individuals retaining some of their ethnic roots. One such advocate of this form of pluralism was Horace M. Kallen.

Kallen accepted the notion of assimilation; however, he also believed that after ethnic minorities had assimilated and had become economically independent, they would rediscover their ethnic roots. According to Kallen, immigrants move through a series of stages.[2] Initially, according to Kallen, the new arrival assimilates and sheds his or her ethnicity. The motive for this initial assimilative act is to attain acceptance into the economic life of the state. Once economic independence is achieved, the assimilation slows to a halt, and the immigrant is "thrown back" to his/her ethnic ancestry.

The next stage includes a change from being a disadvantaged ethnic to a distinctive ethnic. While the "disadvantaged" ethnic is more likely to shed his/her ethnicity, the "distinctive" ethnic takes pride in his/her heritage. The "distinctive" ethnics proceed to integrate aspects of their original cultural heritage into various aspects of American life.

Finally, the former immigrant or his descendants express their distinctiveness in all facets of cultural life. According to Kallen, this expression of ethnicity is Americanization as liberated nationality, as opposed to Americanization as repressed nationality.

The flaw in Kallen's analysis is his failure to understand the dynamic influence of assimilation. For Kallen, the Polish, Irish, Jewish, German, Scandinavian, and Bohemian would remain culturally distinct and contribute to the social, political, economic, and cultural life of the state via their unique ethnic heritages. Today, there are relatively few descendants of European nationalities that maintain such distinctiveness. An overwhelming majority have lost their ethnic roots and have assimilated or amalgamated into the mainstream.

ASSIMILATIONISTS AND INTEGRATIONISTS

Assimilationists. Some individuals, while accepting the basic concept of a "melting pot," conceived of a United States from an assimilationist perspective. The state would consist of a unified nation with somewhat symbolic and private differences ranging from superficial traditions to strong religious convictions. But, on the whole, these citizens would be primarily Americans. Their socialization would emphasize American customs, traditions, history, and the English language. The larger or mass–society was not obligated to stress or even recognize cultural diversity. Ethnic isolationism would be discouraged.

Integrationists. A third perspective of the "melting pot" was reflected by those who might be called integrationists (or melting pot integrationists). The integrationist perspective accepted the notion of a unified nation but with a stronger emphasis on cultural variations than that of the assimilationists. While "integrated" Americans would have a right to participate in the mass–society, they would be able to retain much of their ethnic origins. At a rather naive, theoretical level, they could be isolated on one hand, and assimilated on the other.

However, in cases of conflicts between one's ethnic origins and the mass–society represented by the state, one's allegiance would be to the latter. This view held that American society could be pluralistic only in the sense that ethnic groups would be subculturals or subethnics within, not separate from, a greater American culture. In other words, people would regard themselves as Polish *American* or Americans of Polish Heritage rather than American *Poles*.

All three perspectives of the "melting pot,"—amalgamationist, assimilationist, and integrationist— agree that loyalty, shared decision–making, and uses of power would be for the benefit of the mass American society. All Americans would benefit, because they are all a part of a larger national society. As for those few that sought to remain isolated from the mainstream of America society, they would be tolerated so long as they did not interfere with the greater "good." Coming from the "melting pot" side of the continuum toward the center, the United States was conceived as in complete agreement with the concept, "E Pluribus Unum." The schooling of children was to help create a unified nation with respect and tolerance for those who were culturally and racially different, but the underlying value would be placed on a unified whole.

The Multicultural State

The concept of a multicultural society also recognizes the fact that the United States is composed of people from a variety of racial and ethnic backgrounds. Advocates of multiculturalism tend to embrace one of three perspectives, separatism, co-existence, or integration. We shall first examine the integrationist perspective and move along the continuum, as set forth in figure 1, toward the separatist perspective.

MULTICULTURAL INTEGRATIONISTS.

The multicultural integrationists differ slightly from the melting pot integrationists, and, in some cases, the only difference may
be in the use of either the labels, multicultural and "melting pot," to
describe their perceptions of American society. The term "melting
pot" has been rebuked in popular, liberal circles, especially among
educators. As mentioned earlier, the concept "melting pot" is
shrouded in a history tinged with racism, but this fact is probably
unknown to most educators and other interested parties. Secondly,
unlike the term multicultural, "melting pot" fails to parade the fact
that Americans are represented by a variety of different racial and
ethnic groups.

The multicultural integrationists support the notion of a unified nationality but with respect for cultural differences and the
right for individuals to express these differences. They view integration as the development of goodwill among people of different backgrounds and encourage the sharing of symbolic ethnic traits. Like
other multiculturalists these individuals often tend to accept un-
critically the notion that, "Ethnic and cultural diversity provides a
basis for societal enrichment, cohesiveness, and survival."[3] They fail
to reflect upon the fact that, historically, ethnic and cultural diversity has provided the basis for very violent ethnic and cultural conflicts. Furthermore, they fail to address the phenomenon that most
ethnic groups maintain varying degrees of ethnocentrism (as opposed to symbolic ethnicity)—a major source for interethnic enmity.

Some of these individuals seem to believe that assimilation and
amalgamation are negative outcomes. However, they are oblivious
to the principle that assimilation is a social phenomenon among
ethnic groups living within a larger mass society. The multicultural
integrationist is more often than not a member of the dominant
mass society or a member of a minority group who unwittingly is
assimilated.

Educators who fall into the multicultural integrationist category support a curriculum that emphasizes the cultural diversity of
Americans. Much of this support is probably focused upon symbolic
ethnicity. Wittingly or unwittingly, these educators can be expected
to hold an open assimilationist position. In addition, the multicultural integrationist usually has a very naive notion of the implications of empowerment within the political and economic arena. For
most of these educators, empowerment means a sharing of rights

and opportunities. But this is not the case for those further to the
left of the continuum.

MULTICULTURAL CO-EXISTENCE

The advocates of multicultural co–existence view the United
States as dominated by a power structure that fails to recognize the
rights of minorities. They seek a restructuring of the social, political, and economic system to the extent that minority groups will be
on an equal level with the dominant group. In some cases, this
means creation of a separate socio–economic and political system
that recognizes local autonomy of various groups. Extreme co-
existence advocates will seek a special curriculum for their children. Often this curriculum may include content that expresses a
certain ingroup's ethnocentrism, as opposed to the ethnocentrism of
the mass society. The co-existence perspective seems to conjure up
the notion of a minority use of separate but equal.

MULTICULTURAL SEPARATISTS

The multicultural separatists accept the concept of the United
States, but not as a federal republic. Their solution for maintaining
ethnic diversity may include the concept of a confederation of states
along ethnic or racial lines. Extreme nationalistic minority groups
among Blacks, Hispanics, and American Indians have advocated
this separatism, as have some white supremacist groups. Their
goals seem to be analogous to those of the Commonwealth of Independent States in the former Soviet Union.

Power Behind the Label

The concepts of multicultural and melting pot are part of a
larger and more elaborate scenario being acted out in the American
social drama. This scenario involves a complex interaction regarding power—social, political, and economic. Just as white supremacist groups have political agendas, so do groups advocating co-
existence and separatism for minorities. Not only are they active in
the political arena, but they are also active in stressing their cause
within education. A clear illustration of this is to be found in the
recommendations of the State of New York Task Force on Minorities
(see chapter 3) and in the curriculum African–American Baseline
Essays published by the Portland Public Schools.

The African–American Baseline Essays amount to what is popularly known as an Afrocentric curriculum. According to the booklet accompanying the material,

> The African–American Baseline Essays were written to provide all staff with a holistic and thematic awareness of the history, culture and contributions of people of African descent.[4]

> Notwithstanding its positive aspects, the material is riddled with anti-white, anti-European statements and charged with blatant ethnocentrism. In addition, much of the treatment is totally or partially misleading and unsubstantiated.

> As more ethnic and racial groups compete for power and seek their place in the American state, there will be more pressure exerted on school teachers to teach the "correct" curriculum, and what is deemed correct may depend upon who controls the school board. On a more general plane, the United States may be moving toward a fractionalized state. The state concept of "one from many" may be materializing into a state of "many in one." If this should be the case, then ethnic and racial tensions can be expected to continue to increase. The problem of racism and hate prejudice is not merely a question of reducing hostility among members of different groups. It is intricately woven into the politics of power. This, then, is at least one aspect and perspective of the landscape of American society today.

How Americans Feel

By the 1990s, many white Americans were both fearful of and disgusted with forced busing and the government's policy of affirmative action. This is especially true among many white college students, who only yesterday were seated in high school classrooms. These students are too young to have an immediate understanding or memory of segregation and Jim Crow, of Little Rock, Selma, and Watts. All these young people know is that somewhere down the road there may be an invisible sign reading "Whites need not apply." A few have attempted to form white student unions with the goal of protecting white interests—a response to Black student unions.

This sense of white disenfranchisement can be felt at different strata of society in America today, and reinforces the problem of ethnic and racial hatred. As we have learned from the preceding chapters, racism and ethnic prejudices and violence may permeate an entire society at various levels of intensity. Indeed, ethnic and racial prejudice is the norm in American life. The story of Shawn Slater underscores this feeling of white deprivation and may serve to illustrate how an apparently normal young person may get involved with the ideology of hate.

In 1977, the Slater family arrived in Colorado, when Shawn was eleven-years-old.[5] Shawn spent most of his teenage years in a middle class suburban environment, attending Smokey Hill High School in Aurora. During this time, he developed an affinity for the discipline and order he saw in films about Hitler's Nazi regime. "After seeing the films about Nazi Germany, I began to read about what was going on in America." By this statement, Shawn was referring to what he perceived as the degeneration of the white race and the decline of white rights in the social, economic, and political spheres of society.

Following a brawl with some punk–rockers, he was labelled a Skinhead. Consequently, he became one, and thus began a trek that would result in his emergence as one of the more promising members of the Ku Klux Klan.

On April 20, 1991, Slater organized a Klan rally to celebrate the birthday of Adolf Hitler in front of the state capitol building in Denver. There he appeared for the first time in his Klan robes and hood. Within a few months, Slater was elevated to the rank of Exalted Cyclops of the Knights of the Ku Klux Klan. Slater, along with the other leaders of the KKKK, has directed his attention toward high school students in an effort to recruit youths into the Klan movement.

As of this writing, Shawn Slater is one of the Klan's most promising prospects for future leadership. He is no raving madman. He presents himself cordially, and if one did not know his role as a Klansman, he would appear to be a quite normal and rather pleasant individual—at least on the surface.

Slater's efforts in the targeting of school children are indicative of the "education" program currently employed by virtually all extremist groups in the United States. In addition to hate literature, the KKKK also has produced material that appeals to children and parents on moral grounds. A tee-shirt designed to carry the Klan message along these lines includes the following: "KLAN KIDS KARE, Say no to drugs, Honor your parents, Stay in School."

While white supremacist groups seek empowerment for those they regard as white Americans, there has been a movement among minority groups to do the same for their respective members. These

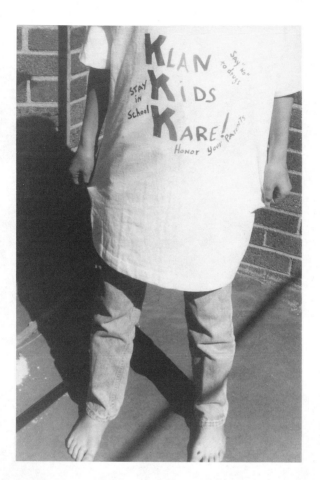

include the American Indian Movement (AIM), Black Muslims, and Black Panthers. This too is a part of the American landscape of intergroup relations.

Many American Indian, Black, and Hispanic students perceive America as a racist, anti-Black, anti-Native American, or anti-Hispanic society. Like many whites, they too fear the possibility of failure in the marketplace and in achieving the American dream or whatever dream they dream. So they too organize and demonstrate against what they view as a continuation of white American domination, the brunt of which existed long before they were born or can remember.

Far left (in black shirt), Mathew Hale, Nazi organizer. In robes, from left, Eugene McCrory, Fresno, California Den; Shawn Slater, Exalted Cyclops, Denver; and Ed Novak, Grand Dragon, Illinois. Denver 1991.

With battle lines drawn, each and every incident that can be interpreted from two such diametrically opposed views becomes a cry to war. Black leaders such as Louis Farrakhan and Jesse Jackson spew racist or anti-Semitic slurs to be lapped up by the frustrated and downtrodden, by pseudo–liberals and pseudo–intellectuals. Statements like Jackson's "hymietown" and Farrakhan's "white devils" complement the attempts of white supremacists—Tom Metzger, Richard Butler, and William Pierce—to preserve the myth of racial purity against the "mud races" and "Z.O.G."

These conditions may explain in part why racial and ethnic violence has spread onto college campuses throughout the United States. The university campus can no longer be regarded as a rational haven in society. Racist incidents have been reported at Rutgers University, Pennsylvania State University, Columbia University, the University of Pennsylvania, the University of Michigan, the University of Colorado, and Syracuse University, to name a few institutions.[6] These acts of racial and ethnic prejudices have included graffiti, name–calling, cross–burnings, and physical assaults. In addition, school papers have published blatantly racist and anti-Semitic items. This too is another aspect of American society.

The Role of Social Educators

It is within this landscape of American society that teachers must decide what and how to teach about intergroup hate prejudice and violence. The question that remains is what can be done to create a more tolerant and integrated world, a world in which individuals will be judged upon their merits and without prejudice based on ethnicity or race.

Certainly the first step in developing an educational strategy is that teachers become well grounded in the subject matter they are expected to teach. Once they have developed at least a basic understanding of the content, they should recognize the complexity of the issue and how it fits into the real world. I have attempted to relate all of these matters in some fashion in the preceding chapters and at the beginning of this chapter. As we have seen, the social–psychological dimensions of this topic are not only complex and laden with emotion; they are further complicated by the diverse goals of various groups. Because of these complexities, teachers should be prepared to engage with students in a high degree of reflective thinking. In addition, the teacher might be well advised to consider the importance of applying principles of effective communication and demonstrating interpersonal and intergroup relations skills.[7]

Aside from the social and psychological aspects of the study of racial and ethnic prejudice and violence, teaching about these topics will require teachers and staff development personnel to locate the missing pages of history. Little will be found in most of today's texts regarding the trials and tribulations of America's racial and ethnic conflicts, as is also the case with texts dealing with European and other world histories. There is, however, a great deal of supplemental material available from publishers. But even this material should be examined carefully for accuracy, appropriate depth, clarity, and balance.

Hate Prejudice and Curricular Strategies

There is no one way by which teachers may design or plan instruction about hate prejudice and its manifestations. In terms of general curricular strategies, a teacher may select one of at least three possibilities. These include: (1) An isolated instructional unit, (2) Integration, and (3) A combined correlated approach.

Isolated Approach

The isolated instructional units may vary depending upon time and depth to be spent on the issue. A major isolated unit may measure from five to ten or more hours of instruction. A minor isolated unit may range from one to three instructional hours. They are isolated in the sense that these units deal with the problem quite apart from the remaining content in the course of study or curriculum. Isolated units often are noticeable when the teacher sets aside the normal course of instruction in lieu of a special lesson. This often is the case when teaching about some current event, the anniversary of some past event, or in remembrance of some notable personality. These isolated units may be designed by teachers or they may be readily available from external sources.

A World of Difference is a case in point, as a recent prejudice reduction packet developed by the Anti-Defamation League of B'nai B'rith. Although the program has not been experimentally tested, many teachers have applauded the work throughout the United States. This supplemental material may be expanded or contracted to meet the individual needs of a given curriculum. Moreover, the *World of Difference* materials are designed by local or regional offices of the Anti-Defamation League and thereby address minority issues and problems pertinent to the particular geographic area.

Integration

Those strategies referred to as integration involve instruction dealing with hate prejudice, racism, and ethnic violence throughout the course of study. In other words, teachers would supplement instruction by presenting sub-topics dealing with intergroup relations related to the period under study. This type of instruction might be called discovering the missing pages of history.

For example, one will be hard pressed to find references to the race wars that plagued American cities during the first quarter of the twentieth century. The concept of race and the history of the rise of racist thought (racism) are generally omitted in history texts and in the social studies curriculum. Where there is mention of racial or ethnic unrest, it amounts to little more than snippets to be easily glossed over. The use of integration calls upon teachers and students to move beyond the common topics traditionally presented and to seek a broader picture of history.

The integrated strategy generally will be factually oriented. It will describe events not usually covered in the text or curriculum guide. At best, it will introduce both concepts and facts, but structuring the concepts through this approach often fails to create a mental mapping of the interrelationships among concepts.

Combined Correlation

The combined correlated approach involves a combination of both the isolation and integration strategies and is the most highly recommended. This approach emphasizes a conceptual approach to learning rather than merely a provision of supplemental, factual information. It also encourages the use of an advance organizer in order to map out the interrelationships among salient concepts. The advance organizer will serve as a framework for examining and reflecting upon events related to hate prejudice and violence throughout the course of study.

Designing a Combined Correlated Strategy

The first step in designing a combined correlated approach might be to identify key concepts related to topic of hate prejudice. A number of these concepts are listed in figure 2 below. Naturally, it is not suggested that all of these concepts be taught at one time. However, at the onset of instruction, a special

1. affirmative action	17. ethnocentrism	32. scapegoating
2. anomie	18. ethnocide	33. segregation
3. anti-locution	19. frustration-aggression	34. selective exposure
4. anti-Semitism	hypothesis	35. selective perception
5. apartheid	20. genocide	36. self-fulfilling prophecy
6. aryan	21. human rights	37. self-hate
7. assimilation	22. integration	38. Social Darwinism
8. attitude	23. (social) majority	39. social distance
9. bifurcation	24. (social) minority	40. stereotype
10. bigotry	25. perception	41. tolerance
11. civil rights	26. projection	42. vicious circle of
12. cultural relativism	27. predilection	discrimination
13. desegregation	28. prejudice	43. xenophobia
14. discrimination	29. race	
15. ethnic group	30. racism*	*including averse and
16. ethnicity	31. relative deprivation	dominative racism

Figure 2. Sample of Concepts.

mini–unit dealing with select concepts should be considered. The mini–unit might include the perception, attitudes, and acts of prejudice. Within each sub-topic the teacher may elect to introduce the following concepts:

I. Perception
    A. Selective perception
    B. Selective exposure
    C. Cultural Relativism
    D. Stereotyping
II. Attitude
    A. Prejudice
    B. Predilection
    C. Tolerance
III. Acts of Prejudice
    A. Discrimination
    B. Aggression and Scapegoating

The introduction of these concepts should include examples from the daily lives of students and current events. The major goal will be for students to understand the concepts in terms of attributes and to be able to distinguish between examples and non-examples. In addition, the presentation of these topics and concepts should permit students to devise concept maps. These maps illustrate how the concepts are related. They also may include examples.

The mini–unit will serve to provide an anchor for future learn-ing as cases of hate prejudice are presented during the normal or usual course of instruction. Additional examples and concepts may be added to the concept map. It is recommended that the original map be redesigned as more data are added. As a result, each new map will contain the information on previous maps and have new information included. By the end of the course of instruction, the student will have produced a concept map portfolio.

Integration of information concerning hate prejudice and its manifestations will vary based upon a particular course of study. In American history, the teacher may elect to introduce ethnicity and ethnic groups as part of the original mini–unit. Another teacher may decide to introduce the concepts when covering the topic of im-migration during the mid- to late-nineteenth century. Regardless of when topics, concepts, and events emerge within the learning pro-cess, it is important to return to the original mini–unit and concept maps previously developed.

The Missing Pages of History Revisited

In the first chapter we noted some of the missing pages of his-tory. Within the context of designing an integrated curricular strat-egy, it may be well to reexamine this issue. Uncovering the "missing pages" more accurately refers to the absence of information gener-ally found in textbooks and consequently in the instruction of his-tory. For practical purposes, there is no limit as to the information that can be uncovered on virtually any topic related to race and eth-nic relations and hate prejudice. It does, however, demand time and research. It also requires a reflective mind.

Peter H. Martorella describes the reflective citizen as one "characterized as having knowledge of a body of concepts, facts, and generalizations concerning the organization, understanding, and development of individual, groups, and societies."[8] He also states that the reflective citizen is "viewed as being knowledgeable about the process of hypothesis formation and testing, problem solving, and decision–making." Providing students with isolated informa-tion in the guise of integration will do little to enhance understand-ing and reflection. Two principles that are recommended in the integration process are the principles of proper perspective and his-torical connection.

It is important that supplemental information and description of events are placed in the proper perspective of time and place. For instance, in William Brandon's *The American Heritage Book of In-dians,* the author notes the June 1637, massacre of Pequot Indians

and the response of the governor of Plymouth upon viewing the results. "It was a fearful sight to see them frying in the fire . . . hor-
rible was the stink and stench thereof. But the victory seemed a
sweet sacrifice and they gave praise thereof to God . . . "[9] Alone, this
response to the attack on the Pequot tells us little. Cases should not
be thrown out as bits of information but rather explored in greater
depth. It is only when we examine the perceptions and beliefs of historical actors that we can reflect intelligently on the role of prejudice and its manifestations. This attempt to understand the social–
psychological environment of an individual or group does not justify
their actions. It does serve to place the event and action into a
proper perspective.

Similarly, when possible, there should be an attempt to connect
events to both the historical past and the historical present. Historical connection is not the same as historical causation. The latter
seeks to find a cause and effect relationship, whereas historical connection indicates a pattern of similar events the sources of which
may or may not be causally related.

For instance, the history of white–black relations in the United
States includes violent conflicts such as riots and lynchings. The
race riots or race wars, as they are labelled by John Hope Franklin,
did not suddenly occur in the twentieth century. They are intrinsically linked to a history of urban violence stemming back to the antebellum period. Between 1829 and 1866, race riots occurred in
Cincinnati (1829–1841), Philadelphia (constantly between 1832 and
1849), New York (July 1, 1834), Detroit, and other numerous Northern cities (1862–1863), and Memphis (1866), to mention a few. Too
often, the events of yesterday or today seem to be singular and out
of the ordinary. As a result they are often treated as aberrations;
things or events that cannot happen again.

Similarly, the massacre of millions of innocent men, women,
and children during the Holocaust has been treated in this manner,
in spite of a definite pattern of genocidal acts committed before and
since. Somehow we seem to fail to connect our history of humankind. This, in turn, limits our ability to engage in more meaningful
reflection.

The Study of Hate Groups: Two Strategies

The examination of the rise of racism and hate groups can be
designed to address those groups and individuals involved in such
activities. In this section, two strategies are presented. To some extent, these strategies overlap, and this will be apparent. On the

other hand, each differs significantly in terms of the treatment of subject matter and the context within which it is presented. One approach focuses upon case studies of hate groups and is guided by the content. This strategy may be referred to as the "Content Centered Strategy." The other approach is guided more by the valuations and decisions of students as well as the content. It is this latter strategy that we shall consider first.

VALUE CENTERED STRATEGY

Educational strategies generally define the overall goals and plans to affect learning. These strategies exist on a general plane and help direct educators in their selection of material, development of lessons, and techniques of instruction. In determining a strategy for the study of hate groups, the teacher might consider the following:

1. Identification and agreement on a core set of values or value base.
2. Presentation of the historical and social context of hate and hate groups.
3. Examination and analysis of hate group rhetoric and beliefs.
4. The development of goals and an action plan by students.

The overriding goal of the strategy is to have students achieve competence in being able to recognize and critically evaluate hate groups and their message. This competency also includes the ability of students to recognize the pitfalls in the apparent "logic" of hate-mongering and to be able to reject the messages of blind and irrational hate in a rational manner.

The Value Base. The first step in developing the strategy involves identifying a value base upon which judgments and evaluations may be made. In the mid-sixties, Oliver and Shaver (1966, pp. 9–12) suggested the concept of human dignity. In addition, the precepts set down in such documents as the Constitution, Declaration of Independence, and Declaration of Human Rights can be used to arrive at list of agreed upon values that should apply to all people regardless of race, ethnicity, or creed.

Naturally, the caveat to this approach is the assumption that students will accept the concept as it applies to themselves and others. Another possible impasse is the fact that what appears to be discriminatory and unfair within one culture may be regarded as just the opposite in another. However, the main focus within which this strategy is designed is limited to the United States, at least at the outset.

During the implementation of this phase of the strategy, concepts such as prejudice, discrimination, and scapegoating can be introduced and examples provided. Various examples of each category or concept will provide a tangible referent for illustrating violations of the principle of human dignity. Similarly, non-examples of each category will strengthen students' understanding and agreements on what does not violate the human dignity standard.

Historical and Social Context of Hate. Once students are equipped with an agreed upon basic standard by which to discern between beliefs and behaviors that support or violate that standard, they can begin to explore the historical and social context of hate. This includes an overview of race and ethnic relations at various intersections of time and geographic place. Topics for instruction include both concepts and historical events.

Among the concepts that can be added at this time are ethnos (ethnic group), race, stereotyping, and xenophobia, along with others. Topics dealing with the historical context of intergroup relations should include a historical overview of the development of race as a biological (scientific) and social (racism) concept.

The history of racial and ethnic bigotry and conflicts within the United States can be divided into six periods. These are: the colonial period; the nineteenth century (Racism Rationalized); 1900 to 1940 (Hate, Resistance, and Violence); 1941–1960 (The Need for Action Mounts); the civil rights movement of the sixties and aftermath; and the Present (where are we now?).

During this phase of instruction, students should constantly refer back to the value standard previously set. They also should be encouraged to carry out independent research in groups of two to four. By employing small group assignments where each group is assigned a specific period and topic, it is not necessary for all students to independently cover every time frame mentioned above.

For example, a particular team or group may be assigned to investigate nativism and its assault against Catholics during the 1800s. Another may be assigned to cover the Klan's activities from 1900 to 1940, and yet another team might investigate the race riots of 1919. Within each team, individual students would be assigned sub-topics to investigate and would prepare a report to be pooled with the reports of other team members.

Each team should be required, in preparation for the valuations of the topic, to describe the historical setting of the period in which their research topic is being made. This aspect of their report can contain an overview of: (1) the political landscape of the time; (2) the social demographics, trends, and conditions; and (3) the economic conditions. The use of newspapers and literature should be encouraged along with scholarly references. Within this structure, the reports should tie together these political, social, economic conditions with the occurrences of hate activities and rise of hate groups.

The next phase of learning requires that each team prepare a master report to be shared and pooled with the reports of other teams. This pooling process requires that students critique the reports of other teams—a sort of reciprocal critiquing. In the final phase, students discuss and clarify issue around a salient question. One such question might be "The American Dream: Did it go astray?" or "America: What Needs to be Done?" Once the team reports are pooled and critiqued, the class produces its final report, linking all team reports into one major report. This master report can be reproduced and distributed to each class member as a mini–text.

The conclusion of the mini–text or class report should address the implications for the present and future. It should also contain goals to be attained in order to improve intergroup relations and activities for reaching these goals. The list of goals and activities can be developed during class discussions of the findings of the various reports. The final class reports represents an agreed summary of the value judgements exercised by students during this study.

Inevitably, students' discussions within the above structure will involve some consideration of the role of hate groups. Once the students have completed their pooled report and have examined the implications of intergroup or race and ethnic relations, they can be directed toward case studies of hate groups. This may occur prior to their publication of the class master report. The process of examining hate groups in-depth would involve teams.

In this case, the investigation teams might consist of four or five students if possible. The examination of hate groups should encompass a review and analysis of their literature as well as reports from such groups as the Southern Law Poverty Center and the Anti-Defamation League of B'nai B'rith. Furthermore, there are a number of special reports on video tape covering hate groups and their activities.

For instance, the Bill Moyers' special, *Hate on Trial,* provides an in-depth coverage of the case of Tom Metzger, leader of the White Aryan Resistance movement. The newsletter and reports from the Center for the Study of Racism and Ethnic Violence in Denver, Colorado also present information on hate groups, including interviews with their leaders and members. Actual hate group publications or excerpts from such publications also can be obtained from the Center, but only are sent to teachers for their screening.

When engaged in the case studies of hate groups, students should continue to evaluate what they are learning in terms of the core value or standard. In addition, they should be provided with a format on how to analyze hate group beliefs, rhetoric, and actions. This can be accomplished through the use of a check list incorporating concepts such as xenophobia, scapegoating, discrimination, and other concepts introduced by the teacher periodically throughout the instructional unit. A sample of such concepts are listed in Figure 2.

In using these concepts, students might raise the question: "Does the particular hate group advocate genocide?" This should be followed by a statement requiring evidence if the answer is positive (e.g., "Cite evidence:") Another question might be whether or not the group under investigation is using scapegoating techniques and if so, again students should be required to cite evidence from the literature or films.

Following the individual and team investigations, information obtained should be shared and pooled among all class members. During this phase, students should closely examine the evidentiary material and clarify or resolve differences of judgment that may arise. For example, one report might classify a group or individual as advocating genocide, but the evidence may be unclear or not supported.

In another case, a student or team may conclude that a particular group does not use stereotyping as an instrument of spreading hate because the group claims that there might exceptions within a certain targeted group. Another student might take exception and refer to the process of bifurcation as a technique to mask overgeneralizations. Once the case studies are completed, polished and edited, they are incorporated into the class report. This may be done as an appendix or as a separate section in the report.

Through the studies, students can be led to devise an social action plan. This plan should serve as a practical guide designed to improve intergroup relations. that can be implementing in their daily lives. The rationale for the plan will take into account student perceptions of reality, which are often most influenced by one's individual experiences and those of his/her peers. It is hypothesized that if decision making develops from the perceptions and concerns of the individual, there is enhanced probability that attitudes will be internalized.

THE CONTENT CENTERED STRATEGY

The Content Centered Strategy can be useful in providing students with a description of the groups in question and in analyzing these groups. Furthermore, the strategy can be developed by students working in groups of two or three. The following format, based on a case study approach, is one suggested way by which students may engage in the study of extremist groups:

I. Background Data
   A. Name of Group:
   B. Date founded:
   C. Location of major activities and main headquarters:
   D. Founder:
   E. Current Leader:
   F. Membership:
   G. Beliefs:
   H. Targets:
   I. Activities (including publications):
   J. Other acquired information:

II. Analysis
   A. Prejudices (if yes to the following illustrate)
      1. Does the group employ stereotyping?
      2. Does the group advocate discrimination?
      3. Does the group rely upon racist ideology?
      4. Does the group advocate violence?
   B. Aggression and Scapegoating (If yes, to either of the first two questions, then continue with questions 3–7 and provide evidence.)
      1. Does the group engage in acts of scapegoating?
      2. Does the group engage of other acts of aggression?
      3. If so, at the anti-locution level?
      4. If so, at the level of vandalism?
      5. If so, at the level of assaults?
      6. If so, at the level of batteries?
      7. If so, at the level of murder?
      8. If so, at the level of genocide?

    C. In analyzing the writings or other activities
       of this group, which of the following apply?
       (Provide evidence for your decision.)
       1. projection:
       2. transference:
       3. frustration–aggression:
       4. displaced aggression:
       5. anti-democratic attitudes:
       6. xenophobia:
       7. Other (specify):
    D. Summarize the above information and provide
       an evaluation of the group.

In addition to these activities, case studies of victims, including groups and individuals, can be used to understand thoroughly the dynamics of hate prejudice. Concepts of self-hate, self-fulfilling prophecy, vicious circle of discrimination, and others can be illustrated through the case study approach.

Another aspect of race and ethnic prejudices and violence includes intergroup conflicts and acts of mass murder and genocide. Again, the case study approach can be used with a format designed to study a particular event. The format in Figure 3 is the same used by the Center for the Study of Racism and Ethnic Violence.

A Concept–Centered–Literary Model

The Use of Literature

The irony of human history has been the failure of so many to realize that the destruction of other humans is a form of suicide at the sub-species level. Social scientists attempt to explain these self-destructive experiences with heuristic models and inferences of statistical probability. Poets and novelists observe the phenomena, but their reflections attempt to create an emotional and intellectual experience for the reader. Whereas the social scientist strives to remove any sense of subjectivity in her/his work, the literary author seeks to implant an affective as well as cognitive influence in the reader.

Indeed, there may be more than a kernel of truth in the notion that poets and novelists are the true psychologists of the human experience. For it is they who integrate feelings, beliefs, and behavior, either directly or symbolically, and provide a holistic approach to

```
CASE STUDY: _____
        (name–event, place, or group)


INVESTIGATOR: _____  Date of Inv. _____
```

1. The Event.
  1.1 Parties involved.
      1.11 Perpetrators.
      1.12 Victims or Target Group.
      1.13 Other Interested Parties.
  1.2 Where.
  1.3 When.
  1.4 What Occurred.
  1.5 Consequences (as result of the occurrence).

2. Background
  2.1 Historical Setting (conditions prior to occurrence and leading up to the occurrence).
  2.2 Perpetrators.
      2.21 Economic Orientation or Condition.
      2.22 Educational Background.
      2.23 Geographical Background.
      2.24 Language Group.
      2.25 Political Orientation.
      2.26 Racial Group.
      2.27 Ethnic Group.
      2.28 Citizenship or National Allegiance.
      2.29 Religion.
      2.210 Social Class.
      2.211 Other Cultural Factors.
  2.3 Victims or Target Group.
      2.31 Economic Orientation or Condition.
      2.32 Education and Occupational Background.
      2.33 Geographical Background.
      2.34 Language Group.
      2.35 Political Orientation.
      2.36 Racial Group.
      2.37 Ethnic Goup.
      2.38 Citizenship or National Allegiance.
      2.39 Religion.
      2.310 Social Class.
      2.311 Other Cultural Factors.
  2.4 Relationship: Perpetrators and Victim or Target Group.
      2.41 Historical.
      2.42 Immediate (just prior to event).
      2.43 Present (today, at time of investigation).

3. Documentation (sources of information).
  3.1 Primary sources.
  3.2 Secondary and Other (specify).

Figure 3. Event Format.

Core	Prejudice	Discrimination	Aggression/ Scapegoating
Primary Concepts:	Stereotype	Segregation	Name–calling
	Ethnocentrism	Majority	Vandalism
	Xenophobia	Minority	Assault
	. . .	. . .	. . .

Figure 4. Sample Illustration of Core/Primary Concepts.

the understanding of this experience. Poetry may penetrate the soul of the reader, and a novel may create empathy and vicarious involvement far beyond the level of cold facts. For this reason, the use of literary works may serve to enhance one's understanding of a critical social issue. The following describes a concept–centered literary paradigm that may prove useful in the study of hate prejudice.

Concept Identification and Classification

The initial step in creating a concept centered literary approach is to identify the basic organizing concepts. These organizing concepts serve as terminals through which other salient concepts and their examples can be interrelated. For example, a teacher might select prejudice, discrimination, and aggression/scapegoating as the organizing concepts for a particular unit. These organizing concepts may be regarded as the core concepts that form the infrastructure of the unit.

The second step is to identify key concepts closely related to the core. These key concepts are labelled primary concepts and are listed below their corresponding core concepts as indicated in Figure 4 above.

Whether a particular concept is a core concept or primary concept may be determined by the teacher or by both teacher and students. In the above example, attitude and behavior could have been selected as core concepts, and prejudice, discrimination, and aggression/scapegoating assigned as primary concepts. Regardless of how one delineates this schema, there should be a clear rationale for determining the relationship between a core concept and its primary concepts. Furthermore, although there should be a distinction between core concepts, there should also be a connection between them. In the illustration given above, prejudice does not require an action and is quite distinct from discrimination or aggression/scapegoating. Discrimination may either lack aggression or, if it is a manifestation of aggression, it is not as overtly violent as those behaviors classified under aggression/scapegoating.

Once the primary concepts have been associated with core concepts, secondary concepts related directly to primary concepts and indirectly to core concepts can be added. Concepts such as integration, desegregation, civil rights, and the like might be listed as secondary concepts. If "murder" were listed as a primary concept under aggression/scapegoating, then genocide may be listed as a secondary concept. The development of primary, secondary, and even tertiary concepts is a matter of perception—the ability to "see" and understand the relationships among concepts. Having each student develop her/his own schema and explain their rationale for it should lead to a greater intrinsic understanding of the issue. Furthermore, the schema developed should be regarded as fluid. In other words, it should be subject to change as the learning experience proceeds. Therefore, the teacher and students will continually revisit their respective schemata and be willing to revise them as the need arises. The source of these revisions will be determined by the examination of examples found in the literature and other information obtained from case studies.

Selection of Literature and Related Information

In a concept centered literary model, examples of concepts can be found in poetry, short stories, novels, or non-literary sources. These non-literary sources may include technical studies by social scientists as well as newspaper reports. They may even include the examination of hate literature.

Technical Studies. Technical studies include those found in scientific journals. They may deal with a variety of issues and concepts such as stereotyping, prejudice, and discrimination. While some articles may require a knowledge of statistical analysis, many do not, and even those that use elaborate statistical operations often contain summaries and conclusions that do not require specialized knowledge.

In addition to journal articles, there are a number of sociological and anthropological ethnographic studies that can be successfully employed. Quite often the teacher may elect to have students read portions of these studies rather than assign the entire work.

News Reports. Hardly a week passes that some event regarding hate prejudice or discrimination is not reported in the news.

More and more local libraries and especially those in nearby universities have data bases that contain articles from hundreds of newspapers, categorized by topics. Most of these will cover events since the mid to late seventies. For earlier news items, the local paper and such major papers as the *New York Times* usually are available in microfiche or microfilm. These can be printed out and copied for classroom use. Newspaper and news magazine reports, editorials, and feature stories may provide a background for understanding the social landscape during a particular time and place. As such they may also provide additional insights to the kind of literature being produced during these times.

Hate Literature. Just as industrial and human wastes pollute the natural environment, a particular type of irrational and ideological waste pollutes the human intellectual environment. Much of this latter pollution is found in hate literature. Having students analyze hate literature may provide a valuable learning experience. However, the teacher should exercise caution when dealing with such sensitive material. It will be prudent for the teacher to prepare students, parents, and the administration before using hate material.

Songs, Poetry, and Novels. The songs of a people often reflect their joy and sadness. Under the guise of entertainment, songs have been used as means of social criticism that otherwise would not be acceptable. The song *Carefully Taught* from the Rogers and Hammerstein musical *South Pacific* is just one example of a musical commentary on the problem of prejudice. Perhaps one of the most cognitive–affective songs for student analysis is "Skip a Rope" by Moran and Tubb, published in 1967. A study of national anthems or various nations, both past and present, may also provide insights into the problems of ethnocentrism and chauvinism.

Finding, recommending, and assigning poems and novels is a main feature of this model. Selections may consist of a variety of poems, ranging from Frost's "Mending Wall" to James Weldon Johnson's "Fifty Years," from Longfellow's "The Jewish Cemetery at Newport" to Langston Hughes' collection in *Shakespeare in Harlem.* It may include the poems of the children in the concentration camp at Terezin and the prayers of the Navajo, Osage, and Pawnee. Novels and nonfictional accounts abound that also range in diversity, including Harper Lee's *To Kill a Mockingbird,* Alice Walker's *The Color Purple,* Richard Wright's *Native Son,* and Ann Frank's *The Diary of Ann Frank.* The works of James Baldwin, John Steinbeck, James Michener, Toni Morrison, Ralph Ellison, Gloria Naylor, and

Herman Wouk can also contribute to the development of understanding regarding the tribulations caused by hate prejudice.

PRESENTATION OF THE MODEL

Presentation of the model may be inductive or deductive. The
deductive approach requires the teacher to present the organizing
concepts in a direct concept instructional mode. One basic concept
lesson approach consists of the following steps: (1) introduction of
the concept; (2) identification of its key attributes; (3) definition of
the concept (using the attributes presented); (4) presentation of examples; (5) presentation of non-examples; and (6) an activity in
which students differentiate between examples and non-examples
of the concept. As this process is carried out, students begin the construction of the core and related concept paradigm.

Once the concepts are presented and understood, students can
engage in the relevant readings. Upon reporting their findings from
readings, students refer to the core and related concepts paradigm
and indicate the relationship between the concepts and what they
have read.

The inductive approach requires that students first carry out
their assigned or selected readings. Upon completion of the readings, students and teacher engage in a directed discussion of the
particular works. In this situation, the teacher directs discussion
toward relating what has been gleaned from the readings to salient
concepts. At this time, the concepts are categorized into the schema
described above.

Regardless of whether the presentation is deductive or inductive, the use of literature in a concept centered approach should
prove beneficial in the study of hate prejudice. Through its highly
descriptive and cognitive–affective nature, literature can provide a
direct and dynamic influence on the study of societal problems.

Conclusion

For Americans, the sixties and seventies were decades of
growth, awareness, disillusionment, pain, and experimentation.
War, Hippies, flower children, Watergate, civil rights, and power—
Black Power, Indian Power, White Power, and power out of the barrel
of the gun—the Kennedy brothers, King, and Kent State, all of
these marked those two decades.

As Americans entered the eighties, the surface of the social landscape seemed to resemble the doldrums regarding public concern for such issues as hate prejudice. Economic woes and international terrorism occupied the media and the minds of the public. But beneath this calm, there was the seething of racial and ethnic hatreds that has plagued the history of civilization since time immemorial. Just as the doldrums occur in an area about the equator, it is the same place from which the tempests of typhoons and hurricanes are spawned. By 1990, America and other nations were at the threshold of a storm after the calm.

As educators, we alone may not be able to prevent the next riot, the next race war. We may not be able to succeed in reaching all of our charges, but for every school child and young adult that we can and do reach, we shall be influencing a world beyond our own. Perhaps we can do our part in seeing to it that children never again have the experiences of Eva Pickova:[10]

• • •

My heart still beats inside my breast.
While friends depart for other worlds.
Perhaps it's better—who can say?
Than watching this, to die today?

No, no, my God, we want to live!
Not watch our numbers melt away.
We want to have a better world,
We want to work—we must not die!

> —Eva Pickova, age 12.
> Perished: At age 14, December 18
> Oswiecim Concentration Camp

NOTES

Preface

1. John Dewey, "The Relation of Theory to Practice in Education," in *The Third Yearbook of the National Society for the Scientific Study of Education,* ed. Charles A. McMurry (Chicago: The University of Chicago Press, 1904), 15.

Chapter 1: On Hate and Social Education.

1. This is no doubt indicative of the ability of humankind to make extraordinary advances in technology and failing to make parallel advances in human relationships. The resultant gap between technology (people-to-things relationship) and human relations (people-to-people relationship) became a potentially catastrophic reality in the twentieth century.

2. Louis Richtol (aka Leizer Richtol), interviewed by Milton Kleg, October 1989– January 1990, Denver, Colorado. Unless otherwise stated, all references to the life of Leizer Richtol are based on the series of interviews during the above period.

3. Yigal Lossin, *Pillar of Fire: The Rebirth of Israel—A Visual History,* trans. Z. Ofer, English text ed. C. Halberstadt (Jerusalem: Shikmona, 1983), 113.

4. W.H. Lawrence, "Poles Kill 26 Jews in Kielce Pogrom," *New York Times,* Friday, 6 July 1946, City edition, p. 1, col. 6. Also see the following articles by the same reporter: "Poles Declare Two Hoaxes Caused High Toll in Pogrom: Boy 9, Admits Story that Jews Slew 15 Children was Lie— Other Victims Lured to Death by Safety Pledge—40 Killed," *New York Times,* Saturday, 7 July 1946, City edition, p. 1, cols. 4 & 5; "Poles Ask Death for Kielce Guilty: Trials to Start Tomorrow—Toll Reaches 43—Second Plot Broken Up," *New York Times,* Sunday, 7 July 1946, City edition, p. 1, col. 7. For other details see "Nine Plead Guilty in Polish Pogrom," *New York Times,* City edition, Wednesday, 10 July 1946, City edition, p. 8, col. 2.

5. Lossin, *Pillar of Fire: The Rebirth of Israel—A Visual History,* 113.

6. Gunnar Myrdal, *An American Dilemma: The Negro Problem and Modern Democracy* (New York: Harper & Row, 1944), lxxi.

7. Francis A. Walker, "Report of Commissioner of Indian Affairs Francis A. Walker, November 1, 1872," in *The American Indian and the United States: A Documentary History,* vol. 1, comp. Wilcomb E. Washburn (New York: Random House, 1973), 179, 183–184.

8. Homer Collins and Felix Snider, *Missouri: Midland State* (Cape Guirado, Missouri: Ramfree Press, 1967), 7.

9. The Chicago Commission on Race Relations, *The Negro in Chicago: A Study of Race Relations and Race Riot* (Chicago: The University of Chicago Press, 1922), 4–5.

10. Ibid.

11. "6,000 Troops Called Out in Chicago to Check New Riots," *New York Times,* Thursday, 31 July 1919, City edition, p. 1, col. 8.

12. The Chicago Commission on Race Relations, *The Negro in Chicago,* 1.

13. John Hope Franklin, *From Slavery to Freedom* (New York: Alfred A. Knopf, 1967), 482.

14. "Troops sent to Omaha; Mob fires Courthouse with Bombs, Attacks Negroes, Lynches One, Nearly Lynches Mayor," *New York Times,* 29 September 1919, City edition, p. 1, col. 8; p.2, cols. 1–2.

15. Ibid.

16. Ibid. According to another version, the mayor was hung twice and each time cut down by police.

17. Ibid. A later report in the *New York Times* 30 September 1919, City edition, p. 5, col. 2, indicates that fellow prisoners shoved Brown to rioters who had entered the building.

18. "Fellow Prisoners Gave Negro to Mob," *New York Times,* 30 September 1919, City edition, p. 5, col. 2.

19. "Gen. Woods Orders the Arrest of Omaha's Rioters," *New York Times,* 1 October 1919, City edition, p. 1, col. 5.

20. "Georgia Mob Burns Two Negroes Alive," *New York Times,* 7 October 1919, City edition, p. 2. col. 6. It was a matter of coincidence that two individuals with the same name of Will Brown were lynched during the same time.

21. Ralph Ginzburg, *100 Years of Lynchings* (New York: Lancer Books, Inc., 1969), 253. The exact number of lynchings probably will never be known. On November 23, 1922, the N.A.A.C.P. reported that 3,436 people had been lynched in the United States from 1889 to 1922. Of these, 28 were

publicly burned between 1918 and 1921. Myrdal (*An American Dilemma,* pp. 560–561) reports that approximately 300 lynchings occurred annually during the 1890s. During the 1930s, Myrdal places the annual average at 30. In an interview with an informant in rural Georgia in the sixties, the author was told that a number of railroad killings—placing a person on the tracks—were actually another form of lynching yet these murders were classified as accidents.

22. Martin Luther King, "I Have a Dream," in *Chronicles of Black Protest,* comp. C. Eric Lincoln (New York: The New American Library, 1968), 186–187.

23. "The Jews and Their Lies", *Aryan Territorial Alliance News Letter,* 1 March 1988, 4.

24. Samuel Totten & Milton Kleg, *Human Rights* (Hillside, New Jersey: Enslow Press, 1989), 47.

25. Anti–Defamation League of B'nai B'rith, *Hate Groups in America: A Record of Bigotry and Violence* (New York, 1982), 44.

26. The Governor's Commission on the Los Angeles Riots, *Violence in the City—An End or a Beginning?* (Los Angeles, 1965), 2.

27. Ibid., pp. 10–11.

28. Ibid., pp. 11–12.

29. Ibid., pp. 23–24.

30. The National Advisory Commission on Civil Disorders, *The Report of the National Advisory Commission on Civil Disorders* (New York: E. P. Dutton and Company, 1968), 69.

31. Ibid., 107

32. Ibid., 113.

33. Ibid., 1.

34. The Civil Rights Commission, *Report of the Civil Rights Commission* (Washington, D. C.: U.S. Government Printing Office, 1959), 547.

35. National Advisory Commission on Civil Disorders, *Report of the National Advisory Commission,* 483.

36. Ibid., 483.

37. The Klanwatch Project of the Southern Poverty Law Center, "Tracking Hate Crimes," *Hate Violence and White Supremacy* 47 (December 1989): 41–45. The incidents listed in this source did not include the bombing deaths in Alabama and Georgia.

38. Brian Duffy, "Days of Rage," *U.S. News & World Report,* 11 May 1992, 21 [21–26] and Tom Mathews, "Siege of L.A.," *Newsweek,* 30. [30-38]

39. Duffy, "Days of Rage," 22.

40. "Race: Our Dilemma Still," *Newsweek* (11 May 1992), 44.

41. Ibid., 48.

42. Shmuel Yerushalmi, *Torah Anthology on the Book of Ecclesiastes,* trans. Zvi Faier (New York: Maznaim Publishing Corp., 1986.), 18.

43. Langston Hughes, "Let America be America Again," in *The Negro Caravan,* eds., Sterling A. Brown, Arthur P. Davis, & Ulysses Lee (New York: Arno Press & the New York Times, 1970), 370–372.

44. Charles P. Taft and Bruce L. Felknor, *Prejudice and Politics* (New York: Anti-Defamation League of B'nai B'rith, 1960), 10–11.

45. Sanford H. Cobb, *The Rise of Religious Liberty in America* (New York: Macmillan, 1902), 177.

46. General Assembly of Maryland, "Act Concerning Religion," (1649) in *The Roots of the Bill of Rights: An Illustrated Source Book of American Freedom,* comp. Bernard Schwartz (New York: Chelsea House Publishers, 1980), 1:93.

47. Taft and Felknor, *Prejudice and Politics,* 13.

48. Ibid., 20.

49. Samuel F. B. Morse, *Imminent Dangers to the Free Institutions of the United States Through Foreign Immigration and the Present State* (New York: E.B. Clayton Printer, 1835), 29.

50. Hermann Hagedorn, Roosevelt in the Bad Lands (Boston: Houghton Mifflin Co., 1921), 355.

51. Woodrow Wilson, *A History of the American People,* 5 vols. (New York: Harper & Brothers, 1902), 212–214.

52. Wyn Craig Wade, *The Fiery Cross* (New York: Simon and Schuster, Inc., 1987), 126.

53. Earl Warren, *The Memoirs of Chief Justice Earl Warren* (Garden City, NY: Doubleday, 1977), 149. Published posthumously.

54. Marion J. Rice, "What is the Meaning of 'Humanizing the Social Studies?'" in *Social Studies: The Humanizing Process* eds. Milton Kleg & John H. Litcher (Winter Haven, FL: Florida Council for the Social Studies, 1972), 18.

55. Donald W. Oliver, "Educating Citizens for Responsible Individualism, 1960–1980", in *Citizenship and a Free Society: Education for the Fu-*

ture, ed. Franklin Paterson (Washington, D.C.: National Council for the Social Studies, 1960), 201–202.

56. Ibid., 202.

57. Ibid., 206.

58. Ibid., 212.

59. Ibid., 227.

60. Peter H. Martorella, *Elementary Social Studies: Developing Reflective, Competent, and Concerned Citizens* (Boston: Little, Brown, & Co., 1985), 12.

61. Ibid.

62. Ibid.

63. Ibid., 201–202.

64. Theodore Kaltsounis, *Teaching Social Studies in the Elementary School: The Basics for Citizenship* (Englewood Cliffs, NJ: Prentice–Hall, 1987), 18.

65. Ibid., 296.

66. James A. Banks, *Teaching Ethnic Studies: Concepts and Strategies* (Washington, D.C.: National Council for the Social Studies, 1973), 1–3. Geneva Gay's chapter (2) does, albeit briefly, discuss some aspects of racism and prejudice. Her definition of racism (p. 30) is actually white racism, an angry and far too narrow approach.

67. Shirley H. Engle and Anna S. Ochoa, *Education for Democratic Citizenship: Decision Making in the Social Studies* (New York: Teachers College Press, 1988), 17–18.

68. Ibid., 23.

69. Ibid., 67.

70. Ibid., 23.

71. These beliefs are shared among a number of racist groups as will be illustrated in chapter 8.

72. The concept of human dignity emerges time and again in the literature of social studies educators. Donald W. Oliver and James P. Shaver provide a criticism and defense for its use and its vagueness in *Teaching Public Issues in the High School* (Boston: Houghton Mifflin Co., 1966), 9–15, 24–25.

73. Anti-Defamation League of B'nai B'rith, *1991 Audit of Anti–Semitic Incidents* (New York: Anti-Defamation League, 1992), 29.

74. "Books: Knowledge is Power," *White Patriot* Issue 88, p. 11. This publication actually had two issue numbers printed, 86 and 88. The issue number 86 appears under the banner and 88 appears on the back page. The correct issue number should be 88 and appeared in the first quarter of 1992.

Chapter 2: Ethnic Groups.

1. Benjamin B. Ringer and Elinor R. Lawless, *Race, Ethnicity, and Society* (New York: Routledge, 1989), 2.

2. Harold A. Larrabee, *Reliable Knowledge: Scientific Methods in the Social Studies,* Revised Edition (Boston: Houghton Mifflin Company, 1964), 162.

3. Stephen Thernstrom, Ann Orlov, and Oscar Hamlin, eds., *Harvard Encyclopedia of American Ethnic Groups* (Cambridge, Massachusetts: Harvard University Press, 1980), vi.

4. Ibid., vi.

5. George Eaton Simpson and J. Milton Yinger, *Racial and Cultural Minorities: An Analysis of Prejudice and Discrimination,* Fifth Edition (New York: Plenum Press, 1985), 11.

6. William Petersen, "Concepts of Ethnicity" in *Harvard Encyclopedia of American Ethnic Groups,* eds. Stephen Thernstrom, Ann Orlov, and Oscar Hamlin (Cambridge, Massachusetts: Harvard University Press, 1980), 238.

7. Ibid.

8. Abraham Kaplan, *The Conduct of Inquiry: Methodology for the Behavioral Science* (San Francisco: Chandler Publishing Company, 1964), 70–71.

9. Brewton Berry, *Race and Ethnic Relations,* Second Edition of *Race Relations* (Boston: Houghton Mifflin Company, 1951), 54.

10. Terrence G. Carrol, "Northern Ireland" in *Ethnic Conflict in International Relations,* eds., Astri Suhrke and Lela Garner Noble (New York: Praeger Publishers, 1977), 21.

11. J. Milton Yinger, "Intersecting Strands in the Theorisation of Race and Ethnic Relations" in *Theories of Race and Ethnic Relations,* eds., John Rex and David Mason (Cambridge, UK: Cambridge University Press, 1986), 21.

12. Thomas C. Holt, "Afro–Americans" in *Harvard Encyclopedia of American Ethnic Groups*, eds. Stephen Thernstrom, Ann Orlov, and Oscar Hamlin (Cambridge, Massachusetts: Harvard University Press, 1980), 7–8.

13. Henry Pratt Fairchild, ed., *Dictionary of Sociology and Related Sciences* 1955 Edition (Ames, Iowa: Littlefield, Adams, and Company, 1955), 201. The first edition appeared in 1945 and was published by Philosophical Library. The definitions of nationality and nation appearing in the 1955 edition were the same as those in the original.

14. Ibid.

15. James Paul Allen and Eugene James Turner, *We the People: An Atlas of America's Ethnic Diversity* (New York: Macmillan Publishing Company, 1988), 51, 69.

16. Eugene K. Keefe, Arsene A. Boucher, Sarah J. Elpern, William Giloane, James M. Moore, Terrence L. Ogden, Stephen Peters, John P. Prevas, Nancy E. Walstrom, and Eston T. White, *Area Handbook for the Soviet Union* (Washington, D.C.: Government Printing Office, 1971), 411–417.

17. Caroline Farrar Ware, "Ethnic Communities" in *Encyclopedia of the Social Sciences*, vols. 5–6, eds. Edwin Seligman and Alvin Johnson (New York: Macmillan, 1937), 607.

18. Milton M. Gordon, *Assimilation in American Life: The Role of Race, Religion, and National Origins* (New York: Oxford Press, 1964), 27.

19. Ringer and Lawless, *Race, Ethnicity, and Society*, 17.

20. Ibid.

21. Berry, *Race and Ethnic Relations*, 54.

22. Israel Rubin, *Satmar: An Island in the City* (Chicago: Quadrangle Books, 1972), 160–179.

23. Paul Lawrence Dunbar, "We Wear the Mask" in *The Negro Caravan* eds., Sterling A. Brown, Arthur P. Davis, and Ulysses Lee (New York: Arno Press and The New York Times, 1970), 310. Dunbar's opening lines are "We wear the mask that grins and lies, It hides our cheeks and shades our eyes,— The debt we pay to human guile; . . . " The contexts in which the phrase is used in the poem and in this work appear diametrically opposed. However, upon further reflection, the two uses may have more in common than at first blush.

24. Herbert J. Gans, "Symbolic Ethnicity: The Future of Ethnic Groups and Cultures in America," *Ethnic and Racial Studies* 2(1) (January 1979):1.

25. Mary C. Waters, *Ethnic Options: Choosing Identities in America* (Berkeley, California: University of California Press, 1990), 7.

26. Ibid., 164.

27. J. Milton Yinger, "Intersecting Strands", 24.

28. James McKay, "An Exploratory Synthesis of Primordial and Mobilizationist Approaches to Ethnic Phenomena," *Ethnic and Racial Studies* 5(4) (October 1982):407.

29. John A. Hostetler and Gertrude Enders Huntington, *The Hutterites in North America* (Fort Worth, Texas: Holt, Rinehart, and Winston, Inc., 1980), 3.

30. The position change from American Cambodian to Cambodian American indicates that in the first instance, the group or individual is Cambodian with American influences. In the second instance, the individual or group is essentially American with Cambodian heritage. During the 1960s and early 1970s, some Black Americans objected to the label of American Negro or American Black claiming that they were Americans like "white Americans"—the emphasis being on American. This was compared to Poles identified as Polish Americans and Italians were referred to as Italian Americans. Jews traditionally were regarded as American Jews. By the mid–1970s, the term Jewish American was being used. The 1973 Yearbook of the National Council for the Social Studies edited by James Banks illustrates this change. Later in chairing the task force on ethnic heritage guidelines, Banks ignored objections to the use of Jewish Americans by a member of the advisory group to the task force. What makes all of this so interesting is the fact that Banks and company were regarded as the champions of multiculturalism and at the same time tended toward treating groups as would an ardent assimilationist.

31. Waters, *Ethnic Options,* 167.

32. Ibid., 168.

33. See Ware, "Ethnic Communities, 607; and Gans, "Symbolic Ethnicity," 1–20. Gans's remarks on religious and ethnic groups were made to the author on May 16, 1991. Israel Rubin disagrees that the Satmar is a cult and, indeed, by virtually any definition of ethnic group, Rubin's view of Satmar as a "religio–ethnic" group has more credibility. It appears that Gans, not unlike Wirth, has allowed personal bias to interfere with his scholarly judgment.

34. In Europe, Jews were generally regarded as members of a separate nationality until the 19th century. Napoleon made a concerted effort to nationalize the Jews as French of Hebraic religion. His creation of the Grand Sanhedrin on February 9, 1807 was designed to meet this objective.

35. Tamotsu Shibutani and Kian M. Kwan, *Ethnic Stratification: A Comparative Approach* (New York: Macmillan Company, 1965), 47.

36. Louis Wirth, *The Ghetto* (Chicago: The University of Chicago Press, 1928), 63–97.

37. Malcolm Wiley, Louis Wirth, and John Wilson, *The Jews: The University of Chicago Round Table* (Chicago: University of Chicago Press, January 28, 1940), 19–20.

38. Ibid., 20.

39. Arthur Compton, Robert Redfield, and Louis Wirth, *Anti–Semitism: A Threat to American Unity?: A University of Chicago Round Table* (Chicago: University of Chicago Press, October 5, 1941), 3–4.

40. Ibid., 4.

41. Ibid.

42. Ibid.

43. Ibid.

44. Iwo Cyprian Pogonowski, *Poland: An Historical Atlas* (Hippocrene Books, Inc., 1987), 17.

45. Based upon a telephone interview between Ravay Snow and Louis Wirth's daughter, Alice Wirth Gray, November 1990.

46. Gans, "Symbolic Ethnicity," 5–13.

47. Solomon Poll, *The Hassidic Community of Williamsburg: A Study in the Sociology of Religion* (New York: Schocken Books, 1969), 15. This study was first published in 1962.

48. Janet B.W. Williams, ed., *Diagnostic and Statistical Manual of Mental Disorder: DSM–III–R,* Thd, (Washington, D.C.: American Psychiatric Association, 1987), 89.

49. Phyllis Dolgin and Milton Kleg, *Who Am I?: Native Americans* Sound Filmstrip (Chicago: Coronet Films, 1975).

50. Document 1417–PS (GB 25B): 1935 Reichsgesetzblatt, Part I. page 1333. This document, defining a Jew, was located in Germany and used at the Nuremburg Trials.

51. Equal Employment Opportunity Commission, *Equal Employment Opportunity: Standard Form 100, Rev. 1–86. Employer Information Report EEO–1: 100–115: Instruction Booklet* (Washington, D.C.: U.S. Government Printing Office, 1986), 5.

52. Ibid.

53. Ibid.

54. James Baldwin, *Notes from a Native Son* (New York: Bantam Books, 1968), 99–135. The original work was first copyrighted by Baldwin in 1949 and published in 1955 by Beacon Press.

Chapter 3: Race: A Biological Concept.

1. John Cassidy, "History Turns Its Back on America's Heroes," *The Sunday Times,* 28 July 1991, sec. 1, p. 15.

2. Arthur M. Schlesinger, Jr., *The Disuniting of America: Reflections on a Multicultural Society* (New York: W.W. Norton & Company, 1992), 17, 113–117.

3. Mary Lefkowitz, "Not Out of Africa: The Origins of Greece and Illusions of Afrocentrists," *The New Republic* (10 February 1992), 29–36.

4. Lawrence Hyman, "Why Liberals Cannot be Politically Correct," (March/April 1992), 5–6.

5. Barbara Dority, "The PC Speech Police," *The Humanist* (March/April 1992), 31–33.

6. Bernard Oritz de Montellano, "Multicultural Pseudoscience: Spreading Scientific Illiteracy among Minorities—Part I," *Skeptical Inquirer* 16 (Fall 1991), 46–50.

7. See Eric Martel, "How Valid are the Portland Baseline Essays?" *Educational Leadership* (December 1991/January 1992), 20–23.

8. Ashley Montagu, *Man's Most Dangerous Myth: The Fallacy of Race,* Fourth Edition (Cleveland, OH: The World Publishing Company, 1964), 23.

9. Synthesized from Walter Schiedt, The Concept of Race in Anthropology and the Divisions into Human Races from Linneus to Deniker in *This is Race: An Anthology Selected from the Literature on the Races of Man,* ed. Earl W. Count (New York: Henry Schuman, 1950), 356; and from Jacques Barzun, *Race: A Study in Superstition,* rev. ed. (New York: Harper & Row and Co., 1965), 45.

10. Aristotle, *Politics* 7.7.1327b20–35 in *The Basic Works of Aristotle,* ed. Richard McKeon (New York: Random House, 1941), 1286.

11. Comte de Buffon, "A Natural History, General and Particular," in *This is Race: An Anthology Selected from the International Literature on the Races of Man,* ed. Earl W. Count (New York: Henry Schuman, 1950), 15.

12. Immanuel Kant, "On the Different Races of Man," in Count, *This is Race,* 17, 23.

13. Johann Frederick Blumenbach, "On the Nature and Variety of Mankind," in Count, *This is Race*, 36.

14. Ibid., 34–38.

15. Georges Cuvier, "Varieties of the Human Species," in *This is Race*, ed. Earl W. Count (New York: Henry Schuman, 1950), 44–45.

16. Ibid., 45.

17. Ibid., 44.

18. Ralph L. Beals and Harry Hoijer, *An Introduction to Anthropology* (New York: The Macmillan Company, 1965), 173–174.

19. Synthesized from Beals and Hoijer, *Introduction to Anthropology*, and from Stanley M. Garn, *Human Races* (Springfield, IL: Charles C. Thomas Publishers, 1961).

20. Garn, *Human Races*, 127–132.

21. Garn, *Human Races*. These are presented throughout Garn's work and not listed as in this current treatment.

22. Ashley Montagu, *Race, Science, and Humanity* (Princeton, NJ: D. Van Nostrand Company, Inc., 1963), 5–6.

23. C. L. Brace and M. F. Ashley Montagu, *Man's Evolution: An Introduction to Physical Anthropology* (New York: The Macmillan Company, 1965), 342.

24. From "Race and Prejudice," reprinted from *The Unesco Courier*, April 1965, 8–11.

25. Henry Pratt Fairchild, "The Truth About Race," in *This is Race*, 688–690.

26. Ibid., 688–689.

27. Ibid., 688–689.

28. Ibid., 690.

Chapter 4: Race and Racism.

1. Eugene D. Genovese, *The Political Economy of Slavery: Studies in the Economy and Society of the Slave South* (New York: Random House, 1965).

2. Herbert Spencer, *Principles of Biology*, vol. 1 (New York: D. Appleton and Company, 1866), 444. He also refers to this in his discussion of the physical attributes of primitive in *The Principles of Sociology*.

3. Herbert Spencer, *The Principles of Sociology*, 3rd edition (New York: D. Appleton and Company, 1897), 95–96.

4. Spencer, *The Principles of Sociology*, 97.

5. Spencer, *The Principles of Sociology*, 48.

6. Spencer, *The Principles of Sociology*, 52.

7. Ibid., 75.

8. Ibid., 87–89.

9. Ibid., 83.

10. Ibid., 89.

11. Ibid., 91.

12. A. Bradford, "Heredity and Environment," *Educational Review,* vol. 1, (1891), 148.

13. This line of thinking was reversed by the Supreme Court in 1954 in *Brown v. Board of Education of Topeka.* The court voted unanimously that segregation of black children in public schools deprives them of equal opportunities, even if physical facilities were equal. This decision was based upon the premise that blacks, as citizens of the United States, are guaranteed by the Constitution, equal protection of the laws. It also pointed out that segregation sanctioned by law generates feelings of inferiority in black children "that may affect their hearts and minds in a way unlikely ever to be undone," as Chief Justice Warren put it. The court also declared that separate educational facilities cannot be equal—they are inherently unequal.

14. Lochner v. New York, 198 U.S. 45, 25 S. Ct. 539, 49 L.Ed. 937 (1905).

15. Pierre L. van den Berghe, "Sociobiology," in *Dictionary of Race and Ethnic Relations,* 2nd edition, eds. E. Ellis Cashmore, Michael Banton, Robert Miles, Barry Troyna and Pierre L. van den Berghe (London: Routledge, 1988), 290.

16. Carl N. Degler, *In Search of Human Nature: The Decline and Revival of Darwinism in American Social Thought* (New York: Oxford University Press, 1991).

17. Donald T. Campbell, "Variation and Selective Retention in Socio–Cultural Evolution," in *Social Change in Developing Areas: A Reinterpretation of Evolutionary Theory,* eds. Herbert R. Barringer, George I. Blanksten, and Raymond W. Mack (Cambridge, MA: Schenkman Publishing Company, 1965), 20. [19–49]

18. See Seymour W. Itzkoff, *The Making of the Civilized Mind* (New York: P. Lang, 1990).

19. Arthur de Gobineau, *The Inequality of Human Races,* trans. Adrian Collins (1915; reprint, New York: Howard Fertig, 1967), 27.

20. Ibid., 27.

21. Ibid., 205–206.

22. Ibid., 206–207.

23. Ibid., 209.

24. Ibid., 210.

25. Ibid., 211–212.

26. Jerome Friedman, "Jewish Conversion, the Spanish Pure Blood Laws and Reformation: A Revisionist View of Racial and Religious Anti-semitism," *The Sixteenth Century Journal* 17, no. 1 (spring 1987): 3–29.

27. Ibid., 28.

28. Leon Poliakov, *The History of Anti–Semitism,* vol. III, trans. by Miriam Kochan (New York: The Vanguard Press, 1968), 20.

29. Norman Cohn, *Warrant for Genocide: The Myth of the Jewish World Conspiracy and the Protocols of the Elders of Zion* (New York: Harper & Row, 1966), 38.

30. Rufus Learsi, *Israel: A History of the Jewish People* (Cleveland: The World Publishing Company, 1949), 279.

31. Abraham Rosenfeld, trans., *The Authorized Kinot for the Ninth of Av* (New York: The Judaica Press, 1979), 168. The elegy was written by Rabbi Joseph of Chartres at about the turn of the 13th century. The actual translation was carried out by Solomon Schechter.

32. Jacob Katz, *From Prejudice to Destruction: Anti-Semitism, 1700–1933* (Cambridge, MA: Harvard University Press, 1980), 14–15.

33. Wilhelm Marr, *Der Sieg des Judentums uber das Germanentum* (Bern:n/p, 1879).

34. Hugo Valentin, *Antisemitism: Historically and Critically Examined,* trans. by A. G. Chater (New York: The Viking Press, 1936), 168.

35. Norman Cohn, *Warrant for Genocide,* 288.

36. Ernst Hiemer, *The Poisonous Mushroom [Der Giftpilz]: A Stuermer Book for Young and Old Fables,* trans. Document 1778–PS (USA 257), (Nurnberg: Der Stuermer, 1938), 6–9.

37. Marie Jahoda, *Race Relations and Mental Health* (Paris: UNESCO, 1960), 6. See the foreword.

38. Juan Comas, *Racial Myths* (Paris: UNESCO, 1958), 7–8. All following references to Comas will be found on page 8.

39. Ferdinand Gregorovius, *The Ghetto and the Jews of Rome,* trans. Moses Hadas (New York: Schocken Press, 1948), 50–51. Gregorovius published his work in German in 1853 the same year that Gobineau published his first work on the inequality of human races.

40. Staff of the Southern Poverty Law Center, "A Hundred Years of Terror," *The Ku Klux Klan: A History of Racism and Violence,* ed. Sarah Bullard (Montgomery, Alabama: Klanwatch, 1988), 7.

41. Paul J. Gillette and Eugene Tillinger, *Inside Ku Klux Klan* (New York: Pyramid Publications, 1965), 24.

42. David M. Chalmers, *Hooded Americanism: The History of the Ku Klux Klan,* 3rd Edition (Durham, NC: Duke University Press, 1987), 19. Also see Wyn Craig Wade, *The Fiery Cross: The Ku Klux Klan in America* (New York: Simon and Schuster, 1987), 59.

43. Wyn Craig Wade, *The Fiery Cross: The Ku Klux Klan in America* (New York: Simon and Schuster, 1987), 90–93. Also see Kenneth M. Stampp, *The Era of Reconstruction: 1865–1877* (New York: Random House, 1965), 199–200.

44. Wade, *The Fiery Cross,* 116.

45. John T. Morgan, "The Race Question in the United States," Arena, vol. 2 (September 1890), 385–398. Reprinted in *The Development of Segregationist Thought,* ed., I.A. Newby (Homewood, IL: The Dorsey Press, 1968), 21–28.

46. See I.A. Newby, *Segregationist Thought,* 24.

47. Hubert Howe Bancroft, *Retrospection* (New York: Bancroft Co., 1912), 367–374. Reprinted in *The Development of Segregationist Thought,* ed., I.A. Newby (Homewood, IL: The Dorsey Press, 1968), 79–83.

48. Lillian Smith, *Killers of the Dream* (revised, 1963: Garden City, NY: Doubleday & Company; W.W. Norton and Company, 1949), 224.

49. Mary Roberts Coolidge, *Chinese Immigration* (New York: Henry Holt Company, 1909), 96.

50. Ibid., 100.

51. See the majority opinion in Chee Chang Ping v. United States (The Chinese Exclusion Case), 130 U.S. 581 (1889).

52. Sidney Lewis Gulick, *The American Japanese Problem* (New York: Charles Scribner's Sons, 1914), 77–80.

53. Eldon R. Penrose, *California Nativism: Organized Opposition to the Japanese, 1890–1913* (Saratoga, CA: R. and E. Research Associates, 1973), 76.

54. Hiram Price, "Report of Commissioner of Indian Affairs Hiram Price, October 10, 1882," in *The American Indian and the United States,* vol. I., 319.

55. Daniel G. Brinton, *The American Race* (New York: N.D.C. Hodges, 1891), 39.

Chapter 5: Prejudice and Attitudes.

1. Wolfgang Stroebe and Chester A. Insko, "Stereotype, Prejudice, and Discrimination: Changing Conceptions in Theory and Research," in *Stereotyping and Prejudice: Changing Conceptions,* eds. Daniel Bar–Tal, Carl F. Graumann, Arie W. Kruglanski, and Wolfgang Stroebe (New York: Springer–Verlag, 1989), 8.

2. Ibid., 8–9.

3. Stephen Crane, "The Wayfarer," in *The Mentor Book of Major American Poets,* eds. Oscar Williams and Edwin Honig (New York: The New American Library, 1962), 232.

4. Ibid.

5. Thomas F. Pettigrew, "Prejudice," in Harvard Encyclopedia of American Ethnic Groups, eds. Stephan Thernstrom, Ann Orlov, and Oscar Handlin (Cambridge, MA: Harvard University Press, 1980), 820.

6. Gordon W. Allport, *The Nature of Prejudice* (Reading, MA: Addison–Wesley Publishing Company, 1954), 9.

7. Ibid.

8. George Eaton Simpson and J. Milton Yinger, *Racial and Cultural Minorities: Analysis of Prejudice and Discrimination,* 5th ed. (New York: Plenum Press, 1985), 21.

9. Ibid.

10. Walter G. Stephan, "Intergroup Relations," in *The Handbook of Social Psychology,* 3rd ed., eds. Gardner Lindzey and Elliot Aronson (New York: Random House, 1985), 600.

11. Ibid.

12. William J. McGuire, "Attitudes and Attitude Change," in *The Handbook of Social Psychology,* 3rd ed., eds. Gardner Lindzey and Elliot Aronson (New York: Random House, 1985), 238–239.

13. Gordon W. Allport, "Attitudes," in *A Handbook of Social Psychology,* ed. Carl Murchinson (Worchester, MA: Clark University Press, 1935), 810.

14. See McGuire, "The Nature of Attitude and Attitude Change," in *The Handbook of Social Psychology,* vol. 2, 2nd ed., eds. Gardner Lindzey and Elliot Aronson (Reading, MA: Addison–Wesley Publishing Company, 1968), 142–144 for a more technical treatment of the mental and neural state attribute of attitude.

15. Robyn M. Dawes and Tom L. Smith, "Attitude and Opinion Measurement," in *The Handbook of Social Psychology,* 3rd ed., eds. Gardner Lindzey and Elliot Aronson (New York: Random House, 1985), 510.

16. Robyn Dawes, telephone conversation with author, 16 July 1991.

17. McGuire, "Attitude and Attitude Change," 553.

18. See Ausubel et al. for an elaboration on cognitive structure in David P. Ausubel, Joseph D. Novak, Helen Hanesian, *Educational Psychology: A Cognitive View,* Second Edition (New York: Werbel & Peck, 1978).

19. Allport, "Attitudes," 807.

20. Ibid. Also see Robert Ezra Park, "Experience and Race Relations," *Journal of Applied Sociology* 9 (1924): 18–24.

21. Allport also quotes Emory S. Bogardus: "An opinion may be merely a defense reaction which through overemphasis usually falsifies consciously or unconsciously a man's real attitude."

22. Allport, "Attitudes," 809.

23. In "The Nature of Attitudes and Attitude Change," William J. McGuire adds "and/" to Allport's definition rather than maintaining the original statement, " . . . directive or dynamic . . . "

24. Kleg, Borgeld, and Sullivan, "An Exploration of Ethnic Attitudes," 4.

25. Allport, "Attitudes," 806.

26. Albert H. Hastorf, David J. Schneider, and Judith Polefka, *Person Perception* (Reading, MA: Addison–Wesley, 1970), 4.

27. Ibid., 15

28. Thomas F. Pettigrew, "Extending the Stereotype Concept," in *Cognitive Processes in Stereotyping and Intergroup Behavior,* ed. David L. Hamilton (Hillsdale, NJ: Lawrence Erlbaum Associates, 1981), 319.

29. Gordon W. Allport, *The Nature of Prejudice* (Reading, MA: Addison–Wesley, 1954), 336.

30. Ibid.

31. Robert P. Abelson, Elliot Aronson, William J. McGuire, Theodore Newcomb, Milton J. Rosenberg, and Percy H. Tannenbaum (eds.), *Theories of Cognitive Consistency: A Sourcebook* (Chicago: Rand McNally, 1968), 769.

32. T. W. Adorno, Else Frenkel–Brunswik, Daniel J. Levinson, and R. Nevitt Sanford, *The Authoritarian Personality* (New York: Harper & Row, 1950), 971.

33. Ibid., 228.

34. Eric Berne, *Games People Play: The Psychology of Human Relationships* (New York: Grove Press, 1964), 23–40.

35. Marinus H. van Ijzendoorn, "Moral Judgment, Authoritarianism, and Ethnocentrism," *The Journal of Social Psychology*, 129, no. 1 (February 1989): 37.

36. Ibid., 37–38.

37. Ibid., 43.

38. Ibid., 44.

39. Theodore M. Newcomb, Ralph H. Turner, and Philip E. Converse, *Social Psychology: The Study of Human Interaction* (New York: Holt, Rinehart, and Winston, 1965), 49.

40. Ibid.

41. William A. Scott, "Attitude Measurement," in *The Handbook of Social Psychology,* vol. 2, 2nd ed., eds. Gardner Lindzey and Elliot Aronson (Reading, MA: Addison–Wesley Publishing Company, 1968), 206.

42. Milton Kleg, Thomas Borgeld, and Nora Sullivan, "An Exploration of Ethnic Attitudes at Three Levels of Social Psychological Interaction." (Paper delivered at the Annual Meeting of the American Educational Research Association Meeting, Chicago, 1974), 17.

43. Ibid., 4.

44. See Scott's article on "Attitude Measurement," 205.

45. See Ausebel and Scott.

46. Scott, "Attitude Measurement," 207.

Chapter 6: Stereotyping.

1. Carl Friedrich Graumann and Margret Wintermantel, "Discriminatory Speech Acts: A Functional Approach," in *Stereotyping and Prejudice: Changing Conceptions,* eds. Daniel Bar–Tel, Carl F. Graumann, Arie W. Kruglanski, Wolfgang Stroebe (New York: Springer–Verlag, 1989), 192.

2. Stroebe and Insko, "Stereotype, Prejudice, and Discrimination," 5.

3. Walter Lippmann, *Public Opinion* (1922; reprint, New York: The Macmillan Company, 1961), 16.

4. Lippmann, *Public Opinion,* 29.

5. Ibid., 29.

6. Ibid., 89.

7. Ibid., 88.

8. Ibid., 91.

9. Ibid., 126.

10. Allport, *The Nature of Prejudice,* 191.

11. Richard D. Ashmore and Francis K. Del Boca, "Conceptual Approaches to Stereotypes and Stereotyping," in *Cognitive Processes in Stereotyping and Intergroup Behavior,* ed. David L. Hamilton (Hillsdale, NJ: Lawrence Erlbaum Associates, 1981), 3. This appears to be the first time that Lippmann's work regarding stereotyping was given more attention than in the previous four or more decades.

12. Ibid., 3.

13. Walter Lippmann, *Public Opinion,* 96.

14. Ibid., 100.

15. Peter H. Martorella, "Knowledge and Concept Development," in *Handbook of Research on Social Studies Teaching and Instruction,* ed. James P. Shaver (New York: Macmillan Publishing Company, 1991), 373–374.

16. Allport, *The Nature of Prejudice,* 191.

17. Ibid., 192.

18. Thomas F. Pettigrew, "Extending the Stereotype Concept," in *Cognitive Processes in Stereotyping and Intergroup Behavior,* ed. David L. Hamilton (Hillsdale, NJ: Lawrence Erlbaum Associates, 1981), 313.

19. Henri Tajfel, "Cognitive Aspects of Prejudice," *Journal of Social Issues* vol. XXV, 4 (1969): 80.

20. Ibid., 83

21. Richard D. Ashmore and Francis K. Del Boca, "Conceptual Approaches to Stereotypes and Stereotyping," 22.

22. Daniel Katz and Kenneth Braly, "Racial Stereotypes of One Hundred College Students," *The Journal of Abnormal and Social Psychology* vol. XXVIII (1933–1934): 280.

23. Ibid., 288.

24. Allport, *The Nature of Prejudice,* 336.

25. Ashmore and Del Boca, "Conceptual Approaches to Stereotypes," 23–24.

26. Shelley Taylor, "A Categorization Approach to Stereotyping," in *Cognitive Processes in Stereotyping,* ed. David L.Hamilton (Hillsdale, NJ: Lawrence Erlbaum Associates, 1981), 84. Taylor lists no less than eight studies during the decade of the seventies.

27. Rose Zeligs, "Children's Intergroup Attitudes," *The Journal of Genetic Psychology* 72 (1948): 105.

28. Ibid., 105.

29. Ibid., 105–107.

30. Taylor, "A Categorization Approach to Stereotypes," 86.

31. For a more comprehensive discussion of this, see Taylor's review.

32. David L. Hamilton, "Illusory Correlation as a Basic for Stereotyping" in *Cognitive Processes in Stereotyping and Intergroup Behavior,* ed. David L. Hamilton (Hillsdale, NJ: Lawrence Erlbaum Associates, 1981), 115–144.

33. Mark Snyder, "On the Self–Perpetuating Nature of Social Stereotypes," in *Cognitive Processes in Stereotyping and Intergroup Behavior,* ed. David L. Hamilton (Hillsdale, NJ: Lawrence Erlbaum Associates, 1981), 184.

34. Ibid., 189.

35. Ibid., 192.

36. Ibid., 198. Research by Snyder and Swan supports this proposition.

37. Robert K. Merton, "The Self-fulfilling Prophecy ," *The Antioch Review,* 8 (1948), 193–210.

38. Gunnar Myrdal with Richard Sterner and Arnold Rose, *An American Dilemma: The Negro Problem and Modern Democracy* (New York: Harper and Row Publisher, 1944), 75–78.

39. Robert E. Park, "The Concept of Social Distance as Applied to the Study of Racial Attitudes and Race Relations," *Journal of Applied Sociology,* 8 (1924), 340.

40. Emory S. Bogardus, "Measuring Social Distance," *Journal of Applied Sociology,* 9 (1925): 301.

41. Ibid., 302.

42. Ibid., 305.

Chapter 7: Discrimination, Aggression, and Scapegoating.

1. Gordon Allport, *The ABC's of Scapegoating,* 5th revised edition (New York: Anti–Defamation League of B'nai B'rith, 1966), 8. The first edition appeared in 1948 and was expanded into the seminal work *The Nature of Prejudice* published in 1954.

2. Ibid., 10.

3. Ibid., 29.

4. Gordon W. Allport, *The Nature of Prejudice* (Reading, MA: Addison–Wesley, 1954), 14–15.

5. Anti-Defamation League of B'nai B'rith, *"A World of Difference: Colorado Teacher/Student Study Guide,* vol. 2 (Denver, CO: Anti-Defamation League of B'nai B'rith, c. 1989), 54, 133–134.

6. See George Eaton Simpson and J. Milton Yinger, *Racial and Cultural Minorities: An Analysis of Prejudice and Discrimination,* 5th edition (New York: Plenum Press, 1985), 23. This position is also reflected by Dovidio and Gaertner in "Prejudice, Discrimination, and Racism: Historical Trends and Contemporary Approaches," in *Prejudice, Discrimination, and Racism,* 3.

7. Carl Friedrich Graumann and Margret Wintermantel, "Discriminatory Speech Acts: A Functional Approach," in *Stereotyping and Prejudice: Changing Conceptions,* eds. Daniel Bar–Tal, Carl F. Graumann, Arie W. Kruglanski, and Wolfgang Stroebe (New York: Springer–Verlag, 1989), 186.

8. Icek Ajen and Martin Fishbein, "Attitude–Behavior Relations: A Theoretical Analysis and Review of Empirical Research," *Psychological Bulletin,* no. 84 (1977): 888–918.

9. Thomas Pettigrew, "Prejudice," in *Harvard Encyclopedia of American Ethnic Groups,* eds. Stephan Thernstrom, Ann Orlov, and Oscar Handlin (Cambridge, MA: Harvard University Press, 1980), 821.

10. Gordon W. Allport, *The Nature of Prejudice,* 50–51.

11. Wolfgang Stroebe and Chester A. Insko, "Stereotype, Prejudice, and Discrimination: Changing Conceptions in Theory and Research," in *Stereotyping and Prejudice: Changing Conceptions,* eds. Daniel Bar–Tal, Carl F. Grauman, Arie W. Kruglanski, Wolfgang Stroebe (New York: Springer–Verlag, 1989), 10.

12. George M. Frederickson and Dale T. Knobel, "History of Prejudice and Discrimination," in *Harvard Encyclopedia of American Ethnic Groups,* eds. Stephan Thernstrom, Ann Orlov, and Oscar Handlin (Cambridge, MA: Harvard University Press, 1980), 830.

13. R. A. Schermerhorn, *Comparative Ethnic Relations: A Framework for Theory and Research* (New York: Random House, 1970), 13.

14. Pettigrew, "Prejudice," 826.

15. Gordon Allport, *The Nature of Prejudice* (Reading, MA: Addison–Wesley, 1954), 51. Actually, this definition was borrowed by Allport from the United Nations Publication, *The Main Causes of Discrimination,* 1949. However, as late as the eighties the definition was still being used by some and attributed to Allport.

16. Stokely Carmichael and Charles V. Hamilton, *Black Power: The Political Liberation in America* (New York: Penguin, 1967), 5.

17. Michael Banton, "Institutional Racism," in *Dictionary of Race and Ethnic Relations,* 2nd edition, E. Ellis Cashmore, ed. (London: Routledge, 1984), 146.

18. William Graham Sumner, *Folkways: A Study of the Sociological Importance of Usages, Manners, Customs, Mores, and Morals* (New York: The New American Library of World Literature, 1960/1906), 27.

19. Sumner, *Folkways,* 27–28.

20. Herbert Hammerman, "Affirmative–Action Stalemate: A Second Perspective," *The Public Interest* 93 (fall 1988), 132.

21. Ibid., 134.

22. Dana Y. Takagi, "From Discrimination to Affirmative Action: Facts in the Asian American Admissions Controversy," *Social Problems,* vol. 27, no. 4 (November 1990), 578–592.

23. Kurt Lewin, "Self-Hatred Among Jews," *Contemporary Jewish Record,* vol. 4, no. 3 (June 1941), 222.

24. Ibid., 225.

25. Ibid., 228.

26. St. Clair Drake and Horace R. Cayton, *Black Metropolis: A Study of Negro Life in a Northern City*, vol. 1 (New York: Harper & Row, 1962/1941), 160.

27. Thomas F. Pettigrew, *A Profile of the Negro American* (New York: D. Van Nostrand, 1964), 179.

28. Blanche Knott, *Truly Tasteless Jokes* (New York: Ballantine Books, 1982), 30.

29. Based upon a review of the following: Blanche Knotts, *Truly Tasteless Jokes X* (New York: St. Martin's Press, 1990) and Blanche Knotts, *Truly Tasteless Jokes* (New York: Ballantine, 1982). The review only covered those chapters specifically indicated as Polish, Black, and Jewish jokes. These were the only ethnic or racial groups specifically identified by chapter headings.

30. Ken Hamblin interviewed by author, 11 November 1991.

31. *Klanwatch Intelligent Report* (February 1991), 21–26 and *Klanwatch Intelligent Report* (December 1989), 41–45.

32. Gordon Allport, *ABC's of Scapegoating*.

Chapter 8: Hate Groups and Haters.

1. For an in–depth case study of the Ayran Nations see James A. Aho, *The Politics of the Righteous: Idaho Christian Patriotism* (Seattle, WA: University of Washington Press), 1990.

2. Richard G. Butler, *Who, What, Why, When, Where? Aryan Nations* (Hayden Lake, Idaho: Church of Jesus Christ Christian, c. 1980?), n.p.

3. Alan M. Schwartz, ed., *Hate Groups in America: A Record of Bigotry and Violence* (New York: The Anti–Defamation League, 1988), 40.

4. Richard G. Butler, *Who, What, Why, When, Where? Aryan Nations*, n.p.

5. Aryan Nations, The Death of the White Race (Hayden Lake, Idaho: Aryan Nations, n.d.) n.p.

6. Flier received from Denver police intelligence section.

7. Kevin Flynn and Gary Gerhardt, *The Silent Brotherhood: Inside America's Racist Underground* (New York: Penguin Books, 1990), 125. All references to the rise and fall of the Silent Brotherhood are taken from this work, along with interviews with Detective Dan Malloy, retired, and Detective William "Bill" Carter of the Denver Police Department. Malloy was interviewed by the author in 1987 and Carter from 1989 to 1991.

8. Andrew Macdonald, *The Turner Diaries* (Hillsboro, WV: National Vanguard Books, 1978/1990). For another hate novel see William L. Pierce (Andrew Macdonald) *Hunter* (Hillsboro, WV: National Vanguard Books, 1989).

9. Interview with Detective Dan Malloy 27 September 1991. This interview was a follow–up to a series of interviews made in 1987.

10. The Covenant, the Sword, and the Arm of the Lord, Newsletter (March 1984), 1. All following quotes are from this newsletter unless otherwise noted.

11. The Covenant, the Sword, the Arm of the Lord, Survival Training School. A brochure and application. n.d.

12. Flynn and Gerhardt, *The Silent Brotherhood,* 308.

13. Ibid., 310.

14. Peter J. Peter, "Personal from the Editor's Pen," *Scriptures for America* 2 (1989), 1. This "Newsletter" appears in the form of a small journal usually between 30 and 40 pages. It is published in LaPorte, Colorado by The LaPorte Church of Christ.

15. Peter J. Peters, "Media Smear," *Scriptures for America* 4 (1989), 4.

16. Flier advertising *Everything You Wanted to Know About Gun Control* (c. 1989).

17. "What's White Power All About?," *The New Order,* January 1979.

18. Rudy "Butch" Stanko, *The Score* (Otto, NC: Church of the Creator, 1989).

19. Bob Scott was interviewed by the author in October 1991.

20. "We are above Ground and Legal," *Racial Loyalty,* 53 (August 1989), 6.

21. Ibid., 9.

22. "The Global Manifesto of the White People," *Racial Loyalty,* 59 (May 1990), 12.

23. White Aryan Resistance "hotline" phone message transcribed by the author on October 5, 1991.

24. Tom Metzger, "Warriors and Priests," *WAR: White Aryan Resistance,* vol. 8, no. 2 (1989?), 2.

25. From: *WAR: White Aryan Resistance,* vol. 8, no. 2 (1989), 6 and vol. 9, no. 2 (n.d.).

26. Southern Poverty Law Center Staff, *The Ku Klux Klan: A History of Racism and Violence,* edited by Sara Bullard (Montgomery, Alabama: Klanwatch Project, 1988), 49.

27. Danny Welch interviewed by author, 3 June 1992.

28. Gillette and Tillinger, *Inside Ku Klux Klan,* 41.

29. The Southern Poverty Law Center, "Klan Power at Its Peak," *The Ku Klux Klan: A History of Racism and Violence ,* 3rd edition, Sara Bullard (ed.) (Montgomery, AL: Klanwatch, 1980), 15.

30. Alan M. Schwartz, Gail L. Gans, Gerald Baumgarten, Irwin Suall, David Lowe, Judith Bolton, Jessica Greenbaum, Susan Berger, James Q. Purcell, and Jerome H. Bakst, *Hate Groups in America: A Record of Bigotry and Violence* (New York: The Anti–Defamation League of B'nai B'rith, 1988), 4. The list of Klan groups is also taken from this source.

31. Information obtained through police intelligence source.

32. "Klansman to Groom Supremacist Politicians," *The Denver Post* Sunday, 17 November 1991. [19A]

33. The Klanwatch Project, *Hate Violence and White Supremacy* (Montgomery, Alabama: Southern Poverty Law Center, 1988), 41–43.

34. Letter from Knights of the Ku Klux Klan Realm of Colorado. Obtained from police intelligence. This letter was part of a packet of racist literature distributed at Smokey Hills High School in a upper middle class suburb of Denver on October 2, 1991.

35. Civil Rights Division, *Extremism on the Right: A Handbook,* new and revised edition (New York: Anti–Defamation League of B'nai B'rith, 1988), 58.

36. Civil Rights Division (ADL), *Extremism on the Right,* 58.

37. Citizen Law Enforcement and Research Committee, *Sheriff's Posse Comitatus Handbook* (Portland, Oregon: C.L.E.R.C., 1970?), 1.

38. Ibid. 10.

39. Fact Finding Department of the Anti-Defamation League of B'nai B'rith, *The American Farmer and the Extremists: An ADL Special Report* (New York: Anti-Defamation League of B'nai B'rith, January, 1986), 6–7. Quote from the pamphlet entitled, "The American Farmer: Twentieth Century Slave," by James Wickstrom.

40. Flier dated October 1966 entitled, "Black Panther Party Platform and Program, WHAT WE WANT WHAT WE BELIEVE."

41. Val Douglas, "The Youth Make the Revolution," *The Black Panther,* 2 August 1969, 12–13.

42. Ibid.

43. Gene Marine, *The Black Panthers* (New York: The New American Library, 1969), 25.

44. Ibid., 23.

45. Clarence Page, "Deciphering Farrakhan," *Chicago* 33 (August 1984): 132.

46. Ibid.

47. Adolph Reed, Jr., "The Rise of Louis Farrakhan," *The Nation* 252 (21 January 1991): 54.

48. "What the Muslims Believe," *Muhammad Speaks,* vol. 10, no. 42 (2 July 1971): 32.

49. "What Muslims Want," *Muhammad Speaks,* vol. 10, no. 42 (2 July 1971): 32.

50. "Brothers in Bigotry," *Time,* 126 (14 October 1985): 41.

51. David Kurapka, "Hate Story: Farrakhan's Still at It," *The New Republic* 198 (30 May 1988): 20.

52. Ibid., 20.

53. "Demoted for Raising Holocaust Doubts, Teacher Sues," *The Denver Post,* 3 December 1990, sec. B. Also see "The 'holohoax' Surrender," *Rocky Mountain News,* 12 March 1991, p. 32.

54. Excerpts of "Swindlers of the Crematoria" reported in the *Denver Post,* Monday, 3 December 1990, section B, 1.

55. Statement provided to author by David VonFeldt Reinhardt, 12 September 1991.

56. Jerry Gray, "Educators Chided for Race Remark," *New York Times,* 24 March 1991, sec. I, p. 34, col. 1. Also see Joseph Berger, "Professors' Theories on Race Stir Turmoil at City College," *New York Times,* 20 April 1991, sec. B, p. 1, col. 2.

57. "Text of Jeffries' July Speech," *New York Newsday,* 18 August 1991, p. 29, col. 1.

58. Joseph Berger, "Professors' Theories on Race Stir Turmoil at City College," *New York Times,* 20 April 1990, sec. B, p. 1, col. 2. Also see: Jerry Gray, "Educators Chided for Race Remarks," *New York Times,* 24 March 1991, sec. I, p. 34, col. 1.

59. Ibid., 29.

60. Ibid., 25.

61. Ibid., 28.

62. Ibid., 29.

63. Ibid.

64. In a telephone conversation with author in 1988.

Chapter 9: Hate Prejudice and Education.

1. See Horace Kallen's article "Democracy Versus the Melting Pot" in two issues of *The Nation,* February 18, 1915, pages 190–194, and February 25, 1915, pages 217–220.

2. Horace M. Kallen, "Democracy Versus the Melting Pot," *The Nation* (February 25, 1915), 218–219.

3. National Council for the Social Studies Task Force on Ethnic Studies Guidelines. "Curriculum Guidelines for Multicultural Education," *Social Education* (September 1992): 276. The Task Force consisted of James A. Banks, Carlos E. Cortés, Geneva Gay, Ricardo L. Garcia, and Anna S. Ochoa.

4. *Using the African–American Baseline Essays* (Portland, Oregon: Portland Public Schools), 1.

5. The following information regarding Shawn Slater was obtained in two interviews with the author and Ravay Snow in November 1991. Information regarding his status within the Klan was obtained in part from Detective Bill Carter of the Denver–F.B.I. Task Force on Terrorism.

6. For a quick overview of the situations regarding racial and ethnic violence on campuses, see *Combatting Bigotry on Campus* by Jane Goldberg with Jeffery Ross (New York: Anti-Defamation League of B'nai B'rith, 1989).

7. For a good introduction to these skills, see *Group Processes in the Classroom* by Richard A. Schmuck and Patricia A. Schmuck (Dubuque, Iowa: William C. Brown, 1988).

8. Peter H. Martorella, *Teaching Social Studies in Middle and Secondary Schools* (New York: Macmillan Publishing Company, 1991), 92.

9. William Brandon, *The American Heritage Book of Indians* (New York: Dell Publishing, Co., 1961), 168–169.

10. Eva Pickova, "Fear" in … *I Never Saw Another Butterfly: Children's Drawings and Poems from Terezin Concentration Camp, 1942–1944,* ed. Hana Volavkova, trans. Jeanne Nemcova (New York: McGraw–Hill Book Company, 1971), n.p.

BIBLIOGRAPHY

Abelson, Robert P.; Aronson, Elliot; McGuire, William J.; Newcomb, Theodore; Rosenberg, Milton J.; and Tannenbaum, Percy H. eds. *Theories of Cognitive Consistency: A Sourcebook.* Chicago: Rand McNally, 1968.

Adorno, T. W.; Frenkel–Brunswik, Else; Levinson, Daniel J.; and Sanford, R. Nevitt. *The Authoritarian Personality.* New York: Harper & Row, 1950.

Aho, James A. *The Politics of Righteousness: Idaho Christian Patriotism.* Seattle, WA: University of Washington Press, 1990.

Ajen, Icek, and Fishbein, Martin. "Attitude–Behavior Relations: A Theoretical Analysis and Review of Empirical Research." *Psychological Bulletin* no. 84 (1977): 888–918.

Allen, James Paul, and Turner, Eugene James. *We the People: An Atlas of America's Ethnic Diversity.* New York: Macmillan Publishing Company, 1988.

Allport, Gordon W. *The Nature of Prejudice.* Reading, MA: Addison–Wesley, 1954.

Allport, Gordon W. *The ABC's of Scapegoating,* 5th rev. ed. New York: Anti-Defamation League of B'nai B'rith, 1966.

Allport, Gordon W. "Attitudes." In *A Handbook of Social Psychology,* edited by Carl Murchinson, 798–844. Worcester, MA: Clark University Press, 1935.

Anti-Defamation League of B'nai B'rith Civil Rights Division. *Extremism on the Right: A Handbook.* rev. ed. New York: author, 1988.

Anti-Defamation League of B'nai B'rith. *Hate Groups in America: A Record of Bigotry and Violence.* New York: author, 1982.

Anti-Defamation League of B'nai B'rith Fact Finding Department. *The American Farmer and the Extremists: An ADL Special Report.* New York: author, January 1986.

Anti-Defamation League of B'nai B'rith. *A World of Difference: Colorado Teacher/Student Study Guide* Vol. 2. Denver, CO: author, n.d.

Anti-Defamation League of B'nai B'rith. *1991 Audit of Anti-Semitic Incidents.* New York: author, 1992.

Anti-Defamation League of B'nai B'rith. *Hate Groups in America: A Record of Bigotry and Violence.* rev. ed. New York: author, 1988.

Aristotle. "Politics." In *The Basic Works of Aristotle,* edited by Richard McKeon, 7.7.1327b20–35. New York: Random House, 1941.

Aryan Nations. "The Death of the White Race." Hayden Lake, Idaho: author. n.d. Mimeo.

Ashmore, Richard D., and Del Boca, Francis K. "Conceptual Approaches to Stereotypes and Stereotyping." In *Cognitive Processes in Stereotyping and Intergroup Behavior,* edited by David L. Hamilton. Hillsdale, NJ: Lawrence Erlbaum Associates, 1981.

Ausubel, David P.; Novak, Joseph, D.; and Hanesian, Helen. *Educational Psychology: A Cognitive View.* 2nd ed. New York: Werbel & Peck, 1978.

Baldwin, James. *Notes from a Native Son.* New York: Bantam Books, 1968.

Bancroft, Hubert Howe. *Retrospection* (New York: Bancroft Co., 1912. 367–374. Reprinted in *The Development of Segregationist Thought,* edited by I.A. Newby. Homewood, IL: The Dorsey Press, 1968. 79–83.

Banks, James A. *Teaching Ethnic Studies: Concepts and Strategies.* Washington, D.C.: National Council for the Social Studies, 1973.

Banton, Michael. "Institutional Racism." In *Dictionary of Race and Ethnic Relations,* edited by E. Ellis Cashmore, 146. London: Routledge, 1984.

Barzun, Jacques. *Race: A Study in Superstition.* Rev. ed. New York: Harper & Row and Co., 1965.

Beals, Ralph L. and Hoijer, Harry. *An Introduction to Anthropology* New York: The Macmillan Company, 1965.

Berger, Joseph. "Professors' Theories on Race Stir Turmoil at City College." *New York Times,* 20 April 1991, sec. B, p. 1.

Berghe, Pierre L. van den. "Sociobiology." In *Dictionary of Race and Ethnic Relations,* edited by E. Ellis Cashmore, Michael Banton, Robert Miles, Barry Troyna and Pierre L. van den Berghe, 290. London: Routledge, 1988.

Berne, Eric. *Games People Play: The Psychology of Human Relationships.* New York: Grove Press, 1964.

Berry, Brewton. *Race and Ethnic Relations*. 2nd ed.. *Race Relations*. Boston: Houghton Mifflin Company, 1951.

Black Panther Party. "Black Panther Party Platform and Program: What We Want, What We Believe." Flier. October 1966.

Blumenback, Johann Frederick. "On the Nature and Variety of Mankind," In *This is Race: An Anthology Selected from the International Literature on the Races of Man,* edited by Earl W. Count, 25–39. New York: Henry Schuman, 1950.

Bogardus, Emory S. "Measuring Social Distance." *Journal of Applied Sociology* 9 (1925): 229–308.

"Books: Knowledge is Power." *White Patriot* 88 (1981): 11.

Brace, C. L., and Montague, Ashley M. F. *Man's Evolution: An Introduction to Physical Anthropology.* New York: The Macmillan Company, 1965.

Bradford, Amory. "Heredity and Environment." *Educational Review.* 1 (1891): 147–159.

Brandon, William. *The American Heritage Book of Indians*. New York: Dell Publishing, Co., 1961.

Brinton, Daniel G. *The American Race*. New York: N.D.C. Hodges, 1891.

"Brothers in Bigotry." *Time.* 126 (14 October 1985): 41.

Buffon, Comte de. "A Natural History, General and Particular." In *This is Race: An Anthology Selected from the International Literature on the Races of Man,* edited by Earl W. Count, 3–15. New York: Henry Schuman, 1950.

Butler, Richard G. "Who, What, Why, When, Where? Aryan Nations." Hayden Lake, Idaho: Church of Jesus Christ Christian, n.d. (circa 1980).

Campbell, Donald T. "Variation and Selective Retention in Socio–Cultural Evolution." In *Social Change in Developing Areas: A Reinterpretation of Evolutionary Theory,* edited by Herbert R. Barringer, George I. Blanksten, and Raymond W. Mack, 19–49. Cambridge, MA: Schenkman Publishing Company, 1965.

Carmichael, Stokely, and Hamilton, Charles V. *Black Power: The Politicals of Liberation in America*. New York: Penguin, 1967.

Carrol, Terrence G. "Northern Ireland." In *Ethnic Conflict in International Relations,* edited by Astri Suhrke and Lela Garner Noble, 21–42 New York: Praeger Publishers, 1977.

Carter, William. Interview with author. 1990 and 1991.

Cassidy, John. "History Turns Its Back on America's Heroes." *The Sunday Times,* 28 July 1991, sec. 1, p. 15.

Chalmers, David M. *Hooded Americanism: The History of the Ku Klux Klan.* 3rd ed. Durham, NC: Duke University Press, 1987.

Chee Chang Ping v. United States. (The Chinese Exclusion Case). 130 U.S. 581 (1889).

Chicago Commission on Race Relations. *The Negro in Chicago: A Study of Race Relations and Race Riot.* Chicago: The University of Chicago Press, 1922.

Citizen Law Enforcement and Research Committee. *Sheriff's Posse Comitatus Handbook.* Portland, Oregon: C.L.E.R.C., circa 1970.

Civil Rights Commission. *Report of the Civil Rights Commission.* Washington, D. C.: U.S. Government Printing Office, 1959.

Cobb, Sanford H. *The Rise of Religious Liberty in America.* New York: Macmillan, 1902.

Cohn, Norman. *Warrant for Genocide: The Myth of the Jewish World Conspiracy and the Protocols of the Elders of Zion.* New York: Harper & Row, 1966.

Collins, Homer, and Snider, Felix. *Missouri: Midland State.* Cape Guirado, Missouri: Ramfree Press, 1967.

Comas, Juan. *Racial Myths.* Paris: UNESCO, 1958.

Compton, Arthur; Redfield, Robert; and Wirth, Louis. *Anti–Semitism: A Threat to American Unity?: A University of Chicago Round Table.* Chicago: University of Chicago Press, 5 October 1941.

Coolidge, Mary Roberts. *Chinese Immigration.* New York: Henry Holt Company, 1909.

Covenant, the Sword, and the Arm of the Lord. "Newsletter" (March 1984), 1.

Crane, Stephen. "The Wayfarer." In *The Mentor Book of Major American Poets,* edited by Oscar Williams and Edwin Honig, 232. New York: The New American Library, 1962.

Cuvier, Georges. "Varieties of the Human Species." In *This is Race: An Anthology Selected from the International Literature on the Races of Man,* edited by Earl W. Count, 44–47. New York: Henry Schuman, 1950.

Dawes, Robyn. Interview with author. 16 July 1991.

Dawes, Robyn M., and Smith, Tom L. "Attitude and Opinion Measurement." In *The Handbook of Social Psychology.* 3rd ed., edited by

Gardner Lindzey and Elliot Aronson, 509–566. New York: Random House, 1985.

Degler, Carl N. *In Search of Human Nature: The Decline and Revival of Darwinism in American Social Thought.* New York: Oxford University Press, 1991.

"Demoted for Raising Holocaust Doubts, Teacher Sues." *The Denver Post* (3 December 1990), sec. B.

Dewey, John. "The Relationship of Theory to Practice in Education," in *The Third Yearbook of the National Society for the Scientific Study of Education,* ed. Charles A. McMurry, 9–30. Chicago: The University of Chicago Press, 1904

Dolgin, Phyllis, and Kleg, Milton. *Who Am I?: Native Americans* Sound Filmstrip. Chicago: Coronet Films, 1975.

Dority, Barbara. "The PC Speech Police." *The Humanist* (March/April 1992), 31–33.

Douglas, Val. "The Youth Make the Revolution," *The Black Panther,* 2 August 1969, 12–13.

Dovidio, John F., and Gaertner, Samuel L. "Prejudice, Discrimination, and Racism: Historical Trends and Contemporary Approaches." In *Prejudice, Discrimination, and Racism,* edited by authors. Orlando, FL: Academic Press, 1986.

Drake, St. Clair, and Cayton, Horace R. *Black Metropolis: A Study of Negro Life in a Northern City.* Vol. 1. New York: Harper & Row, 1962/1941.

Duffy, Brian. "Days of Rage." *U.S. News & World Report* (11 May 1992): 21–26.

Dunbar, Paul Lawrence. "We Wear the Mask." In *The Negro Caravan,* edited by Brown, Sterling A.; Davis, Arthur P.; and Lee, Ulysses, 310. New York: Arno Press and The New York Times, 1970.

Engle, Shirley H., and Ochoa, Anna S. *Education for Democratic Citizenship: Decision Making in the Social Studies.* New York: Teachers College Press, 1988.

Equal Employment Opportunity Commission. *Equal Employment Opportunity: Standard Form 100, Rev. 1–86. Employer Information Report EEO–1: 100–115: Instruction Booklet.* Washington, D.C.: U.S. Government Printing Office, 1986.

"Everything You Wanted to Know About Gun Control." Flier distributed by Pete Peters. n.d. (circa 1989).

Fairchild, Henry Pratt, ed. *Dictionary of Sociology and Related Sciences.* Ames, Iowa: Littlefield, Adams, and Company, 1955.

Fairchild, Henry Pratt. "The Truth About Race," In *This is Race: An Anthology Selected from the International Literature on the Races of Man,* edited by Earl W. Count, 688–690. New York: Henry Schuman, 1950.

"Fellow Prisoners Gave Negro to Mob." *New York Times,* 30 September 1919, City edition, p. 5, col. 2.

Flynn, Kevin, and Gerhardt, Gary. *The Silent Brotherhood: Inside America's Racist Underground.* New York: Penguin Books, 1990.

Franklin, John Hope. *From Slavery to Freedom.* New York: Alfred A. Knopf, 1967.

Frederikson, George M., and Knobel, Dale T. "History of Prejudice and Discrimination." In *Harvard Encyclopedia of American Ethnic Groups.* edited by Stephan Thernstrom, Ann Orlov, and Oscar Handlin, 829–847. Cambridge, MA: Harvard University Press, 1980.

Friedman, Jerome. "Jewish Conversion, the Spanish Pure Blood Laws and Reformation: A Revisionist View of Racial and Religious Antisemitism." *The Sixteenth Century Journal* 17, no. 1 (spring 1987): 3–29.

Gans, Herbert. Interview with author, 16 May 1991.

Gans, Herbert J. "Symbolic Ethnicity: The Future of Ethnic Groups and Cultures in America." *Ethnic and Racial Studies* 2, no. 1 (January 1979): 1–20.

Garn, Stanley M. *Human Races.* Springfield, IL: Charles C. Thomas Publishers, 1961.

"Gen. Woods Orders the Arrest of Omaha's Rioters." *New York Times,* 1 October 1919, City edition, p. 1, col. 5.

General Assembly of Maryland. "Act Concerning Religion" (1649). In *The Roots of the Bill of Rights: An Illustrated Source Book of American Freedom.* Compiled by Bernard Schwartz, 5 vols., 1:93. New York: Chelsea House Publishers, 1980.

Genovese, Eugene D. *The Political Economy of Slavery: Studies in the Economy and Society of the Slave South.* New York: Random House, 1965.

"Georgia Mob Burns Two Negroes Alive," *New York Times,* 7 October 1919, City edition, p. 2, col. 6.

Gillette, Paul J., and Tillinger, Eugene. *Inside Ku Klux Klan.* New York: Pyramid Publications, 1965.

Ginzburg, Ralph. *100 Years of Lynchings.* New York: Lancer Books, Inc., 1969.

Gobineau, Arthur de. *The Inequality of Human Races*. Translated by Adrian Collins. New York: Howard Fertig, 1915/1967.

Goldberg, Arthur. Interview with author, 1988.

Goldberg, Jane with Ross, Jeffery. *Combatting Bigotry on Campus*. New York: Anti-Defamation League of B'Nai B'rith, 1989.

Gordon, Milton M. *Assimilation in American Life: The Role of Race, Religion, and National Origins*. New York: Oxford Press, 1964.

Graumann, Carl Friedrich Graumann, and Wintermantel, Margret. "Discriminatory Speech Acts: A Functional Approach." In *Stereotyping and Prejudice: Changing Conceptions*, edited by Daniel Bar-Tel, Carl F. Graumann, Arie W. Kruglanski, Wolfgang Stroebe, 182–204. New York: Springer-Verlag, 1989.

Gray, Alice Wirth. Interview with Ravay Snow. November 1990.

Gray, Jerry. "Educators Chided for Race Remarks." *New York Times*, 24 March 1991, sec. I, p. 34.

Gregorvious, Ferdinand. *The Ghetto and the Jews of Rome*. Translated by Moses Hadas. New York: Schocken Press, 1948.

Gulick, Sidney Lewis. *The American Japanese Problem*. New York: Charles Scribner's Sons, 1914.

H. Kristina. "Being White is Not a Crime." *War: White Aryan Resistance 8*, no. 2 (n.d.): 6.

H. Kristina. "Let Us Forever Banish the Myth." *War: White Aryan Resistance 9*, no. 2 (n.d.): 2.

Hagedorn, Hermann. *Roosevelt in the Bad Lands*. Boston: Houghton Mifflin Co., 1921.

Hamblin, Ken. Interview with author. 11 November, 1991.

Hamilton, David L. "Illusory Correlation as a Basic for Stereotyping." In *Cognitive Processes in Stereotyping and Intergroup Behavior*, edited by David L. Hamilton, 115–144. Hillsdale, NJ: Lawrence Erlbaum Associates, 1981.

Hammerman, Herbert. "Affirmative–Action Stalemate: A Second Perspective." *The Public Interest* 93 (fall 1988):130–134.

Hastorf, Albert H.; Schneider, David J.; and Polefka, Judith. *Person Perception*. Reading, MA: Addison–Wesley, 1970.

Hiemer, Ernst. *The Poisonous Mushroom [Der Giftpilz]: A Stuermer Book for Young and Old Fables*. Nurnberg: Der Stuemer, 1938. English Translation. Evidence of the International Military Tribunal (Nurnberg). Document 1778–PS (USA 257).

Hitler, Adolf; Frick, Wilhelm; and Hess, Rudolf. "First Regulation to Reich Citizenship Law of 14 November 1935." Evidence of the International Military Tribunal (Nurnberg). Document 1417–PS (GB 25B): 1935 Reichsgesetzblatt, Part I. p. 1333.

Holt, Thomas C. "Afro–Americans." In *Harvard Encyclopedia of American Ethnic Groups,* edited by Stephen Thernstrom, Ann Orlov, and Oscar Hamlin, 5–23. Cambridge, Massachusetts: Harvard University Press, 1980. 7–8.

Hostetler, John A., and Huntington, Gertrude Enders. *The Hutterites in North America.* Fort Worth, Texas: Holt, Rinehart, and Winston, Inc., 1980.

Hughes, Langston. "Let America be America Again." In *The Negro Caravan,* edited by Sterling A. Brown, Arthur P. Davis, & Ulysses Lee, 370–372. New York: Arno Press & the New York Times, 1970.

Hyman, Lawrence. "Why Liberals Cannot be Politically Correct." (March/April 1992), 5–6.

Ijzendoorn, Marinus H. van. "Moral Judgment, Authoritarianism, and Ethnocentrism." *The Journal of Social Psychology,* 129, no. 1 (February 1989): 37–45.

Itzkoff, Seymour W. *The Making of the Civilized Mind.* New York: P. Lang, 1990.

Jahoda, Marie. *Race Relations and Mental Health.* Paris: UNESCO, 1960.

Kallen, Horace M. "Democracy Versus the Melting Pot, I." *The Nation,* 18 February 1915, 190–194.

Kallen, Horace M. "Democracy Versus the Melting Pot, II." *The Nation.* 25 February 1915, 217–220.

Kaltsounis, Theodore. *Teaching Social Studies in the Elementary School: The Basics for Citizenship.* Englewood Cliffs, NJ: Prentice–Hall, 1987.

Kant, Immanuel. "On the Different Races of Man." In *This is Race: An Anthology Selected from the International Literature on the Races of Man,* edited by Earl W. Count, 16–24. New York: Henry Schuman, 1950.

Kaplan, Abraham. *The Conduct of Inquiry: Methodology for the Behavioral Science.* San Francisco: Chandler Publishing Company, 1964.

Katz, Jacob. *From Prejudice to Destruction: Anti–Semitism, 1700–1933.* Cambridge, MA: Harvard University Press, 1980.

Katz, Daniel, and Braly, Kenneth. "Racial Stereotypes of One Hundred College Students." *The Journal of Abnormal and Social Psychology* 28 (1933–1934): 280–290.

Keefe, Eugene K.; Boucher, Arsene A.; Elpern, Sarah J.; Giloane, William; Moore, James M.; Ogden, Terrence L.; Peters, Stephen; Prevas, John P.; Walstrom, Nancy E.; and White, Eston T. *Area Handbook for the Soviet Union.* Washington, D.C.: Government Printing Office, 1971.

King, Martin Luther, Jr. "I Have a Dream." In *Chronicles of Black Protest,* compiled by C. Eric Lincoln, 186–187. New York: The New American Library, 1968.

"Klansman to Groom Supremacist Politicians." *The Denver Post,* Sunday, 17 November 1991. 19A.

Klanwatch Project of the Southern Poverty Law Center. "Klan Power at Its Peak." *The Ku Klux Klan: A History of Racism and Violence,* 3rd ed., edited by Sara Bullard, 14–18. Montgomery, AL: author, 1980.

Klanwatch Project of the Southern Poverty Law Center. "Tracking Hate Crimes." *Hate Violence and White Supremacy,* 47 (December 1989): 41–45.

Klanwatch Project of the Southern Poverty Law Center. *Intelligence Report.* (December 1989): 41–45.

Klanwatch Project of the Southern Poverty Law Center. *Hate Violence and White Supremacy.* Montgomery, Alabama: Southern Poverty Law Center, 1988.

Klanwatch Project of the Southern Poverty Law Center. *Klanwatch Intelligent Report.* (February 1991): 21–26.

Kleg, Milton; Borgeld, Thomas; and Sullivan, Nora E. "An Exploration of Ethnic Attitudes at Three Levels of Social Psychological Interaction." Paper presented at the Annual Meeting of the American Educational Research Association, Chicago, April 1974.

Knotts, Blanche. *Truly Tasteless Jokes X.* New York: St. Martin's Press, 1990.

Knotts, Blanche. *Truly Tasteless Jokes.* New York: Ballantine, 1982.

Kurapka, David. "Hate Story: Farrakhan's Still at It." *The New Republic* 198 (30 May 1988): 21–19.

Larrabee, Harold A. *Reliable Knowledge: Scientific Methods in the Social Studies.* Rev. ed. Boston: Houghton Mifflin Company, 1964.

Lawrence, W.H. "Poles Kill 26 Jews in Kielce Pogrom," *New York Times,* Friday, 6 July 1946, City edition, p. 1, col. 6.

Lawrence, W.H. "Poles Ask Death for Kielce Guilty: Trials to Start Tomorrow—Toll Reaches 43—Second Plot Broken Up," *New York Times,* Sunday, 7 July 1946, City edition, p. 1, col. 7.

Lawrence, W.H. "Poles Declare Two Hoaxes Caused High Toll in Pogrom: Boy 9, Admits Story that Jews Slew 15 Children was Lie—Other Victims Lured to Death by Safety Pledge—40 Killed," *New York Times,* Saturday, 7 July 1946, City edition, p. 1, cols. 4 & 5;

Learsi, Rufus. *Israel: A History of the Jewish People.* Cleveland: The World Publishing Company, 1949.

Lefkowitz, Mary. "Not Out of Africa: The Origins of Greece and Illusions of Afrocentrists." *The New Republic* (10 February 1992), 29–36.

Lewin, Kurt. "Self–Hatred Among Jews." *Contemporary Jewish Record.* 4, no. 3 (June 1941): 219–232.

Lippmann, Walter. *Public Opinion.* 1922; reprint, New York: The Macmillan Company, 1961.

Lochner v. New York, 198 U.S. 45, 25 S.Ct. 539, 49 L.Ed. 937 (1905).

Lossin, Yigal. *Pillar of Fire: The Rebirth of Israel—A Visual History.* Translated by Z. Ofer. Edited by C. Halberstadt. Jerusalem: Shikmona, 1983.

Macdonald, Andrew. *The Turner Diaries.* Hillsboro, WV: National Vanguard Books, 1978/1990.

Macdonald, Andrew. *Hunter.* Hillsboro, WV: National Vanguard Books, 1989.

Malloy, Dan. Interviews with author. 1987 and 27 September 1991.

Marine, Gene. *The Black Panthers.* New York: The New American Library, 1969.

Marr, Wilhelm. *Der Sieg des Judentums uber das Germanentum.* Bern, author, 1879.

Martel, Eric. "How Valid are the Portland Baseline Essays?" *Educational Leadership* 49, no. 4 (December 1991/January 1992): 20–23.

Martorella, Peter H. *Elementary Social Studies: Developing Reflective, Competent, and Concerned Citizens.* Boston: Little, Brown, & Co., 1985.

Martorella, Peter H. *Teaching Social Studies in Middle and Secondary Schools.* New York: Macmillan Publishing Company, 1991.

Martorella, Peter H. "Knowledge and Concept Development." In *Handbook of Research on Social Studies Teaching and Instruction,* edited by James P. Shaver, 370–384. New York: Macmillan Publishing Company, 1991.

Mathews, Tom. "Siege of L.A.." *Newsweek* (11 May 1992), 30–38.

McGuire, William J. "The Nature of Attitude and Attitude Change." In *The Handbook of Social Psychology.* Vol. 3, 2nd ed., edited by Gardner Lindzey and Elliot Aronson, 136–314. Reading, MA: Addison–Wesley Publishing Company, 1968.

McGuire, William J. "Attitudes and Attitude Change." In *The Handbook of Social Psychology,* 3rd ed., edited by Gardner Lindzey and Elliot Aronson, 233–246. New York: Random House, 1985.

McKay, James. "An Exploratory Synthesis of Primordial and Mobilizatist Approaches to Ethnic Phenomena," *Ethnic and Racial Studies* 5, no. 4 (October 1982):395–420.

Merton, Robert K. "The Self-fulfilling Prophecy." *The Antioch Review* 8 (1948): 193–210.

Metzger, Tom. "Warriors and Priests." *WAR: White Aryan Resistance* 8, no. 2 (1989?): 2.

Montagu, Ashley. *Race, Science, and Humanity.* Princeton, NJ: D. Van Nostrand Company, Inc., 1963.

Montagu, Ashley. *Man's Most Dangerous Myth: The Fallacy of Race.* 4th ed. Cleveland, OH: The World Publishing Company, 1964.

Montellano, Bernard Oritz de. "Multicultural Pseudoscience: Spreading Scientific Illiteracy among Minorities—Part I." *Skeptical Inquirer* 16 (fall 1991), 46–50.

Morgan, John T. "The Race Question in the United States." *Arena.* 2 (September 1890): 385–398. Reprinted in *The Development of Segregationist Thought,* edited by I.A. Newby, 21–28. Homewood, IL: The Dorsey Press, 1968.

Morse, Samuel F. B., *Imminent Dangers to the Free Institutions of the United States Through Foreign Immigration and the Present State.* New York: E.B. Clayton Printer, 1835.

Myrdal, Gunnar; with Sterner, Richard; and Rose, Arnold. *An American Dilemma: The Negro Problem and Modern Democracy.* New York: Harper and Row Publisher, 1944.

National Advisory Commission on Civil Disorders. *The Report of the National Advisory Commission on Civil Disorders.* New York: E. P. Dutton and Company, 1968.

National Association for the Advancement of Colored People. "Lynchings." *New York Times* 22 November 1922, City edition, p. 19.

National Council for the Social Studies Task Force on Ethnic Studies Guidelines. "Curriculum Guidelines for Multicultural Education," *Social Education* (September 1992): 276.

Newcomb, Theodore M.; Turner, Ralph H.; and Converse, Philip E. *Social Psychology: The Study of Human Interaction.* New York: Holt, Rinehart, and Winston, 1965.

"Nine Plead Guilty in Polish Pogrom," *New York Times,* City edition, Wednesday, 10 July 1946, p. 8, col. 2.

Oliver, Donald W. "Educating Citizens for Responsible Individualism, 1960–1980." In *Citizenship and a Free Society: Education for the Future,* edited by Franklin Paterson, 201–227. Washington, D.C.: National Council for the Social Studies, 1960.

Oliver, Donald W., and Shaver, James P. *Teaching Public Issues in the High School.* Boston: Houghton Mifflin Co., 1966.

Page, Clarence. "Deciphering Farrakhan." *Chicago* 33 (August 1984): 130–135.

Park, Robert Ezra. "Experience and Race Relations." *Journal of Applied Sociology* 9 (1924): 18–24.

Park, Robert E. "The Concept of Social Distance as Applied to the Study of Racial Attitudes and Race Relations." *Journal of Applied Sociology,* 8 (1924): 339–344.

Penrose, Eldon R. *California Nativism: Organized Opposition to the Japanese, 1890–1913.* Saratoga, CA: R. and E. Research Associates, 1973.

Peters, Peter J. "Personal from the Editor's Pen," *Scriptures for America* 2 (1989): 1.

Peters, Peter J. "Media Smear," *Scriptures for America* 4 (1989): 4.

Petersen, William. "Concepts of Ethnicity." In *Harvard Encyclopedia of American Ethnic Groups,* edited by Stephen Thernstrom, Ann Orlov, and Oscar Hamlin, 234–242. Cambridge, Massachusetts: Harvard University Press, 1980.

Pettigrew, Thomas F. "Extending the Stereotype Concept." In *Cognitive Processes in Stereotyping and Intergroup Behavior,* edited by David L. Hamilton, 303–331. Hillsdale, NJ: Lawrence Erlbaum Associates, 1981.

Pettigrew, Thomas F. *A Profile of the Negro American.* New York: D. Van Nostrand, 1964.

Pettigrew, Thomas F. "Prejudice." In Harvard Encyclopedia of American Ethnic Groups. edited by Stephan Thernstrom, Ann Orlov, and Oscar Handlin, 820–829. Cambridge, MA: Harvard University Press, 1980.

Pickova, Eva. "Fear" in ... *I Never Saw Another Butterfly: Children's Drawings and Poems from Terezin Concentration Camp, 1942–1944,* edited by Hana Volavkova. Translated by Jeanne Nemcova. New York: McGraw–Hill Book Company, 1971.

Pogonowski, Iwo Cyprian. *Poland: An Historical Atlas*. New York: Hippocrene Books, Inc., 1987.

Poliakov, Leon. *The History of Anti-Semitism*, vol. 3. Translated by Miriam Kochan. New York: The Vanguard Press, 1968.

Poll, Solomon. *The Hassidic Community of Williamsburg: A Study in the Sociology of Religion*. New York: Schocken Books, 1969.

Portland Public Schools. *Using the African–American Baseline Essays*. Portland, Oregon: author, 1989.

Price, Hiram. "Report of Commissioner of Indian Affairs Hiram Price, October 10, 1882." In *The American Indian and the United States*, Vol. I. Compiled by Wilcomb E. Washburn, 315–344. New York: Random House, 1973.

"Race and Prejudice." In *The UNESCO Courier*, April 1965, 8–11.

"Race: Our Dilemma Still," *Newsweek* (11 May 1992), 44.

Reed, Adolph, Jr. "The Rise of Louis Farrakhan." *The Nation*. 252 (21 January 1991): 37, 51–56.

Rice, Marion J. "What is the Meaning of 'Humanizing the Social Studies?' " In *Social Studies: The Humanizing Process*, eds. Milton Kleg & John H. Litcher, 17–20. Winter Haven, FL: Florida Council for the Social Studies, 1972.

Richtol, Louis. Interviews with author. October 1989–January 1990.

Ringer, Benjamin B., and Lawless, Elinor R. *Race, Ethnicity, and Society*. New York: Routledge, 1989.

Rosenfeld, Abraham, trans. *The Authorized Kinot for the Ninth of Av*. New York: The Judaica Press, 1979.

Rubin, Israel. Interview with author. 1991.

Rubin, Israel. *Satmar: An Island in the City*. Chicago: Quadrangle Books, 1972.

Schermerhorn, R. A. *Comparative Ethnic Relations: A Framework for Theory and Research*. New York: Random House, 1970.

Schiedt, Walter. "The Concept of Race in Anthropology and the Divisions into Human Races from Linneus to Deniker." In *This is Race: An Anthology Selected from the Literature on the Races of Man*, edited by Earl W. Count, 354–391. New York: Henry Schuman, 1950.

Schlesinger, Arthur M..Jr. *The Disuniting of America: Reflections on a Multicultural Society.* New York: W.W. Norton & Company, 1992.

Scott, Bob. Interview with author. October 1991.

Scott, William A. "Attitude Measurement." In *The Handbook of Social Psychology.* Vol. 2, 2nd ed., edited by Gardner Lindzey and Elliot Aronson, 204–273. Reading, MA: Addison–Wesley Publishing Company, 1968.

Shibutani, Tamotsu, and Kwan, Kian M. *Ethnic Stratification: A Comparative Approach.* New York: Macmillan Company, 1965.

Simpson, George Eaton, and Yinger, J. Milton. *Racial and Cultural Minorities: Analysis of Prejudice and Discrimination.* 5th ed. New York: Plenum Press, 1985.

"Six Thousand Troops Called Out in Chicago to Check New Riots," *New York Times,* Thursday, 31 July 1919, City edition, p. 1, col. 8.

Slater, Shawn. Interview with Ravay Snow and author. November 1991.

Smith, Lillian. *Killers of the Dream.* Revised, 1963: Garden City, NY: Doubleday & Company; W.W. Norton and Company, 1949.

Snyder, Mark. "On the Self–Perpetuating Nature of Social Stereotypes," In *Cognitive Processes in Stereotyping and Intergroup Behavior,* edited by David L. Hamilton, 183–212. Hillsdale, NJ: Lawrence Erlbaum Associates, 1981.

Southern Poverty Law Center Staff. "A Hundred Years of Terror." *The Ku Klux Klan: A History of Racism and Violence,* edited by Sarah Bullard. Montgomery, Alabama: Klanwatch, 1988.

Spencer, Herbert. *The Principles of Sociology.* 3rd ed. New York: D. Appleton and Company, 1897.

Spencer, Herbert. *Principles of Biology.* Vol. 1. New York: D. Appleton and Company, 1866.

Stampp, Kenneth M. *The Era of Reconstruction: 1865–1877.* New York: Random House, 1965.

Stanko, Rudy "Butch." *The Score.* Otto, NC: Church of the Creator, 1989.

Stephan, Walter G. "Intergroup Relations." in *The Handbook of Social Psychology.* 3rd ed., edited by Gardner Lindzey and Elliot Aronson, 599–659. New York: Random House, 1985.

Stroebe, Wolfgang, and Insko, Chester A. "Stereotype, Prejudice, and Discrimination: Changing Conceptions in Theory and Research." In *Stereotyping and Prejudice: Changing Conceptions,* edited by Daniel Bar–Tal, Carl F. Graumann, Arie W. Kruglanski, and Wolfgang Stroebe, 3–34. New York: Springer–Verlag, 1989.

Sumner, William Graham. *Folkways: A Study of the Sociological Importance of Usages, Manners, Customs, Mores, and Morals.* New York: The New American Library of World Literature, 1960/1906.

"Swindlers of the Crematoria" reported in the *Denver Post,* Monday, 3 December 1990, section B, 1.

Taft, Charles P., and Felknor, Bruce L. *Prejudice and Politics.* New York: Anti-Defamation League of B'nai B'rith, 1960.

Tajel, Henri. "Cognitive Aspects of Prejudice." *Journal of Social Issues* 25, no.4 (1969): 79–97.

Takagi, Dana Y. "From Discrimination to Affirmative Action: Facts in the Asian American Admissions Controvers." *Social Problems* 27, no. 4 (November 1990): 578–592.

Taylor, Shelley. "A Categorization Approach to Stereotyping." In *Cognitive Processes in Stereotyping,* edited by David L. Hamilton, 83–114. Hillsdale, NJ: Lawrence Erlbaum Associates, 1981.

"Text of Jeffries' July Speech," *New York Newsday,* 18 August 1991, 3, 25–29.

"The Covenant, the Sword, the Arm of the Lord, Survival Training School." A brochure and application. n.d.

"The Global Manifesto of the White People," *Racial Loyalty,* 59 (May 1990), 12.

The Governor's Commission on the Los Angeles Riots. *Violence in the City— An End or a Beginning?* Los Angeles, 1965.

"The 'holohoax' Surrender," *Rocky Mountain News,* 12 March 1991, p. 32.

"The Jews and Their Lies", *Aryan Territorial Alliance News Letter,* 1 March 1988, 4.

Thernstrom, Stephen; Orlov, Ann; and Hamlin, Oscar; eds. *Harvard Encyclopedia of American Ethnic Groups.* Cambridge, Massachusetts: Harvard University Press, 1980.

Totten, Samuel, and Kleg, Milton. *Human Rights.* Hillside, New Jersey: Enslow Press, 1989.

"Troops sent to Omaha; Mob fires Courthouse with Bombs, Attacks Negroes, Lynches One, Nearly Lynches Mayor," *New York Times,* 29 September 1919, City edition, p. 1, col. 8; p.2, cols. 1–2.

Valentin, Hugo. *Antisemitism: Historically and Critically Examined.* Translated by A. G. Chater. New York: The Viking Press, 1936.

VonFeldt, David. Statement provided to author. 12 September 1991.

Wade, Wyn Craig. *The Fiery Cross.* New York: Simon and Schuster, Inc., 1987.

Walker, Francis A. "Report of Commissioner of Indian Affairs. Francis A. Walker, November 1, 1872." In *The American Indian and the United States: A Documentary History*. Vol. 1. Compiled by Wilcomb E. Washburn, 176–190. New York: Random House, 1973.

Ware, Caroline Farrar. "Ethnic Communities." In *Encyclopedia of the Social Sciences*. Vols. 5–6, edited by Edwin Seligman and Alvin Johnson, 607. New York: Macmillan, 1937.

Warren, Earl. *The Memoirs of Chief Justice Earl Warren*. Garden City, NY: Doubleday, 1977.

Waters, Mary C. *Ethnic Options: Choosing Identities in America*. Berkeley, California: University of California Press, 1990.

"We are Above Ground and Legal," *Racial Loyalty*, 53 (August 1989), 6.

Welch, Danny. Interviewed by author. 3 June 1992.

"What the Muslims Want," *Muhammad Speaks* vol. 10, no. 42 (2 July 1971): 32.

"What the Muslims Believe," *Muhammad Speaks* vol. 10, no. 42 (2 July 1971): 32.

"What's White Power All About?," *The New Order* (January 1979), 8.

White Aryan Resistance "hotline" phone message. Transcribed by the author on October 5, 1991.

Wiley, Malcolm; Wirth, Louis; and Wilson, John. *The Jews: The University of Chicago Round Table*. Chicago: University of Chicago Press, 28 January 1940.

Williams, Janet B.W. ed., *Diagnostic and Statistical Manual of Mental Disorder: DSM-III-R*. Washington, D.C.: American Psychiatric Association, 1987.

Wilson, Woodrow. *A History of the American People*. 5 vols. New York: Harper & Brothers, 1902.

Wirth, Louis. *The Ghetto*. Chicago: The University of Chicago Press, 1928.

Yerushalmi, Shmuel. *Torah Anthology on the Book of Ecclesiastes*, translated by Zvi Faier. New York: Maznaim Publishing Corp., 1986.

Yinger, J. Milton. "Intersecting Strands in the Theorisation of Race and Ethnic Relations." In *Theories of Race and Ethnic Relations*, edited by John Rex and David Mason, 20–41. Cambridge, UK: Cambridge University Press, 1986.

Zeligs, Rose. "Children's Intergroup Attitudes." *The Journal of Genetic Psychology* 72 (1948): 101–110.

INDEX

I

Belmont University Library

39

Belmont University Library

NOV 02 1995

NOV 24 1995

NOV 27 2004

NOV 06

DEC 06 REC'D

DEC 17 2008

DEC 0 9 REC'D

GAYLORD

PRINTED IN U.S.A.